Mic

CW01301423

CRIME AND MUSLIM BRITAIN

Marta Bolognani completed her PhD in Sociology at the University of Leeds. She wrote this book while Assistant Professor of Anthropology at Lahore University of Management Sciences in Pakistan. She is now Head of Sociology, Criminology and Popular Culture at the University Of Wales Institute, Cardiff, UK.

CRIME AND MUSLIM BRITAIN

Race, Culture and the Politics of Criminology among British Pakistanis

Marta Bolognani

TAURIS ACADEMIC STUDIES
an imprint of
I.B. Tauris Publishers
LONDON • NEW YORK

Published in 2009 by Tauris Academic Studies
an imprint of I.B.Tauris & Co Ltd
6 Salem Road, London W2 4BU
175 Fifth Avenue, New York NY 10010
www.ibtauris.com

Distributed in the United States and Canada Exclusively by Palgrave Macmillan
175 Fifth Avenue, New York NY 10010

Copyright © 2009 Marta Bolognani

The right of Marta Bolognani to be identified as author of this work has been asserted by the author in accordance with the Copyright, Designs and Patent Act 1988.

All rights reserved. Except for brief quotations in a review, this book, or any part thereof, may not be reproduced, stored in or introduced into a retrieval system, or transmitted, in any form or by any means, electronic, mechanical, photocopying, recording or otherwise, without the prior written permission of the publisher.

Library of Crime and Criminology 1
ISBN: 978 1 84511 833 4

A full CIP record for this book is available from the British Library
A full CIP record for this book is available from the Library of Congress

Library of Congress catalog card: available

Printed and bound in India by Thomson Press
camera-ready copy edited and supplied by the author

To my Mum and Dad

CONTENTS

List of Tables   xi

Acknowledgements   xiii

Introduction   1

1. The Taboo of Criminological Research amongst Minority Ethnic Groups   7
1.1 The Origins of Interest in Race and Crime   8
1.2 Crime and Culture   9
1.3 Race and Crime in Britain: Discrimination, Policing and the Criminal Justice System   11
1.4 Taking Culture out of the Picture: Alexander's Study   13
1.5 Colonial and Post-Colonial Criminology: Tatum's Theoretical Framework   16
1.6 'Blacks Don't Have Culture': Pryce's Participant Observation in Bristol   18
1.7 De-Essentialising and De-Pathologising: Benson vs Werbner   21
1.8 The Structural Bias: Deprivationism According to Ballard   23
1.9 Conclusion: Towards a 'Minority Criminology'   24

2. Theoretical and Methodological Solutions to the 'Race and Crime' Taboo   27
2.1 Criminality as a Migration Stage: Mawby and Batta   28
2.2 Bringing Religion into the Picture: Macey's Bold Attempt   30
2.3 Islam and its 'Betrayal': Quraishi's Transnational Study   32
2.4 The Anthropological Gaze: Lien's Ethnography of Deviance   33

2.5 Masculinities and Identity: Webster and Imtiaz	35
2.6 Attachment and Commitment to the Community: Wardak's Approach	37
2.7 Ethnographic Information as a Working Whole: the 'Emic' Approach	38
2.8 Access and Multi-sited Fieldwork as the Key to the 'Working Whole'	40
2.9 The Sampling and Labelling of Sub-groups	42
2.10 Breaking the Taboo through Methodology: Criminology, Minority Perspectives and Anthropology	45

3. Bradford as a Case Study — 47

3.1 A 'BrAsian' City	48
3.2 Ethnic Disadvantage	50
3.3 The Migration History	52
3.4 Ethnic Resources and Networks: the Peculiarities of the *Biraderi* System	57
3.5 'From Textile Mills to Taxi Ranks' (Kalra 2000)	62
3.6 Assertiveness, Self-defence and Political Struggles in the 1980s	64
3.7 The Rushdie Affair and Vigilantism	65
3.8 The Climax of Tension: 2001	67
3.9 Local and Global: Bradford Post-9/11	70
3.10 A Community caught between *Biraderi* and the *Umma*?	71

4. Criminological Discourses: Labelling — 74

4.1 Crime in the Community: an Endemic Problem?	75
4.2 The Labelling Process: Crime within and without the Community	77
4.3 Many Problems, One Name: Drugs in the Community	80
4.4 Drug-dealing, Drug-taking and the Chain of Criminal Activities	81
4.5 'Poisoning the Community'	85
4.6 Purity and Contamination: *Haram*, *Halal* and *Makkru*	88
4.7 Crime as a Threat to Community Stability	91

5. Criminological Discourses: Aetiologies of Crime — 95

5.1 The Asian Economic Niche	96
5.2 Deprivation, Discrimination and Unemployment	98
5.3 'The Lure of Big Things': Strain Theory	102

5.4 Demography and Education	104
5.5 The Interplay of Ethnic Resources and Networks: the 'Out of Place Culture'	106
5.6 The Erosion of Ethnic Networks: the Generation Gap, Vertical and Horizontal Ties, and *Khidmat*	108
5.7 The Risks of Excessive Bonding and *Biraderism*	112
5.8 Competing Sources: Culture, Islam and the West	115
5.9 Conclusion: Theories of Community Criminologies	120
6. Criminological Discourses: Gender and Deviance	**124**
6.1 Pathologising Young Men: Subcultural Studies in the British Pakistani Context	125
6.2 'Double Consciousness' or 'Torn between Two Cultures'?	130
6.3 Women and Deviance: Unveiling the Problem	132
6.4 Victimhood, Agency and Double Deviance	134
6.5 Women as an Indicator of the Level of Deviance in the Community	137
6.6 Rude Boys' Lifestyles: Appearances, Locations and 'Sharifisation'	138
6.7 From Self Defence to Heroes: the Growth of a 'Mafia Mentality'	144
6.8 Conclusion: Young People and Moral Panic	147
7. Criminological Discourses: Informal Social Control	**150**
7.1 Social Control through the Family: Prevention for Girls, Retrieval for Boys	151
7.2 Social Control through the Family: Three Case Studies of Parental Strategies	154
7.3 The Mother's Roles	160
7.4 'Home-made Rehabilitation': 'Village Rehab' and the 'Marriage Cure'	162
7.5 Means of Social Control: Gossip and Scandal	165
7.6 Importing a Communal System of Social Control	168
7.7 Between Culture and Religion: Taweez	172
7.8 Religion as a Protective Factor	174
7.9 Purification, Reintegration and 'Reconversions'	175
7.10 Popular Preaching: Sheikh Ahmed Ali – a Case Study	180
7.11 Conclusion: Informal Control as a Partial Solution	182
8. Criminological Discourses: Formal Social Control	**184**

8.1 Mosques: Caught between the Local and the Global	185
8.2 Madrassas and the Understanding of Islam	190
8.3 Mosques as Community Centres	192
8.4 Media	194
8.5 Local Institutions	196
8.6 Schools	198
8.7 Prisons	200
8.8 Policing	202
8.9 Conclusion: Complementarity of Formal and Informal Social Control	205
9. The Politics of Criminology: from *Biraderi* to Community	**207**
9.1 Breaking the Taboo, through Empirical Considerations beyond Anti-Essentialism	208
9.2 Notes for Researchers and Funding Bodies about Breaking the Taboo of Race and Crime	212
9.3 A 'Community Criminology'	213
Notes	219
Bibliography	227
Glossary	246
Index	251

LIST OF TABLES

Table 3.1: Asian Population in Bradford, 1961–2001   50

Table 5.2: Theories of Community Criminologies   122

Table 6.1: Comparison of British Pakistani Male Sub-Cultural Models 128

ACKNOWLEDGEMENTS

I strongly believe that no work can be produced by one's own effort alone, and this work is no exception. However, it is impossible to thank all the people who have helped me in so many different ways. The ones who made this project possible, the research participants, are too many to be individually mentioned, but my thanks go to them all. Amongst my rich 'social capital', first of all I am indebted to the City of Bradford, which has not only proved to be a fruitful research ground but has become something of a home to me too. Its intricate dynamics of love and the controlling grip which affects whoever decides to enter it make it so difficult to leave.

I was able to write this thesis thanks to a University of Leeds scholarship, something that I would have never been awarded in my home country. Malcolm Harrison was an exemplary supervisor, continuously pushed me to do better and kept mentoring me in spheres of life that go much beyond academia. I wish one day I can give to my students how much he gave me.

Teela Sanders and Virinder Kalra, respectively my internal and external PhD examiners, contributed to the writing of the book with their very helpful comments, and took time out of their busy schedules to read this work a second time in the form of a book draft.

I must acknowledge the contribution to my intellectual development from 'The Muslims in Britain Research Network' (in particular Sean McLoughlin and Philip Lewis) and the 'Pakistan Workshop' (in particular Pnina Werbner and Stephen Lyon).

In the field, I firmly believe that Arif Mehmood made all the difference to my contacts and my way of dealing with distressing events. This book would have never come out had I not met Arif.

I have to thank my current employer, the Lahore University of Management Sciences, for encouraging me to publish and giving me funding for proofreading. During the writing-up stages I managed to keep (relatively) sane thanks to my colleagues and friends Sadaf Ahmad and Ali Khan; their affection and their humour always make everything bearable and they are one of the best 'things' that ever happened to me. My thanks must also go to Dr. Steven Gardiner and Nida Haseeb Khan who gave me much needed help with practical stuff.

INTRODUCTION

This book is about men, women, the young, the old, those who have 'made it' and those who are 'underdogs'. It is not about each single one of them, but about all of them and how their interaction makes what we know as 'British Pakistanis'. If qualitative anthropological research cannot cover large numbers—and has never seen the scope of such a numerical endeavour—on the other hand it is the duty of an anthropologist to try to be in touch with as many components as possible from the community under scrutiny, and to make sense of that working whole.

This book is based on research conducted in Bradford between 2003 and 2006. Bradford has long been considered the thermometer and the thermostat of Muslim political issues in Britain: the thermometer, because what happens in Bradford is widely considered a reliable symptom of what is or will soon be affecting the rest of the Muslim world (see for example the Rushdie affair, exposed in Bradford before it was known about in Iran, and the 2001 riots anticipating, as a cause of distrust and prejudice, 11 September 2001); and a thermostat because the temperature of events in Bradford often sets the tone for policy makers in other parts of Britain (see for example the recommendations of the Ouseley Report in 2001).

Whether or not British Pakistanis can be considered as a relatively homogenous group, with more or less consolidated problems and objectives, is still debatable; the question will be tackled throughout this book. Whether they are in any way representative of what faces British Pakistanis in general is even more controversial. My belief, however, is that most recent writings on them have focused on one segment of this population at a time, thus avoiding issues of representations altogether. They have focused alternatively on young men, 'underdogs' or women, rarely on the well-to-do or the (at least at a local level) famous. This fragmented approach does not do justice to the social commentaries that British Pakistanis make about themselves and their localities, and does not record the discourses constructed through elders' experiences, challenged by the young and often resisted by alternative springing pockets of resistance to traditional community discourses such as the ones of Islamists or left-wing activists. These commentaries—here lies a surprise in this book—are often the result of the trickling down or trickling out of national or local-authority policies. Bradford Pakistanis are less angry, 'other' and disenfranchised than most of us would expect. All these voices contribute to the formation of discourses about community that are much more articulate that may appear at first glance. With a tradition still very much alive of passing knowledge on in an informal way through gossip and narration of events that have been heard as three, four or five removes, these informal social commentaries made in grocers' shops, outside mosques and on street corners have become the core of the book. The present research shows how these fine analyses emerged from the intertwining of inter-generational, formal and informal debates as they figure in the conversations of Pakistanis in Bradford.

One of the main intents behind the present research has been to give voice to these commentaries and to contextualise them in the history and the cultural and social capitals of the community. My desire to do so came about through a long relationship with Bradford, which started in the late 1990s, surviving the 2001 riots and all the local side-effects of terror and of the 'war on terror'. In the tense atmosphere surrounding British Pakistanis in the first decade of the new millennium, I was granted a PhD bursary from Leeds University to study crime in Bradford. My interest as an anthropologist, however, prevented me from producing a survey of the recorded problems affecting the city and analysing it from an established criminological, theoretical point of view. My aim was instead to engage with the insiders' informed account of the development of the problem across time, generation and gender and to collect the protagonists' discourses on the solutions they envisaged.

My hope is that I will be able to combine all these layers in a whole. At the moment, in fact, the vast amount of literature produced on British Pakistanis can be broadly divided into three fields: cultural, socio-economic and religious studies. However, rarely have these three fields been combined, and research has struggled to produce significant inputs for policy makers, at a time when moral panic about British Muslims is of growing concern. At the same time, an open criminological analysis that considers both cultural and socio-economic variables operating in British Muslim communities has been neglected, allegedly because of a taboo (discussed in Chapter One) connected to the likely charge of racism when studying crime and deviance in relation to one specific ethnic group. The underlying aim of the research as it unfolded related crime and deviance in this context to much more general topics discussed at a national level, including whether British Pakistanis are really insular, separate, angry, antagonistic and 'other'. This book therefore focuses on issues about criminality, but is grounded in diasporic studies and problems of citizenship and multiculturalism.

Another problem encountered is that there is a tendency to construct the British Pakistani community as pathological. Outside academia, racialisation of crime is very popular, with the media being concerned about relating crime, more or less subtly, to cultural specificities, not least by making headlines about the ethnic background of the criminals as well as about their crime. Inside academia, on the other hand, the taboo discussed in Chapter One on making connections between race and crime has meant that the knowledge held by minority ethnic groups has been overlooked. Cain (2000) has described this process as 'Occidentalist', referring to the practice of standardising certain Western criminological theories as though they were universals, in spite of the many cultural and social differences that must inform labelling and social control amongst non-Western societies.

Concerns about increasing public pathologisation and racialisation risk removing cultural analysis altogether, rather than reforming it in non-essentialist terms. All those who have tried to breach the taboo, especially in respect of Muslims, have failed, at least partially, to disseminate information on how specific cultural capital may potentially contribute to the solution of problems. Although there is a body of ethnographic studies related to crime amongst Muslims in Europe, this is unfortunately still far from giving a voice to insiders' theories of what is wrong, how it went wrong and what should be done (see Chapter Two). The main thrust of the research may be summarised as a concern to explore how far Bradford Pakistanis today might have rather distinctive outlooks and particular ways of living that might be regarded as generating their own community criminology, rather than one likely to be shared by the rest of British society. Behind this question there is by no means a belief that there is a unified Bradford Pakistani community that is homogenous in its way of life. Nor did the researcher place herself in a dual dimension such as either insider or outsider. The Indian anthropologist André Beteille, addressing the 2006 Association of Social Anthropologists (ASA) conference, invited his colleagues to reject dichotomies such as insider/outsider or we/other: within each group there is a wide range of points of view. It is in this belief that the present research is grounded: there are no homogenous communities, but there are common experiences that lead groups of people to be cohesive and find similar solutions to certain problems. In particular, in a diaspora, members of such groups continuously negotiate different influences in order to find the most adequate solutions to their problems.

This book is also an attempt to fill in the gap identified in criminology by Philips and Bowling in 2003. They argued that minority ethnic groups' knowledge of crime has been marginalised by the discipline in order to avoid sensitive discussions such as the one on the link between race and crime. This book tries to fill this empirical gap as far as British Pakistanis are concerned.

Through participant observation and 'reciprocal exposure' (Bolognani 2007b) this research has been able to relate changes in the conviction rate of Bradford Pakistanis, and to contextualise crime and deviance, in their migration and settlement history (see Chapter Three). If the first aim of the research was to investigate the relevance of a study of minority ethnic perceptions about crime, the second was to follow a set of methodological approaches that would allow the researcher to prioritise local grassroots' views rather than deductive theoretical accounts, and thus to analyse how practical concerns, cultural and religious beliefs and moral dilemmas play a part in the construction of the idea of crime.

For this reason the book will appear as a piece of work thick with dialogues and quotes from the field, to give maximum space to the way community members view and transmit their beliefs and mediate information about crime. Following the basic tenets of the Chicago School, the first to study crime in relation to community and cultures in the urban West, this book has an ecological approach. And while the epistemology refers to ecology, the ontology dictates that in the system of concentric rings which delineate their membership of groups, an ecological model of British Pakistanis includes their ethnic group, their city, their nation and the virtual global umbrella of the Muslim Umma. Individuals within those groups who commit crimes must be studied in a socialised context; when they break the law they are aware of doing so, and in fact of breaking one of the rules of 'their own' society.

In this research it has also emerged that the main preoccupations of the community under study are not necessarily those portrayed by institutions or the media. In Chapter Four we will see that there is a high degree of consistency in in relation to the labelling of crime, depending on the level that it is considered to affect the community. The interviewees were not concerned about possible future rioting, for instance, but were in some instances considering moving out of their areas because of the drug problems and the gun crime they often encountered, issues that have not been particularly highlighted by the media in relation to this ethnic group.

Once the book has established how the process of labelling works, it will move towards analysing the discourses that inform the aetiologies of crime. Chapter Five will discuss both the structural and the cultural variables that have been mentioned by interviewees as factors leading to the rise in crime over the last ten years. Very little has been written lately on the older generation, whether men or women, although the underlying assumption is that the cause of the younger generation's many problems may lie with their parents. The four main aetiologies reported to me during the research do blame the elders to an extent, but especially in relation to their parenting inadequacy at times of economic recession, which led them into 'family-unfriendly' occupations. What at least three aetiological discourses have in common ('out-of-place culture', 'erosion of ethnic networks' and '*biraderism*') is that they bear at their core the notion of community and how the sense of service to it has gone missing. These different discourses seem to add an important element to what will be discussed here as the core of community criminologies: the threat to the community itself. This element is the consideration of a split between *biraderi* (extended family) and community, where families appear no longer necessary to the stable functioning of the community, and the exclusiveness of intra-familial bonding may jeopardise collectivity. Families' strong ties—'a combination of the amount of time, intimacy and reciprocal services' (Granovetter 1973:1361)—and once perceived as the pillar of internal cohesion may now be an agent of fragmentation wherever the particular interests of a family are in conflict with the common good of the community.

Chapter Six will attempt to study gender and gendered constructions of deviance in relation to the community context. The limelight recently endured more than enjoyed by British Pakistanis has significantly cut out women, for instance. While an increasing number of publications look in detail at the activities of young British Pakistani men in terms of employment (or crime), education (or underachievement) and religion (or extremism), only a little has been written that systematically considers them in relation to their communities, and how their communities interact with them. Even less has been written about their relations with young women. Young women have often been portrayed as passive victims of perverse family systems. The first consequence of this approach is that tackling one gender and age group at a time assumes that the aetiology of whatever social condition we are discussing does not involve the family structure so embedded in the Pakistani heritage, especially in that of the Pakistani Kashmiri. With the assumption that British Pakistanis are problematic in terms of community cohesion (given the recent experience with rioting in the northern towns), young men are often studied separately from their family and from their communities. If reports are accurate (but statistics are biased by data-collection methods, and it is a well known fact that stop-and-search policies and investigations are more likely to be triggered against the young and the male rather than the old and the female) in claiming that young males are the main perpetrators of crime both within their ethnic boundaries and the larger community, then this book is constructed around the belief that the interaction of the perpetrators with their environment is crucial. Chapters Seven and Eight, however, will argue that in terms of social control, the environment relevant to the process of change is not only the ethnic one. British Pakistanis have a sense of community that incorporates local institutions as main players in their localities. Far from being completely disenfranchised and 'other', they engage with mainstream criminological and policy discourses in a way that might well be considered a kind of reflection representative of the position of their diaspora: the community for them does not only include their traditional structures but all the intra-communal and inter-communal relations that are meaningful to them, both as resources and constraints; this is illustrated in Chapter Nine.

1
THE TABOO OF CRIMINOLOGICAL RESEARCH AMONGST MINORITY ETHNIC GROUPS

[There is] a need to *reconcile* criminological data with the 'lived experiences' and subjectivities of minorities. . . . Reconciling these conflicting perspectives can be partially achieved through *both* improvements in the collection, analysis, interpretation and dissemination of such criminological data *and* by making central to our understanding the knowledges provided by minority communities themselves. This, however, does not go far enough. There must be also a critical deconstruction of the process of knowledge production about minorities . . . (Phillips and Bowling 2003:270)

The link between race and crime can be said to have been a recurrent feature of criminological studies. Social scientists in different times have wondered whether there is a special connection between belonging to a group and involvement in deviant behaviour (Russell 1992:669; Gabbidon and Taylor Greene 2005:50). For example, Cesare Lombroso, founder of the school of Positivist Criminology, was persuaded that organised crime in post-unified Italy had to do both with biology and with the legacy of the Oriental conquerors in Southern Italy.

While the original positivists mainly focused on the relation between a group and its members' tendency to break laws, a growing number of scholars nowadays would take into consideration both victims and perpetrators' ethnic background as significant in the study of the dynamics of crime and its prosecution. Race, culture and ethnicity have in fact emerged as a very important variable in the investigation and prosecution process (see for example Shallice and Gordon 1990). This book aims to go further, as the research on which it is based investigates how culture influences not only victimisation and the criminal justice processes, but also crime-labelling and informal social control. This chapter's scope, in particular, is to argue that involving cultural variables in the study of crime is not a racist practice, but instead consists of re-affirming the importance of diversity in understanding and controlling the community that each and every human society has established over its history.

The first part of this chapter will discuss the early days of the study of race and crime in the light of both biological and cultural studies. We will then consider how in the 1980s many British criminologists started looking at the debate mainly from the point of view of fair treatment for minorities in the criminal justice system. It will be argued that by focusing policy on urgent needs—made more cogent by events such as the Brixton riots—dealing with the cultural specificities of ethnic minorities slowly became a taboo (cf. also Russell 1992; Phillips and Bowling 2002). Priority was given instead to studies that focused on discrimination, both in policing and sentencing, rather than to the study of what minorities had to say about crime in their neighbourhoods. Here it will be argued that the fear of essentialising minority ethnic groups in relation to crime by including cultural analysis made room for mostly structural accounts in which the agents' point of view was neglected (Phillips and Bowling 2003), as shown by a selection of works that represent different perspectives on the subject (Alexander 2000; Tatum 2000; Pryce 1979, 1986). By comparing these studies with classic debates in the field of ethnic studies in general (Benson 1996; Werbner 1996), this chapter will legitimise the practice of incorporating (cultural) knowledge 'by minority ethnic groups' (Phillips and Bowling 2003:270, my emphasis) as an important step both for criminological and diaspora studies.

1.1 The Origins of Interest in Race and Crime
One of the first scholars to make a clear and systematic analysis of the link between race and crime was Cesare Lombroso (Gabbidon and Taylor Greene 2005:50; Gibson 2002:99; Phillips and Bowling 2002:580).

Lombroso's positivistic theory is interesting as a key study, presenting as it does certain human physical features as indicators of a predisposition to crime. According to racial paradigms, therefore, certain physical features would automatically be the signs of a predisposition to deviance (Gabbidon and Taylor Greene 2005:50). These biological accounts, however, were also supported by 'ethnical' elements (ibid) such as the belief that African or Oriental influences had impacted on brigands' criminal behaviour in Southern Italy. Although Lombroso was mainly interested in the study of race, as shown in his essay *White Man and Coloured Man* (1871, cited in Gibson 2002), there was also room in his writings for speculations on social environment and its impact on the criminal mind (Gibson 2002:98). These nuances were overlooked when Lombroso's work was exported to the Anglo-Saxon world (ibid:249; Gabbidon and Taylor Greene 2005:58). Lombroso's theories were used to support social Darwinism (Gibson 2002:98) and therefore after the Second World War were widely dismissed as racist and ideologically dangerous. Assumptions about eugenics were at that time still visible in some studies of deviance, but overt reference to Lombroso was avoided (Wootton 1959:45). In America, however, exponents of right realist criminology, Wilson and Herrnstein, published a book in 1985 that appeared to revive some of Lombroso's attitudes towards the anthropological study of criminals. Their *Crime as Human Nature* argues that some biological differences must be taken into account when studying crime in different ethnic groups (Gabbidon and Taylor Greene 2005:59). For example, it is argued that a general higher muscularity amongst black men could be one of the factors that lead to a higher number of offences if compared to white men's. Although Wilson and Herrnstein openly refer to Lombroso (1985:75) and look at the aetiology of crime also in terms of genetics (ibid:90) and factors such as IQ, it would be unfair to summarise their work only in these terms. In *Crime as Human Nature* factors such as inadequate socialisation (ibid:470), sub-cultural deviance (ibid), ecology (ibid:289), attachment (ibid:218) and deprivation (ibid:467) appear as some of the causes of crime. It is interesting, however, to see that some of Lombroso's positivistic approaches to the study of crime survive today. Overall, although some of the biological theories may survive—see for example theories about women committing crime at certain stages of their menstrual cycle (d'Orban 1991)—nowadays the positivistic approach seems to be mostly accompanied by other sociological or psychological explanations, especially, as in the case of Winston and Herrnstein, when biology is connected to race. While biological or positivistic criminology was widely dismissed after the Second World War because of its connection with eugenics (ibid:250), the study of the link between groups as cultural (rather than biological) units and their relation to crime may at first sight may appear less contentious. However, this can turn out to be equally problematic, as shown by the critique of Malinowski's work.

1.2 Crime and Culture

One of Malinowski's studies, published in 1926, dealt with the question of crime and its link to different groups from a specific point of view: the socio-cultural. In *Crime and Custom in Savage Society*, Malinowski described norms and their violation in the Trobriand Islands. In this work, adherence to norms and labelling processes was seen as strictly connected to what he called the 'civic law' of the islands (ibid:38). The possibility of committing a crime was not seen either as the product of biological predetermination or as structural compulsion; rather, the chances of an individual deviating from positive norms were seen in terms of a cultural paradigm. This bore a double significance: first, the rational choice behind an action would be informed by the surrounding cultural context; secondly, deviance might be only labelled as such according to a specific customary law. According to Malinowski, therefore, crime and deviance could only be studied by setting their definition and the consequential norms in a cultural context. The study of the Trobriands, however, was that of a bounded community that appeared to Malinowski as extremely homogenous. In his view, 'the Melanesian' (Malinowski 1926:64, my emphasis) followed the rules of nature as the laws to be respected. The innovation in Malinowski's study seems to lie in the critique of 'modern anthropology' and its belief that 'sheer inertia' constrained 'the savage' to exert civic law (ibid:63), while ignoring social arrangements and psychological motives. Such an approach was considered a victim of 'the mere glamour of tradition' (ibid:65), alluring to some anthropologists. However, Malinowski was not advocating more attention to individual agency; although personal choices were considered, they were seen as subject to one supreme rule: reciprocity (ibid). Networks of obligations and mutual service appear in this text as the single and all-encompassing rule amongst Trobriandeses. Their behaviour and their law infringement were therefore to be understood through the parameters of the rule of reciprocity, and the Trobriandeses were considered to relate to crime and punishment in a way that was essential for a part of their cultural identity.

This poses a dilemma: if we deny Lombroso's biological connection between certain (racial) groups and crime, the question of whether some cultures are likely to be more violent than others will still be unanswered. At the same time, however, if we agree with Malinowski and think that the particular structure of a group's culture regulates social control, we may still think that some groups, because of their culture, are more prone to break or construct some rules than others.

Melossi (2000:296) argues that both approaches may be reduced to Lombroso's positivism. The only difference would be that the latter is based on group culture, rather than somatic traits. Melossi's argument reproduces in criminology the discussion that has taken place elsewhere in the social sciences about 'cultural racism'. Some have in fact argued that in the last 30 years racist ideologies have abandoned the emphasis on 'immutable biological differences' and transferred their attention from 'pigmentation to culture' (Back 1996:9). This statement may shed some light on the taboo that some have observed in criminological studies over considering race as a variable (Russell 1992:669; Phillips and Bowling 2003:271): by considering the specific link (albeit cultural and not biological) between a group and crime there may be a danger of constructing some groups as prone to deviance. In 1992 Russell argued that there was as much need for a 'black criminology' as there had been for a feminist one. Although Russell acknowledged the emancipatory and positive developments of criminology towards minority ethnic groups (for example in the study of discrimination), on the other hand she argued that the picture was always incomplete. For example, racial identity[1] was still confused with ethnic, and there was a lack of social-ecological sensitivity that took into account ethnic diversity (ibid:671).

Even the inclusion of a plethora of variables in criminological studies on minority ethnic groups, argued Russell, such as age, gender, socio-economic status and employment status did not consider ethnic background adequately (ibid:673). In 2003, Phillips and Bowling were still manifesting the same concerns, proving with their writing that criminological theory was much ahead of its empirical counterpart, still uncomfortable with tackling ethnicity in full. They argued that empirical criminology had primarily focused on issues of discrimination against minority groups, based on statistics, while abandoning the opportunity of dealing with their agency; 'this historical contextualization of minority experiences has a direct bearing on our understanding of victimization, offending and criminal justice in the contemporary period' (Phillips and Bowling 2003:278). Recently Garland et al. (2006) have argued that not investigating ethnic variables may be a result of taking the 'white condition as normal' (ibid:423) and Cain (2000) denounced the occidentalist biases of criminology after a lecturing experience at the University of the West Indies in Trinidad.

1.3 Race and Crime in Britain: Discrimination, Policing and the Criminal Justice System

In Britain, by avoiding drawing any link between race, ethnicity and crime (Phillips and Bowling 2003:270), criminologists have often focused on discrimination towards minority ethnic groups in policing and in the criminal justice system.

Phillips and Bowling (2002:583) describe such developments by analysing the historical context of the 1960s. Enoch Powell and other MPs contributed towards increasing the moral panic that White British media were developing against 'coloured immigrants'. When Margaret Thatcher was elected in 1979 her government sympathised with these fears, and at the same time started her tough campaign against crime. In this tense climate, disorder occurred, in Bristol (1980) and Brixton (1981). These events were classed as somehow 'not English', as aberrations in the national context (Rowe 1998:1; McGhee 2005:15). McGhee (2005:22) argues that, while public opinion was reinforcing the widespread idea of a connection between Afro-Caribbeans and crime, the Scarman Enquiry and its report slightly changed these parameters: Afro-Caribbeans were not seen as inherently destabilising, but as destabilising in the light of the history of their settlement, allegedly a switch from biological to historical or cultural racism. According to McGhee, Scarman registered the experience of oppressive policing that Afro-Caribbeans had encountered thus far, and highlighted the level of social and economic exclusion in the areas where many minority ethnic groups lived. However, in spite of the general praise for the report's efforts in mentioning over-policing and police under-protection in respect of Afro-Caribbeans (see for example Phillips and Bowling 2002), McGhee argues that Scarman's report was still constructing race rather than racism as a social problem (2005:16).

At present, British data (Kalra 2003:142) show that some minority ethnic groups are over-represented in prison. Whether this is caused by over-policing of certain groups or over-offending due to structural constraints is at the centre of the debate (Phillips and Bowling 2002:579). According to some commentators (Phillips and Bowling 2003:270; Chakraborti et al. 2004), what seems to be missing in most literature, however, is knowledge held *by* minorities.

In the growing interest in the race and crime debate in the 1980s, there is at least a study showing how race can be very meaningful in the understanding of crime. Secret and Johnson's provocative American study in 1989 hypothesised how race, and not other variables such as socio-economic background, influenced attitudes towards crime control. Their conclusion was that race did influence those attitudes because different groups had developed different attitudes towards the police depending on how they had been treated in the past. Race was therefore an important element of studies in criminality, as the perceived background of individuals deeply affected their chances, rights, interactions and consequential patterns of behaviour, and the construction of the criminal justice system. At the same time, Secret and Johnson argued that whenever the police had a good general awareness about a certain group, relations between them and such a group had more chances of being positive.

In the following pages we will present three different approaches to the study of race and crime, and work towards a conclusion that will illustrate their connection to wider debates about the study of ethnicities.

1.4 Taking Culture out of the Picture: Alexander's Study

Alexander's *The Asian Gang* is an ethnographic study of young Bengali men in South London. It reflects on the complexities and dangers of what Alexander fears are all-encompassing notions of culture and ethnicity in relation to urban tension, violence and deviance. Here, any study that tries to link race and crime is seen as a pathologising one. For this reason, rather than studying the 'gang', Alexander argues that such definition is a media construction coming as much from the *Daily Mail* as from the *Guardian* (Alexander 2000:5). The author's aim is to bring individual stories into the academic gaze and to de-construct what she calls 'the "othering" process' in a way that has been repeated in other studies on Muslim men (Archer 2001, 2003). According to Alexander, in media accounts about episodes of violence affecting young Bengali men, both as victims and as perpetrators, race is automatically seen as negative; if a group of friends have a fight and they all belong to the same 'race', they become a gang.

> The spectre of 'race' with its implications of absolute and hostile difference, conflict and 'nihilistic . . . violence' is left to speak for itself—at once cause, effect and justification. (Alexander 2000:4)[2]

Here, 'race' seems to blur with 'ethnicity', as it refers to cultural dynamics as well as to bodily or biological features. Individual reasons and choices fade into the background because ethnic origin radicalises any behaviour (ibid:102): if more than two men involved in violence are of the same origin they are automatically described as a gang. This is one of the crucial points of Alexander's critique of representations of young Asian men: racialisation can hide other important variables such as masculinity, peer group (friendship) or individual histories. In retrospect, Alexander defines the inclusion of these multiple factors as the key characteristics for a new generation of ethnographers with 'fragmented lenses' (2006:402). The concern to include those variables is shared also by those who claim there is a need to open up the race and crime debate. For example, Phillips and Bowling agree that focusing on ethnicity may obscure other important factors, such as gender, class, sexuality and religion (Phillips and Bowling 2003:272).

Alexander's concerns about narratives which racialise the gang, popular in the media (2000:5), appear to be reflected in the fieldwork findings on which the present study is based. However, in the attempt to fill the gap between ethnicity and criminality, it can be argued that the over-estimation of such concerns may contribute to the formulation of the taboo mentioned by Phillips and Bowling (2002:271). If compared to the studies reviewed here and in the following chapter, Alexander's is the one that most strongly points to the dangers of explaining patterns of deviance by incorporating race and culture in the analysis. What is called the 'narrative' of Alexander's study—instead of a theoretical framework (2000:xv)—is based on observing processes of including or excluding family and peer groups, and the dynamics of masculinity and age. According to Alexander, these are the dimensions that are forgotten by the 'old ethnicity approach' (ibid:240, referring for example to Shaw's seminal 1988 study of Pakistanis in Oxford). On the other hand, masculinity, adolescence and peer groups are the dimensions that are more likely to work towards the construction of Asian youth as 'folk devils' (ibid). While criminological studies that focus on race are blamed for the racialisation of the topic, the sociologists who have tried to include masculinity and age as relevant variables end up, according to Alexander, constructing even more pathological images (ibid:20). Combining race and culture with masculinity and age (thus young Bengali men = Asian gang) is seen by Alexander as the peak of the racialisation process, leading to widespread moral panic (ibid). Goodey's (1999) and Macey's innovation (1999, see following chapter) of bringing youth into the picture of ethnic studies is blamed for maintaining a 'cultural twist' (Alexander 2000:18). Masculinity and age would be subjected to essentialist and hegemonic views on Asian young men: 'Asian youth is in trouble and out of control' (ibid).

Alexander's only possible solution seems to be to take culture out of the picture altogether. The actions of young Bengali men in South London should thus be seen in a cultural vacuum. It seems that in the deconstruction of the Asian gang, family, peer groups, masculinity and age are seen as the only significant layers of the complex identity of individuals, and all these variables are independent of the group's culture and traditions. This is an attempt to create a space in which commonality between individuals, and not their difference from the majority, is important.

Much of Alexander's critique is centred on the increasing attention given by the media to Muslim communities. However, not only the media are caught in the accusation, but the whole of the 'race relations industry', with anthropologists as its allies. Alexander argues that only after the Salman Rushdie affair and the first Gulf War did Asians become a heterogeneous fragmented front and 'problem youth' emerge (Alexander 2000:6; see also Modood 1992; Samad 1996). These two main events are seen as the milestones of the critique of the Asian 'culture-rich/culture-bound' nature that contributed to 'othering' individuals of such backgrounds (Alexander 2000:13). After the 1995 riots in Bradford, furthermore, Asian Muslims' culture has been seen as *backward* in opposition to *modern* British culture (ibid:10). If the assumption is that a culture is backward, studies thus generated may result in being patronising and in pathologising. The solution would therefore be:

> to argue for a more nuanced, local and historically situated account of identity formation, which encapsulates often contradictory processes of continuity and change, constraint and agency, solidarity and diffusion, representation and re-imagination. (Alexander 2000:23)

Whether the race relations industry and 'accomplice' anthropologists have really neglected change and agency will be discussed later. Here, it is important instead to highlight that according to Alexander contextualisation in time and space must be considered. In the following chapter, in fact, it will be explained that the Bradford context and the post-9/11 era impacted on this study in terms of motivation, methods and findings. According to Alexander, however, basing an analysis on a 'community', whatever meaning we might attribute to such an abused word, means essentialising a group (ibid:13)[3]. Alexander's arguments are therefore two: the main one is that including race and ethnicity in the study of deviance is necessarily a pathologising process; the second is that grounding research in a 'community' is an arbitrary process that refers to outsiders' construction of such an entity. Alexander therefore appears as a strong supporter of maintaining the taboo of race/ethnicity and crime because such a link would not enlighten any study but only contribute to the pathologisation of a group.

However, some of the statements in the second half of *The Asian Gang* seem to contradict the alleged solution of leaving race/ethnicity out of the study of deviance. For example, it is argued that the deep respect for one's family and community (*sic*) is one of the main tenets of young Bengali men in South London (Alexander 2000:129). Getting to know each other through one's family status as portrayed by one's parents in relation to the background in Bangladesh is also considered important (ibid). Ethnicity is also described as one of the axes of alliance for the making of peer groups, as much as age, gender, territory, history, geography and personality (ibid:166). Ultimately, culture seems to make its way into *The Asian Gang*. Even more clearly:

There is a need to reassert the constitutive nature of structure in the formation of cultural identities, the play of power and history, but also to recognize the only partial circumscription of marginal identities, the potential for disruption and the imagination of 'Other' sensibilities and alliances . . . Recognising the complex and shifting nature of identity also demands the recognition of solidarity and belonging; not the stasis of stagnant absolutes but the necessary emotional touchstone of family, friends and community. (Alexander 2000:248)

Alexander seems to recognise that 'cultural identities', 'belonging' and 'community' are 'necessary emotional touchstones'. Her critique is of 'the stasis of stagnant absolutes' that seems to be conveyed by whoever deals with collective forms of identity. Her protest against the rise of a media and public pathologisation of young Asian men risks removing cultural analysis altogether, rather than reforming it in non-essentialist terms. Alexander, however, analyses the relation between race and crime as it is presented in the media and by sociologists: in a problem-orientated way. She is not tempted to ask whether ethnicity may be a potential resource for the fight against crime. This question does not seem to be raised because of the taboo mentioned by Phillips and Bowling (2003) about including ethnicity amongst the variables to consider in the study of crime.

However, in addition to the effort of including individuals with their personal stories under the academic gaze, there is another merit of Alexander's work: her choice of de-pathologising masculinity and age and considering them as part of the complex set of variables that may influence one's behaviour. This is not what happens with Tatum's grand theory, which may be considered a step backwards in the discussion of ethnicity and crime.

1.5 Colonial and Post-Colonial Criminology: Tatum's Theoretical Framework

In Tatum's *Crime, Violence and Minority Youth* (2000) the main focus is on acknowledging the apparent failure of mainstream structural perspectives in explaining high crime-rates amongst minority ethnic youth in America (Tatum 2000:xi). By 'mainstream structural perspectives', Tatum means both 'strain theories' emerging from Durkheimian traditions—anomie, opportunity theories and the theory of delinquent subcultures (ibid:3)—and the 'colonial model' (ibid).

By 'colonial model' Tatum indicates a framework that privileges class over race, which can be traced back to Fanon (Tatum 2000:6). In colonial theories, the alienation from one's cultural capital (whatever it is) and from political praxis are considered paramount in explaining social mechanisms of exclusion and oppression. In the following section we will see how Pryce's idea of loss of cultural capital and of sectarianism in Jamaican churches in Bristol might be seen as part of such a colonial model.

In the colonial model, some youths resist the dominant culture of 'internal colonies' (i.e. colonies within the boundaries of the nation) (Tatum 2000:7). Their resistance is a reaction to oppression, and the colonial model recognises that race and racism play an important role in the history of internal colonies by examining alienation and frustration (ibid:13). In the economy of the present chapter, albeit Tatum does not refer to it in these terms, an analysis that starts from the relation of a subject to the oppressors rather than from the subject as an autonomous being becomes very important for the discussion of the role of the 'race relations industry' in studying minority ethnic groups (see below). Modood has expressed a relevant concern very assertively:

> Most ordinary people wish to be defined in terms of a historically received identity . . . they wish to be known for what they are, not for what others find problematic about them. (1988:398)

> Muslims are wiser here than anti-racists: in locating oneself in a hostile society one must begin with one's mode of being [ethnicity] not one's mode of oppression [race] for one's strength flows from one's mode of being. (1990a:92)

According to Tatum (2000:16), the major faults of colonial theory are not grounded in the initial standpoint, as may be Modood's view, but in three other arguments:
- it does not consider multiple alienations;
- it does not analyse differential responses to oppression; and
- it does not account for class variables in the impact of racism.

The criminological neo-colonial model coined by Tatum, therefore, aims at including such reflections. For example, alienation is investigated through a multiple model based on 'self-alienation', 'alienation from the racial or social group', 'alienation from the general other' and cultural alienation (ibid:56). It is important to notice how alienation itself, and not one's very culture, is the most significant aspect of this model applicable to any minority ethnic group. Again, cultural systems are pushed aside to make space for structural ones.

One of the main points of Tatum's neo-colonial theory is that deviance studies should focus on differential responses to oppression, especially through social support systems (ibid:69). Considering class variables in the impact of racism on constrained choice related to committing crime, on the other hand, implies that one's class aspirations might dictate the perception of discrimination and oppression (ibid:87).

According to Tatum and the model tested through her quantitative survey, race, social class and their interaction with structural and perceived oppression are the main variables that should help in successfully investigating the relation between crime and minority ethnic groups (2000:27). These, however, cannot be enough if they are not paired with an analysis of the availability of specific ethnic social support systems (ibid). Here we find a contradiction similar to Alexander's: by moving (a specific) culture out of the academic gaze, it is possible to analyse 'the family forms that have developed and their impact on perceptual, affective, and behavioural adaptations of its members' (ibid:23). The unchallenged consequential assumption, then, seems to be that families and social support systems exist in a cultural vacuum and that they owe more to economic and racial constraints rather than to a resourceful deployment of heritages. However, Tatum herself argues that they are not: black families have in fact 'generally been regarded as deviant or pathological because they differ from the family structure of Whites' (ibid).

Again, even in Tatum's post-colonial theory, culture cannot be avoided, in spite of the struggles of her grand theory. The difference with Alexander's, however, is that in this example of neo-colonial theory a proper analysis of multiple variables, including age and gender, seems to be neglected. A combination of neo-colonial theory with multiple variables can however be found in a British monograph (Pryce 1979).

1.6 'Blacks Don't Have Culture': Pryce's Participant Observation in Bristol

Pryce's 1979 study of West Indian lifestyles in Bristol could be considered a British example of Tatum's neo-colonial model, although the data are collected through qualitative methods such as participant observation, and deviance is only one of the aspects investigated.

The basis of Pryce's monograph *Endless Pressure* is the belief that history has had a very important role in shaping West Indians' lifestyles. He originates six typologies of men's lifestyles that have probably inspired much later work on male youth identities (see Chapter Six). According to these typologies, West Indians in Bristol can be mainly grouped under two categories: 'stable law-abiding' and 'expressive-disreputable' (those who work and those who hustle, Pryce 1979/1986:xii). Other sub-categories are 'hustlers', 'teenyboppers', 'proletarian respectables', 'saints', 'mainliners' and 'in-betweeners' (ibid). Much criticism of *Endless Pressure* came, after its publication, from black radicals. They argued that Pryce's two main typologies were practically saying that some blacks were merely criminals instead of 'closet politicos' (ibid:16).

The study mainly analyses the causes of estrangement from legal work. All social tensions in Pryce (even the ones between West Indian men and women) are analysed principally in terms of exploitation and class. However, the analysis is not based on an all-encompassing vision of class overlapping race; rather, as argued by Tatum in terms of a neo-colonial approach, a range of resistance strategies to oppression, based on different class backgrounds, are revealed.

In the discussion of the taboo of race/ethnicity and crime it is very interesting to see how Pryce's neo-colonial approach deals with culture. It may be worth pointing out here that Pryce's work is based on participant observation, but in spite of the popularity of this method in anthropology, he is a sociologist. The responsibility for a certain discourse around culture is placed by Benson on anthropology (see below), but here we have an example of how a sociologist may be accused of a similar fault. In a section titled 'Culture, poverty and the West Indian family', Pryce argues that some of the problems of the sub-category labelled as 'teenyboppers' have to do with the traditional family system back home:

> The aetiology of the teenybopper problem extends back to the peculiarities of family life in the West Indies, which in turn owe their origin to practices evolved under conditions of slavery and colonialism and to macro-structural patterns of underdevelopment as reflected in the sub-standard educational facilities of the masses. (1979/1986:108)

According to Pryce, therefore, the 'peculiarities of family life' are such because of the structural and historical constraints that have affected life in the West Indies. An anti-essentialist cultural approach might agree with this statement (cf. Werbner 1996), but in *Endless Pressure* culture is taken out of the picture again, at least as far as West Indians are concerned:

> In England, some black youths (like teenyboppers) do not succeed in the struggle for survival because of *the failure of West Indians in general to develop a distinctive culture of their own* that is strong enough to counteract the disorienting effects of poverty and the frustrations of

social rejection in a white-dominated society like Britain. This is a predicament which contrasts sharply with the situation of *Indian and Pakistani youths who tend to have a very strong sense of identity based on distinctive language, a distinctive religion in a highly normative family system*. The net effect on the West Indian young of the absence of a rooted sense of identity, capable of giving guidance and direction in times of crisis, is psychic and cultural confusion and lack of confidence in coping with the stress of racial rejection. (1979/1986:112, my emphasis)

It is almost as if Pryce gives cause to Benson's famously provocative statement: 'Asians have culture, West Indians have problems' (Benson 1996:47). A very clear example of this approach is to be found when the 'subalternity' of women is discussed by drawing on the story of Bang-Belly and his girlfriend Pamela. Pamela is not jealous of the white prostitutes' Bang-Belly pimps, but would be if they were 'coloured' (*sic*) (Pryce 1979/1986:80). Here this tension is seen in terms of exploitation and class, and not much in terms of beliefs, aspirations, ideals and cultural capital—that would be impossible, as the author argues that Bristol West Indians lack these attributes (ibid:112). They appear not to have a culture strong enough to be used as a resource, a very essentialist statement:

[This] clearly reveals the weaknesses of West Indian family life and demonstrates vividly how, in the resultant collapse, it is the young who invariably suffer. . . . West Indians still lack a self-contained folk culture and a tight communal form of group life. (1979/1986:119).

It is important to note how in all the three studies reviewed here family plays an important role, as in the present research (see Chapters Five and Seven). However, it is their problems and not their culture that make generalisations possible: 'the problems of West Indians in Britain are uniform enough to permit generalisation' (ibid:271).

The premises seem therefore to be consistent with a colonial model based on alienation from cultural capital and from political praxis. At the same time the acknowledgement of different class-based strategies to fight oppression and build alternative support systems—such as the ones of 'mainliners' (ibid:223)—are enough to inscribe Pryce's work in the neo-colonial framework as defined by Tatum.

The most controversial part of his work, however, appears to be the idea that an entire population has been deprived of a specific culture due to colonial oppression. A reverse essentialism of this kind (a celebration of culture-rich/culture-bound cultures in a post-colonial context) is the core of the contention discussed below.

1.7 De-Essentialising and De-Pathologising: Benson vs Werbner

Above we have seen how both Tatum and Alexander are critical of an approach explicitly drawing on cultures to develop an understanding of crime in certain groups. Alexander very openly criticises the 'race relations industry' and especially anthropologists for 'disguising [their] voice as the legitimate voice of the other' (Alexander 2000:225). In the late 1990s similar accusations grew to the point of accusing academics (and in particular anthropologists) of having started to support a second colonial indirect-rule system within the national borders:

> These cultural forms [i.e. music] continue to be imbued with an exoticised, othered status in the West and our primary goal has been to break out of the Orientalist tradition of making knowable these cultural productions for an ever-eager academic audience and other agencies of control... We recognise interest in a sociology of South Asian culture in Britain, and especially youth cultures, as having close ideological connections with the disciplines of command that police inner-urban neighbourhoods, close down Black clubs, collude in immigration control and so on. (Sharma et al 1996:2)

And again:

> It must be acknowledged that the anthropological silence on questions of racism, power and domination had some uncomfortable resemblance to that earlier silence on questions of racism, power and domination in the colonial encounter... Each people or minority is analysed in terms of a set of cultural practices and institutional arrangements proper to itself, or compared and contrasted in some particular respect with another people or minority. (Benson 1996:50)

This debate was discussed thoroughly in an edited collection, *Culture, Identity and Politics* (Terence et al 1996). Here, Werbner refused to accept that anthropology in Britain was an accomplice of orientalism and colonialism (Werbner 1996:74). The debate between Benson and Werbner that appeared in the same edited collection seemed to be pivoted on essentialism and anti-essentialism. Benson argued that anthropologists were inclined to work with South Asian communities because while doing fieldwork on the doorstep they were still able to map 'predictable patterns' that 'fit well with questions of caste, religion, marriage systems and so on' so typical of the classics of the discipline (Benson 1996:54). On the other hand, Afro-Caribbeans were considered lacking in these cultural practices and seen as fragmented and 'disordered' (ibid). Fluidity, change, re-invention were, according to Benson, too disturbing for anthropologists[4]. Benson described Afro-Caribbeans' culture as one 'that makes itself up, and in some important respects knows that it makes itself up' (Benson 1996:54). The implication of this statement seems to be that other cultures may not 'make themselves up' and that anthropologists choose to study only those that tend to be more static. In her reply to Benson, Werbner used her own seminal work *The Migration Process* (1990) to demonstrate how anthropological approaches were not essentialist, took account of structural constraints as well as cultural ones, and took into serious consideration the study population's vantage points:

> In *The Migration Process*, it is not assumed from the beginning that there is a clearly bounded and homogenous community. Rather, it is discovered that people who come from different backgrounds choose to make certain friends rather than others. They (the subjects) make up a level of homogeneity, this level is not imposed by the anthropologist... It is a process (not a pre-given static condition).... It is not only supportive but powerfully coercive, disturbing, conflictual. (Werbner 1996:68–9)

Again, adding a strong argument about the use of 'community' as a label to refer to a heterogeneous whole:

> Community had become, in effect, a kind of argument through practice: an argument of images between those different knots of friends with their different lifestyles, consumption patterns and visions of what their community should be like, by comparison to other communities, seen from a particular vantage point. (Werbner 1996:70)

Werbner argues that other subjects, such as nation states and 'those who draw on the past to think about the future and mobilise for action' (Werbner 1996:75), are inclined to essentialise communities. For this very reason culture is a very contested field, and demands to be taken more into consideration in any study that involves communities (ibid:76). Werbner, however, does not fully tackle another accusation by Benson about anthropology in Britain: the lack of consideration for racism, power and structural constraints (Benson 1996:50), all elements that according to the three studies analysed above should never be overlooked. However, this particular criticism had already been tackled by Ballard in 1992.

1.8 The Structural Bias: Deprivationism According to Ballard

Ballard seems to have written one of the most outspoken criticisms of the 'race relations industry' in his 1992 paper 'New clothes for the emperor? The conceptual nakedness of Britain's race relations industry'. Here Ballard argues that authorities such as the Commission for Racial Equality (since October 2007 subsumed under the new Equality and Human Rights Commission) now still cannot make sense of ethnicity, and prefer to stick to race and connected general disadvantage for any analysis they attempt to make. He argues that

> an analysis which limits itself solely to an exploration of deprivation will inexorably suggest that the victims of exclusionism lack the capacity to take charge of their own destiny. (1992:484)

Ballard suggests that the 'race relations industry' should have started looking at the resistance to disadvantage rather than disadvantage itself. By doing this, not only would the dignity of active subjects be returned to ethnic minorities, but also attention would be switched to a 'creative process' that will reveal much more about the existences of minority ethnic groups. Although 'multiple resistance' is a concept used by Tatum to support her neo-colonial model, here Ballard's statement aims much further than neo-colonial theory. By analysing 'the construction of an alternative moral and conceptual vision' (ibid:485), policy makers would access 'a set of values, expectations and understandings which are wholly unfamiliar to [minority ethnic groups'] oppressor' (ibid). The membership of a specific ethnic network is considered by Ballard as vital to the structural dynamics of multicultural societies. The pejorative label of 'deprivationism' is therefore given to the stream that apparently seeks to study groups in terms of economic disadvantage and pigmentation (ibid:492), but fails to consider sufficiently aspects of agency amongst minority ethnic groups in Britain. The concern around deprivationism appears to parallel that discussed by theoretical criminology (Russell 1992; Phillips and Bowling 2003; Garland et al 2006) about the taboos of race and crime affecting empirical research. In educational research, Modood (2004) has addressed the same deficiency: minority ethnic groups have been considered by deprivationists as on the whole under-achieving (ibid:88). This all-encompassing notion has neglected the analysis of why there are some pockets of over-achievement. Modood argues that 'the system' (society-wide economic forces) must be analysed alongside 'community forces' (minorities' trajectories and dynamics) (ibid:97). Community forces provide networks, skills and aspirations that shape action and resistance in society. By considering as dynamic and fluid anything that has to do with ethnicity, this notion combines internal resources with resistance to the system, and should provide a basic field of analysis for those concerned with minority ethnic groups.

1.9 Conclusion: Towards a 'Minority Criminology'

In this chapter we have seen how interest in the study of race and crime in Europe has original examples, in Lombroso's positivistic accounts on the one hand and the culturally grounded observations on Melanesia by Malinowski on the other. Both these approaches carry the risk of essentialisation, and the use by Lombroso of eugenics has especially contributed to creating widespread suspicion of any study that may link aspects of crime to a certain group. We have also seen how essentialisation is not necessarily pathologising: Malinowski's 'bon savage' narrative can be for example considered consistent with British stereotypes such as 'law-abiding Indians', or 'Leicester Gujaratis' (Modood 2004:101), versus 'underachieving Muslims', or 'Bradford Pakistanis' (ibid). On the other hand, many cultural stereotypes carry a negative connotation, like the one leading to the construction of the 'Asian gang' (Alexander 2000). The studies discussed above try to answer the question of why certain groups commit crime in a certain way and tend to find a solution to the riddle in limiting the role of any specificity related to a group. For example, Alexander uses her 'fragmented ethnographic lenses' (Alexander 2006), implying that there is no connection between the way individuals engage in crime and their belonging to an ethnic group.

In Britain the race and crime debate amongst scholars has mainly been characterised by an emancipatory approach that has tended to study discrimination within the criminal-justice system. According to Phillips and Bowling this has contributed to the creation of a gap in criminology where there should have been developed an understanding of how issues are *perceived by* minority ethnic groups (2003:271). Miller (2001:2) has argued that often public discussion about the link between crime and minority ethnic groups has been very negative for race relations in Britain. This can be considered the result of what has been condemned as a new indirect rule system in Britain, where social scientists' knowledge is functional to social control agencies (Sharma et al 1996:2). Innovative criminological approaches, on the other hand, are more likely to insert any variable in their study but the ethnic one—see for example 'reintegrative shaming theory' (Braithwaite 1989:9)—unless it is to illustrate a victimisation study. Information presented by the police deploys ethnicity, but mainly in terms of statistical concerns (Kalra 2003:140).

The taboo (Russell 1992:671; Phillips and Bowling 2003:271) about minority ethnic groups and crimes seems to reflect the debate in ethnic studies that flourished in the 1990s (see especially Ballard 1992; Benson 1996; Werbner 1996). Then, the discussion was about the alleged essentialisation of certain cultures and the alleged neglect of power, economics and deprivation in ethnic studies. Some criminologists now seem to be asking themselves similar questions. This study aims to shed some light on how Bradford Pakistanis view and 'live' crime within their 'territory', not on whether and how they differ from others in the extent or character of their criminal activities; such activities will not be the focus of the study, but rather its concern will be with how Bradford Pakistanis as active subjects construct crime and react to it. Knowledge held *by* them, instead of knowledge *on* them, should include analysis of their ethnic resources and networks, not as an obstacle to the amelioration of their status in society, but as a basis for different standpoints that may produce different constructions and understandings from White British ones. So far this type of awareness (that presupposes the idea that they may hold specific knowledge containing parts of the solution) has been unexplored. This hypothesis cannot be ruled out before research is done, although the result may be that cultural difference does not impact on this specific labelling process.

This book will attempt empirically to fill the gap detected by Phillips and Bowling's theoretical speculation (2003). This should not obscure other factors, as both Phillips and Bowling (ibid:272) and Alexander point out (2000:102), such as gender, age and structural constraints, for instance. However, as Ballard (1992), Werbner (1996), Kalra (2000) and Modood (2004) have argued, structural constrains may be 'cultural' or 'ethnic', not only economic. Ethnic resources and ethnic networks must be acknowledged as generating important changes in the social world. Anthropology and its traditional methods can help understand this process, provided that they do not become victims of the 'mere glamour of tradition' (Malinowski 1926:65). Anthropology should help in trying to discover how culture may be a resource and a constraint, maintaining an equal distance between pathologisation and hagiography.

An analysis of Bradford Pakistanis' values, labelling processes and perceived solutions to crime might reveal specific influences and implications for the city and its fight against crime. One hypothesis could be that these minority ethnic views may turn out to be the same as the ones of the white majority, but until studies are completed in this field we cannot be sure. Until then, if serious anthropological, sociological and criminological accounts fail to deal with the relations between ethnic capitals and networks and crime, the primary analysis taking them into consideration will be a pathological one that depicts some groups and sub-groups as folk devils and excludes *a priori* the possibility that in this relation may lie a great potential for the fight against crime. In the next chapter some attempts to deal with this problem will be explored, taking into consideration methodology as an important variable in any research involving race (Kalra 2006:467).

2

THEORETICAL AND METHODOLOGICAL SOLUTIONS TO THE 'RACE AND CRIME' TABOO

> The value of an emic study is, first, that it leads to an understanding of the way in which . . . a culture is constructed, not as a series of miscellaneous parts, but as a working whole. Second, it helps one to appreciate not only the culture . . . as an ordered whole, but it helps to understand the individual actors in such a life drama—their attitudes, motives, interests, responses, conflicts, and personality developments.
> (Pike 1954:11)

In the previous chapter we have established that so far criminology and sociology have tended to concentrate on certain aspects of the relationship between race/ethnicity and crime. This chapter will critically examine some attempts at engaging with the Pakistani diaspora and crime. The amount of literature produced in this field is quite impressive, although some of the material may be considered only tangential to criminology and includes in-depth analysis of other factors such as religion and masculinities.

This chapter will develop through a thematic and methodological analysis of a selection of some relevant academic works. This will allow us to see how, so far, scholars have dealt with the aforementioned 'race/ethnicity and crime' taboo, and will give us the opportunity to open a debate on how research methodology can contribute to the defeat of such a taboo.

The first study presented is Mawby and Batta's (1980), which reflects on how the experiences of migration and settlement impact on crime rates. Here, although cultural diversity is seen as relevant to the way the system decides to deal with Asian offenders, the specificity of the Pakistani heritage is only marginal to the analysis, and religion does not appear in the text unless it is mentioned as a cause for insularity. Male youth is not considered a 'problem', as it is in more recent studies.

It will be argued that the first substantial attempt to highlight religion in the study of crime and violence is Macey's (1999a and 1999b). In Macey's work religion seems to be closely connected to the behavioural dynamics of male youth. In general, religion seems to be included in analysis whenever external circumstances encourage analysts to focus on it: Macey as well as Imtiaz (2002) are writing after the Rushdie affair, while another author who focuses on religion and crime, Quraishi (2005), is writing after 11 September 2001 ('9/11'). Amongst those who, rather than focusing on religion, base their research on a 'thick description' of certain sub-groups as problematic, there is Lien's ethnography (2005) on Pakistani gangs in Oslo. Webster's (1997) and Wardak's (2000) studies deal with religion and culture, but at the same time include multiple variables. Again, male youth is at the centre of attention. In the conclusion to this chapter it will be argued that the danger of pathologising minority ethnic groups when discussing crime has not been completely avoided by these studies, especially when male youth is discussed, but also that the solution to the problem of the race and crime taboo mentioned by Phillips and Bowling (2003) could lie within methodology. It is within methodology, in fact, that the present research was able to develop and pursue the task of combining insiders' views and policy-relevant observations in the context of the Bradford Pakistani community.

2.1 Criminality as a Migration Stage: Mawby and Batta

The first study about crime and Pakistanis in Britain known to the present author is Mawby and Batta's *Asians and Crime: The Bradford Experience* (1980). Although this work is based on the very limited sample of the Mirpuri community of Bradford (Quraishi 2005:29), it attempts to explain changes in patterns of deviance according to a general paradigm connected to the stages of settlement of any relocating community. The migration process (Werbner 1990) and the many adjustments that individuals have to undergo through it are, therefore, considered paramount for the analysis, in what Tatum (2000:6, see previous chapter) would describe as a 'colonial model'. Here, the alienation from one's cultural capital (whatever it is) and from political praxis are considered paramount in explaining social mechanisms of exclusion and oppression. The level of *attachment to one's culture* is considered an important variable for crime prevention, but *not the culture itself,* apart from exceptions (such as the mafia) that do not seem to apply to

Pakistanis:

> [The] strength of the culture of the migrant group has an important impact on social control and crime. This is not necessarily the case where a criminal tradition is imported, as in the case of the Mafia. But where a culture is able to provide a cushion against difficulties experienced in migration, or where the social structure of the country of origin is retained by the migrant group in the new society, a degree of insularity may 'protect' the migrants for a not inconsiderable time . . . where an immigrant group maintains its ethnic identity, for example through its religion, or where migration is seen as temporary and social control as imposed by the homeland is a meaningful reality crime rates may remain low. (Mawby and Batta 1980:18)

Asians (*sic*) in Bradford were said to be protected from the worst structural and racist inequalities by their family system (ibid:26), and this idea was reflected in how the criminal-justice system dealt with young offenders: they were generally given care orders rather than other types of sentence, reflecting the idea of an efficient Asian system of informal social control (ibid:41). In general, the study argues that in migrant communities the first generation tends to have low crime rates, but that in the second generation they might increase (ibid:31).

Mawby and Batta seem to be very much aware of an Asian 'specificity' in terms of the authorities' perception, and also partly in terms of some objective differences in offending (such as the lower rate of female crime) in comparison to other groups. However, most of their attention is focused on the process of disruption of norms and values in general rather than the study of specific norms and values. The background of this study is in fact based in social-disorganisation theory. The belief behind this approach is that offences are more likely to take place where traditional norms and values, of any cultural origin, are being disrupted (Eadie and Morley 1999; Lederman et al. 2002: 514). In the process of settlement, therefore, disruption of traditional values can lead to an increment in crime in the second generation. These considerations appear to be relevant not only to criminology but also to studies of migration, diaspora and identity. Inter-generational differences and tensions, and the breaching of some important social and cultural norms (as well as consequent sanctions), could reflect and even explain the process of cultural changes at different stages of settlement. Deviance and crime could then be considered almost as a natural stage of the migration process.

One of the most interesting aspects of *Asians and Crime* is that religion is not considered as a crucially important element in the study of crime in that community. In 1980, studies of minority ethnic groups were focusing on issues of race and pigmentation, while at the time of the present research culture and religion play a much more significant role. Then, Islam was not considered a key factor. Religion, and in particular Islam, only started to become much more prominent in ethnic studies with the Rushdie affair (cf. Modood 1992). While a number of publications have reflected this shift of interest within ethnic studies (see Lewis 1994), research on deviance has maintained some degree of distance from religion. According to Spalek (2002:51) criminology has done so because people's beliefs do not fit with 'its claim of objectivity and rationalism'. If we follow Phillips and Bowling's argument (2003) we may be persuaded that such dismissal of religion could derive from a fear of pathologising a group. Below, two examples of how religion was included in the sociology of deviance will be illustrated.

2.2 Bringing Religion into the Picture: Macey's Bold Attempt

The strongest impetus given to the study of religion and crime so far has probably come from Macey (1999a; 1999b). She writes after two very important events in Bradford's and British Asian history: the 1995 riots and the 1989 Rushdie affair[5]. Macey's article in *Ethnic and Racial Studies* (1999a) was written in response to Burley and Reid's (1996) account of the these riots. According to Macey, these authors neglected social class and religion (Macey 1999a:845), but had the merit of giving greater attention to gender differences within the group they were studying, while most of the sociology of deviance had supposedly, up to then, left gender aside (cf. also Archer 2001:79). Material deprivation, poor educational provision, police brutality, institutional racism and masculinity, albeit present in the Bradford Pakistani community, are according to Macey in themselves inadequate explanations for the types of violence which occurred (ibid: 846). She suggests instead that patterns of crime are also influenced by 'ethnic, religious, gender, generational and socio-economic influences that intersect and interact with each other (and wider social structures) in dialectical formation (ibid:852). While these factors are common coinage when processes of identity construction are debated (see amongst others Wallman 1979; Ericksen 1993; Sarup 1996; Kalra 2000), they still often fail to enter discussions about criminality. Macey is persuaded, however, that the 'manipulation of cultural and religious resources to achieve desired ends' (ibid) is very common in the community.

Macey refers mainly to two examples, one 'public' and one 'private' (ibid:855). The example of public violence, where religion is manipulated in order to justify or threaten actual violence, was the campaign to chase the prostitutes out of Manningham, which took place just before the 1995 riots. At the time, a religious ethos was very clearly and publicly attached to the violent action[6]. This followed years of frustration, asking the police, without result, to put an end to street prostitution in the area (Siddique 1993:119; Burlet and Reid 1996:146). The 'private' example was a consideration that arose from Macey's interviews. According to her data, much domestic violence in the Bradford Pakistani community was justified through an *ad hoc* interpretation of Islam.

The most contentious part of Macey's work is her linking of the high number of Muslims in prison (cf. also Wilson 1999 and Kalra 2003:142) to Islam (Macey 1999a:856). However, her argument is not that Islam has intrinsic elements that lead young men to violence:

> Whether this type of Islam is theologically legitimate is irrelevant: as long as men use Islam to justify violence, religion must be considered a significant variable in its analysis. (Macey 1999a:960)

This has been also quite a common reading of the relationship between post-2001 terrorist attacks in Europe and Islam. While some commentators were keen to deprive the suicide bombers of Muslim identity, others argued that the very fact that Islam was used to articulate their message was *ipso facto* a reason for demanding an analysis which included Islam (in whatever interpretation) as one of the factors that might lead to these acts (Siddiqui 2005).

Macey is particularly sensitive to a possible connection between certain manipulations of Islam and those versions that are often described as its illiterate or rural forms (cf. the 'religion vs. Culture' debate, Chapter Five) practised by the majority of the Mirpuri Bradford Pakistani population (ibid:859). However, as elsewhere (Furbey and Macey 2005), the inclusion of religion in a sociological analysis appears judgemental insofar as there is no analysis of its positive potential. Religion, and in particular Islam, has emerged as a 'protective factor', for instance in other studies that focus on addiction, (Orford et al. 2004:23). Macey's understanding of religion, however, has the advantage of being a complex one, and of avoiding an essentialist view of Islam. Quraishi (2005), on the other hand, is based on an all-encompassing and de-culturalised idea of Islam.

2.3 Islam and its 'Betrayal': Quraishi's Transnational Study

Although the title of Quraishi's book is *Muslims and Crime*, his analysis contains the comparison of two very precise geographical settings: Haslingden in Lancashire (with a community mainly of Sylethis and Chachchis[7]) and a residential area in Karachi (2005:69). The aims of his book are to analyse how Islamic criminal law impacts on the understanding of crime of these communities, to explore how 'Islamophobia' impacts on the victimisation of Muslims, and to give some policy-orientated suggestions (ibid:vii). Quraishi's book is firmly grounded in a post-9/11 context. At the outset he gives more attention to Islam than to any other cultural practices, unlike Macey's attempt to disentangle a plethora of aspects of religious belief and practice. The first chapter describes Islam, sectarianism and Islamic jurisprudence as an objective whole. This is supposed to give the reader the benchmarks against which to measure the level of impact of religion on crime in both Haslingden and Karachi. Quraishi's main criticism of previous literature about Muslims and crime is very heavily based on the alleged neglect of religion. When he reviews the work of Mawby and Batta (see above), for example, there is no acknowledgement of the study of resistance to racism at the time, in spite of the work being based on research done just before the creation of the Bradford Twelve (see Chapter Three). Rather, Quraishi's preoccupation is with their overlooking of Islam. Quraishi's choice, instead, is to outline Islam's supposed stance with regard to criminal law and to test the perceptions and behaviour of his two sample groups against it. Although his sample is very ethnically varied (from Sylethis and Chachchis in Lancashire to Mohajjirs[8] in Karachi), this is not taken into account, as he believes that they are all to be classed in the same way as Muslims. Not only is Quraishi oblivious to geographical differences in Islamic practices and to the 'religion vs. Culture' debate (see Chapter Six), but he also assumes that Islamic criminal law speaks to everybody in the same way, ignoring the notion of *ijtihad*[9]. To make this even clearer, it is interesting to note his response to Webster's Keighley study. While Webster argues that:

> Islam as such cannot explain how Muslims behave, or how they might/ought to behave. Other factors outside Islam must be invoked. (1997:79)

Quraishi replies:

> Any cursory evaluation of Islamic hadith will provide, according to

Muslims, the perfect role model for ideal behaviour, certainly at least how they ought to behave. Considering the majority of Webster's research population are Muslim, a detailed assessment of religious teachings, practice and influence upon youth conformity and community self-identity would substantially contribute towards deconstructing the Asian offending puzzle. (2005:30)

While in the previous chapter we have seen how essentialising can undermine attempts to include culture in the discussion of race and crime, Quraishi seems to fall into the same trap by not acknowledging culture in his work, and imposing on his sample an essentialised idea of Islam. This attempt, however, seems to fail, as in his conclusion he is forced to acknowledge that Islam is not the most prominent element influencing perceptions of acceptable and unacceptable behaviour in his sample, but 'an individual interpretation . . . inspired partly by Islamic and partly by secular culture' (ibid:123). However, most of the authors who have attempted to fill the gap about race and crime in the Pakistani diaspora, have acknowledged, unlike Quraishi, a cultural system other than Islam and British culture. This is often simply labelled 'culture' with reference to one's parents' heritage. Anthropological research by Lien (2005) is pivoted around this.

2.4 The Anthropological Gaze: Lien's Ethnography of Deviance

While studies by Mawby and Batta and by Macey have focused on ecological factors behind patterns of deviance amongst Bradford Pakistanis, Lien's study provides us with a description of these very patterns. Lien's study was based in Oslo, and benefits from the author's 20 years' research on Pakistan and its Norwegian diaspora. Lien, as a member of the European network for the study of gangs, is interested in providing an investigation that highlights the intersection of general gang traits and the specificities of the 'Pakistani gang'. The universal aspects of gang life are described through reference to age group, symbols, self-definitions, territory, continuity, norms, types of violence and types of crime (2005a:2). Lien provides two case studies of Pakistani gangs in Oslo, articulating general gang traits through their specific cultural background. For example, the specific structure of the Pakistani kinship system (*biraderi*) strengthens participation in the gang (ibid:12), and sometimes this becomes the very reason that attracts people to join: the whole *biraderi* (even up to some 40 members) may have to face repercussions because of the acts of one member and of calls for self-defence. While most literature on gangs describes them as a substitute for families, Lien argues that in this case they overlap (ibid:15). Where the literature talks about power and status, in the context of Pakistani gangs in Oslo this becomes a concept intertwined with specific notions of family honour (ibid:17). The fact that there are gang members of Indian, Vietnamese and cross-caste origin is seen more as a constructive functional bridging of social capital rather than a permanent characteristic of the structure of the gang (ibid:9). Gangs can also opportunistically liaise from time to time with influential elites (for example journalists) and the welfare system (ibid:19). Members of the gang may also use family traditions to achieve their goals: this is the case with traditional elders' mediation to resolve gang rivalries (ibid:15). Lien capitalises on sociological and psychological theories of deviance, drawing on notions of power, emotion and social bonds (2005b:7). *Izzat*[10], for example, is treated as a psychological trigger that is translated into action through culturally specific manifestations of what is nothing other than the universal sentiment of pride. At times the description of culturally specific behaviours may appear more as an ethnographic curiosity rather than a useful tool to unravel criminological issues. For example, Lien describes in detail how members of a gang humiliate rivals by forcing them to touch their feet, a sign of submission and respect typical of the *sufi* tradition. Such descriptive excursuses do not shed much light on the relationship between a specific group (one considered highly criminogenic by the Norwegian press) and crime. Liens's study seems to be split between her ethnographic concerns, which often appear to end up as mere curiosity, and sociological and psychological theories that use cultural specificities in order to confirm 'etic'[11] theories promoting a universal pattern of involvement in crime. Two criticisms amongst those posed for anthropology in the previous chapter could be addressed to Lien's work: the orientalist and the 'indirect-rule' arguments. Said's orientalist argument (1985) has been used also in criminology to define the fascination, 'otherisation' and essentialisation of another group and their perceptions of crime (Cain 2002). By indulging in descriptions, such as of the rituals of reciprocal humiliation amongst gang members, Lien may be found close to an orientalist approach. By the indirect-rule argument we refer to the accusation that was made against anthropologists such as Evans-Pritchard when their studies were used to subjugate new peoples under British colonial rule. Lien, in her split between ethnographic concerns and outsider theoretical abstractions, may be accused of producing knowledge relevant to controlling agencies (see Sharma et al. 1996:2, quoted in Chapter One). The ethnographic aspects of her research, therefore, seem to support universal-frameworks arguments rather than insiders' analysis, leaving very little room for minority ethnic perceptions and interpretations of criminal issues.

In the ethnographic sections, Lien does not seem too concerned about why young Pakistani men in Oslo are actively involved in gangs, but rather about how they become involved. Heritage becomes important in the deviant action primarily when it appears as a manifestation of an etic psycho-social theory, not in its prevention or even in the more abstract terms of social construction of deviance and labelling. Lien denies that there is a cultural specificity in the criminogenesis, and her conclusion is that 'crime is the cause of crime' (2005b:23). Lien argues that this is the only possible way of including these young men in programmes of rehabilitation: it is important to understand what crime acts do to individuals, not what their heritage does. The cultural study of the dynamics of the gangs appears therefore as an exercise imposing etic psycho-social frameworks on a specific cultural context. In Lien's work, even *izzat* seems to be discussed more as a universal feature of masculinity than as an aspect of a culturally specific dimension.

In all the studies mentioned above, young men, with their identities and masculinity, play a very important part in the literature dealing with deviance in the Pakistani diaspora. In particular, the following two studies dwell on masculinity and identity it as the most important factors when studying deviance amongst British Pakistanis.

2.5 Masculinities and Identity: Webster and Imtiaz

The studies discussed in the following focus more on broader ideas of deviance rather than on crime. They focus on men, and mention ecological causes of deviance as well as more psychological causes and those more related to identity construction, keeping on the edge between identity studies and the sociology of deviance[12]. Webster's study (1997) is based on research in the Bradford district. While he had dealt with the problem of crime in earlier work (1995, 1996), here he broadens the scope of his analysis to a classification of male types in relation to their adherence to, or deviance from, the behavioural expectations according to their parents' perceptions. Amongst the typologies, the two categories of *experimenters* (1997:77) and *go-betweens* (ibid:78) are those which include people who break the law. Breaking or abiding by the law, however, is not the only benchmark for classifying deviance or 'propriety' (ibid:74): further categories are the *conformists* —those who adhere to family and community expectations (ibid:77); *vigilantes*—older people, frustrated by the lack of police intervention and of protection against 'public improprieties; and *Islamists*—those able to distinguish 'between a Muslim and an Islamic identity'[13]. Both *experimenters* and *go-betweens* would guarantee stability to the community through the preservation of some norms, but would accommodate other emotional, social and psychological needs through a 'double life'. This typology is clearly inspired by Pryce's 1979 work, but also includes a model similar to Tatum's neo-colonial one based on 'self-alienation', 'alienation from the racial or social group', 'alienation from the general other' and 'cultural alienation' (2000:56). It is important to notice how alienation itself, and not the degree of detachment from the legacy of a certain culture or group, is the most significant aspect of this model, which is applicable to any minority ethnic group. The main difference between Webster's work and that of Pryce and Tatum is that exploitation and class are only two of the factors that cause the different typologies to arise. By bringing religion and culture in, Webster in fact seems to go beyond their models.

A similar approach, that however tackles crime only marginally, is the very clearly contextualised study of Bradford Pakistani identities during and directly after the Rushdie affair. Imtiaz's doctoral thesis (2002) in social psychology is mainly an analysis of the politics of representations of identity, and its relevance to this chapter lies with the fact that young men are seen as the problematic focus of the Bradford Pakistani community. Imtiaz argues that external representation, ideologies and hegemony play a crucial part in the process by which the identity of young Pakistani men is generated. Imtiaz's model hence envisages three categories of reaction to a triple discrimination (racial, cultural and religious), by the different articulation of one's cultural capital: *coconuts, rude boys* and *extremists* (Imtiaz 2002:124). These categories are claimed to be representations from inside (ibid:125), gathered among 'specialists' or members of the community who are engaged in paid or voluntary work with young men. The label *coconuts* refers to those young men said to be 'brown outside and white inside' (ibid:125); they are seen as having benefited from a certain degree of social mobility and from having distanced themselves from tradition, even by moving away from their own families. They would apparently have internalised the external stereotype and created distance from its source (ibid:147), and supposedly reject whatever is looked down upon by outsiders. Through this process they tend not to engage with illegal activities (although their rejection of their heritage might be read by some as deviant and destabilising for the community in general).

The other two categories, instead of internalising the stereotype, resist it either by capitalising on the difference or by challenging external constructions (ibid.). *Rude boys* in fact are seen as generating a tradition between 'Bollywood and bhangra' (Imtiaz 2002:147) and 'Mirpur and LA' (ibid:127) and revitalise pride in their identity in spite of unemployment and disaffection from the wider society (ibid.) However, they do not distinguish between their culture and their religion, about which knowledge is not very deep (cf. the 'religion vs. culture' debate in Chapter Five). *Rude boys* are considered more likely to breach norms. Finally those labelled *extremists* base their identity representation on the search for a 'pure' religion, relieved from the cultural medium of their parents (ibid:21). *Extremists* are considered agents of the preservation of 'order' in the community (ibid:133), a notion that overlaps with that of stability (and will be mentioned in Chapter Four). The categories outlined by Imtiaz are said to be very fluid, but at the same time delineate their members' potential for deviance or for adherence to norms. According to Imtiaz, the major factor in explaining patterns of deviance is not any form of attachment to one's heritage (as in Hirschi's theory of social control), but the key element is rather the constructive use and translation of a *certain* religious and cultural heritage, together with historical pressures. Here a study on identity manages to bring together the various aspects that Alexander considered as the most meaningful variables of deviance: age, gender, cultural influences and economic/political resources and constraints. This seems not to have been achieved yet by criminologists, although Wardak seems to get closer than anybody else.

2.6 Attachment and Commitment to the Community: Wardak's Approach

Wardak's study of young men and deviance in an Edinburgh mosque draws on typologies similar to those described above, at the same time combining them with a universal criminological theory, such as Hirschi's control theory. Here attachment and belonging are the most important variables to classify research participants within an analytical framework that can be reproduced in any other context. Wardak calls *conformists* the young men who follow their family's transmitted social norms (2000:155–6). Their inherited cultural capital is upheld as ideal, and deployed in the real world; members of this group are trouble-free, and relational proximity between them, their families and the community acts to deter crime, as hypothesised by supporters of social control theory (Hirschi 1971:17; Burnside and Baker 1994:21). The category of *conformists* is followed by *accommodationists*, those who believe some compromises with the family norms are acceptable to accommodate their individual needs (ibid:156). Their compromises are not inherently destabilising for the group they still feel they belong to. The category of *part-time conformists* repeatedly breaks social rules, but makes sure to preserve family reputation by complying in some token activities (ibid:157), such as attending mosque on Fridays or for funerals, behaviours that are consistent with the 'double lives' mentioned in Webster 1997. Finally, the group violating and challenging most of community 'propriety' are labelled *rebels*.

The main argument is that amongst Edinburgh Pakistanis, represented by the 'Pilrig boys', there is a widely shared notion of what 'public propriety' is: 'appropriateness, seemliness, decency, conformity with good manners, conformity with convention of language and behaviour' (Cohen 1979:124, quoted in Webster 1997:74). However, propriety often consists of adherence to family tradition, and is not independently forged by young men: agency is mostly neglected. Rather than studying how households perceive deviance and engage in their choices, Wardak classifies them according to his own etic benchmark—attachment to their parents' culture. He does not agree with Alexander about the opportunity of studying young men in a cultural vacuum (Alexander 2000:18,102,140), but rather he is only able to see them in a cultural context, that founded by the older generation of those settling in Edinburgh. Although faith and religious practice are important variables in the study (whose participants were all attending a madrassa), this did not seem to produce a sub-group, as in Imtiaz and Webster's works. This may be because in the Pilrig mosque exclusivist influences (such as Tableegh Jamaat, see Chapter Seven) were not present. The tension between Islam and the traditional cultural background is not registered; the only conflict represented is seen as the one smoothed out by the double lives of the young men. We have to remember, however, that Wardak's is an etic account. While at times reference to the boys' own constructions of propriety and deviance are analysed, his categories are based on his own analysis of the data collected amongst the Pilrig boys, based on Hirschi's social control theory, and giving only limited space to insiders' comments.

2.7 Ethnographic Information as a Working Whole: the 'Emic' Approach

So far we have seen how applying universal frameworks to study minority ethnic groups and their relation to crime carries an implicit risk of reaching conclusions not necessarily shared or comprehended by the research participants. On the other hand, multi-sited fieldwork, collecting viewpoints from a variety of sample groups, as carried out by Macey, may unwillingly contribute to the pathologisation of the group when a mainly ethnographic interest guides the research, as in the case of Lien. Restricting one's research instead to a single sub-group, as in the case of Webster (and to some extent Imtiaz), loses the opportunity of contextualising the mingling of generations, cultural capital and ecology—which is not necessarily passively accepted, but rather actively negotiated and acted upon by the various social actors.

One of the main aims of the present work is to give voice to alternative points of view, or *Weltanschauungen* ('views about the world'), in the context of the Bradford Pakistani community. Instead of evaluating external analyses that have so far investigated the criminal problems in this setting through class and deprivation, the emic approach 'seeks experience from within . . . and attempt(s) to capture the meanings and experiences of *interacting* individuals' (Denzin 2001:40, my emphasis).

As pointed out in Chapter One, the criminological debate on race and crime tends to focus on deprivation and class, while the combination of these structural factors with cultural ones (cf. Macey 1999a; Phillips and Bowling 2003) sometimes goes almost unnoticed. The emic standpoint seems to be adequate to represent agency, to give room to the expression of outsiders' voices and to make them active research participants rather than the objects of one of the established criminological analyses, thus starting to fill in the gap in criminology about minorities' perspectives (Phillips and Bowling 2003:272).

> The terms 'etic' and 'emic' were coined by Pike and were brought to the attention of Anthropology with his 1954 work. The terms were constructed through the study of linguistic (specifically phonological) analysis, and relate to the terms 'phonemic' and 'phonetic'. Pike was arguing that the study of any kind of complex human activity could not rely only on that specific activity, but should analyse it in the whole of a 'unified set of terms and a unified methodology' (Pike 1954:1)[14].

From this starting point, and building on the linguistic analogy, Pike says that examining the structural whole of human behaviour can imply either an emic or an etic approach. The latter assumes that there is always a possible degree of abstraction in the analysis of a behavioural structure, and that through abstraction the social scientist can impose alien models on a specific structure: a theoretical framework constructed in totally different situations may be applied to a community that has a very distinct history, for instance.

An etic approach is thus concerned with making generalised statements about the data in order to compare them with others (Pike 1954:8). An emic approach, on the other hand, is concerned with only one 'relatively homogenous' culture (ibid). While etic research aims at comparison and generalisation, emic research attempts to make sense of various elements of a culture in relation to their functioning with each other, rather than to explain them through an *a priori* theoretical classification (Pike 1954:8), as for example, Quraishi does by applying the alleged encompassing Islamic criteria as benchmarks of deviance in his research.

It is evident, therefore, that an emic approach is clear of any deductive inference, and can be consistent with inductive strategy and grounded theory; emic units are discovered by the analyst in the specific reality of a study, not created by her/him *a priori* or by imposing categories created for other settings (ibid:20).

It is important to highlight how a social scientist who subscribes to this approach may not be able to neglect any aspect of the lives that are being observed, as they all contribute to making the culture in question function as it does. So in studying patterns of social control, for example, family structure, economic strategies, gender relations and the interplay of all these among insiders will all be considered meaningful and inter-functioning parts of the analysis.

Consequently the emic scientist will be as close as possible to the structure in question, while an etic analytical standpoint (which, on the contrary, might be called 'external' or 'alien') requires the analyst to stand farther away from, or even 'outside', a particular culture 'to see its separate events of other cultures' (ibid:10)[15]

2.8 Access and Multi-sited Fieldwork as the Key to the 'Working Whole'

Awareness of the multiple influences shaping the experiences of this particular social world is grounded in an anti-essentialist standpoint that recognises the presence of multiple influences on and experiences of the individuals involved in the research. In this piece of work, saying that the community holds its own set of meanings does not simplistically mean that there is a homogenous and static entity, where all the individuals behave very similarly (see Alexander's critique in Chapter One). This will be particularly clear when the sampling strategy is discussed: individuals inform their behaviour through information coming from the community experience and draw on their ethnic resources and networks, but their choices in the end are motivated also by their individual histories.

Although the focus of this research is on emic sets of meanings, the role of the researcher in the building of relevant knowledge should not be underestimated. The epistemology of this research is grounded in the process of the researcher's engagement with social actors, as what is initially spontaneous and natural to them is de-stratified and discussed dialogically (Geertz 1973).

As this research mainly focuses its interest on three variables (economic and general disadvantage, ethnic resources and networks, and agency the methodology had to reflect this approach. In previous studies where the interaction between culture and structure has been investigated, the choice of methods has been seen as problematic (Metcalf et al. 1996). While the choice of a large-scale quantitative survey is more capable of abstracting from general local economic factors, a qualitative and ethnographic approach enables the researcher to explore a multitude of experiences. Also, no quantitative strategy would be suitable for an interpretive approach, where the thoughts and interpretation of facts are relevant (Fabietti, 1991; Herzfeld, 1982). Furthermore, qualitative, interpretive research on a sensitive topic in the extremely suspicious Bradford Pakistani community (McLoughlin, 2000) demands a very high grade of involvement on the part of the researcher to gain first-hand interpretation. This was also one of the reasons why a variety of methods were employed for data collection: each and every technique had in fact to suit the research participants and their personal and communicative preferences. I therefore used participant observation, unstructured and semi-structured interviews, and focus groups.

In this research a qualitative ethnographic approach allowed the researcher to collect a considerable amount of material about insiders' points of view on the topic in question, and also helped in establishing a bond of trust with them in order to gain access. It could be argued that an impersonal, quantitative approach would never have guaranteed me the trust and consequently the access that I was able to gain through the anthropological strategy. Although anthropology has been accused of being incapable of explaining very recent social phenomena where there is a high level of intertwining of factors (for an account of this debate see Werbner 1987), the methodology of this research is grounded in the belief that without anthropological methods the researcher would have not been able to gain access in the community and to collect reliable data.

Participant observation was a tool to build access before becoming the means of collecting data. Bradford's Pakistani community, where most of the information system is based on word of mouth, has always required a very high level of involvement on the part of the researcher to gain first-hand information (Murphy 1987; McLoughlin, 2000). After 2001, such involvement has become indeed the only way to defeat suspicions about the research and to negotiate access. This denotes a significant change in strategy for the researcher, as global politics affect what happens in the field (Bolognani 2008). The researcher's dilemma lay in the affiliation to a group or an institution that would have at the same time created an automatic personal reference, but also the idea that I belonged to a certain group, given the fragmentation of the Bradford Pakistani grass-roots' scene (McLoughlin 1998c).

The researcher-respondent rapport is however built on many more levels than simply economic or practical help (Sanders 2004:27) where 'norms of reciprocity' (Alder and Alder 1991:175) had to be observed, and I had to expose my research persona as well as myself as much as I could in order to become visible, transparent and recognisable. The researcher's identity had thus to become public and liable to observation (Harrington 2003:597) if the research was to succeed.

It was essential that I accepted becoming 'public'; I had to go through a 'scan' in order to be 'let in', not only by individuals but by the community at large. This is why the fieldwork was built on a series of activities that were not necessarily directly functional to the data collection (such as attending a particular gym, watching Bollywood movies in local cinemas, shopping at the local green grocer's, textile shops and mobile-phone shops and going to Cannon Mill market to attend concerts and public events (cf. Bolognani 2008).

According to Macey (1999b), multi-sited fieldwork was what in her case guaranteed a reliable set of data, as she could prove a high level of congruence between experiences recounted by very disparate informants and thus confirmed that her material was not impressionistic but grounded in the lived reality of Bradford people. In the present case, in addition to this and to the target of including groups that are normally left out in rapid 'survey raids' by public agencies, 'hanging around' or waiting to be approached by passively stating one's interest has been considered key to gaining access.

Physical proximity was the first step towards access and was built over a long time span, capitalising on networks built up since 2001. The danger of getting too close to the sample was real, but this level of interaction was the only one that guaranteed access and trust during the interviews.

2.9 The Sampling and Labelling of Sub-groups

As this study aimed from the beginning to be an anti-essentialist account of the Bradford Pakistani community, at the start of the research a theoretically guided sampling-strategy was created in order to guarantee the representation of different sub-groups. In order to set up the snowballing process and to create benchmarks for further stock-taking, some sub-groups had to be identified as previous research and a literature review seemed to suggest (i.e. by accounting for generational differences). Subsequently the selection of these theoretically constructed groups was adjusted through ethnographically derived, rather than etic, categories.

First of all the sampling strategy had to take account of the representation of different generations and times of settlement in Bradford. Generational studies have been increasingly popular in sociology (cf. Edmunds and Turner 2002), as they are supposed to reflect an important component of change in society. The question of generations for the Bradford Pakistani community can be controversial, as the majority of marriages are organised between England and Pakistan[16] (Shaw 2001:319). If we consider individuals coming from Pakistan and gaining permanent residence in the UK as 'first-' and their children as 'second-generation', a problem of 'dilution' will occur in the definition of an individual born of two parents each from a different generation. For this reason, the generation-based sampling appeared soon to be problematic [17] or even irrelevant for the representation of the individuals in the sample. See for example:

> I think there is quite a divide between the elders who are generally quite religious and generally good people, you know, and then there seems to be boys ... the second and third generation ... I am first generation, really, because I was born in ... my father came here and I was born here, I am the first generation who was born here. So we sort of grew up as the first generation of this country, but the second or third generation that came along, they ... just their general outlook, just their cockiness, and that kind of stuff, their demeanour is different from what mine is. (Zameer, community worker in his early thirties)

Rather, the experiences and organisation of daily lives, beliefs and level of integration in the community and in Bradford seemed, according to the first interviewees, to be far more significant variables.

Two sample groups were initially identified as 'young people' and 'parents' groups. The latter was supposed to provide the points of view of individuals who were likely to be seriously engaged in the safety and moral issues concerning their children's upbringing. The second sample group was therefore chosen on two criteria: age and position in the community.

At the end of the pilot stage, though, two issues emerged as far as the second sample group was concerned. The first issue was about the language barrier between the researcher and the first generation; the first two members of which who were approached for an interview agreed to answer my questions provided that their son would do the interpreting; this intercession by a related subject could have undermined the reliability of the data. The second problem concerned the finding that interviewees seemed to regard marriage as a more important threshold than age and parenthood. Marriage was often described as a rite of passage for most of the individuals (see Chapter Seven) who apparently tended to change their life style after the nuptial rites. Therefore, after the pilot stage, the second sample group became more an age-cum-marriage group, and relied on an English-speaking sample.

The popular debate about ethnic segregation in the city (see Chapter Three) had originally led the research to include only individuals who could be defined as 'Pakistanis' (although the majority of the population classified by the census in Bradford as of Pakistani origin are actually from Azad Kashmir, which holds a special status within the geo-political boundaries of Pakistan). Four months into the fieldwork the author was presented with the opportunity to include in the sample some willing Muslims of Gujarati origins. Gujarati Muslims seemed to be in most cases profoundly socialised within the Pakistani community (they live in the same areas, are invited to weddings, exchange visits, attend the same mosques and share patterns of marriage; mosques with Gujarati imams are attended by Pakistani people in spite of the usual ethnically-based congregations (cf. Lewis 1994). One individual of Bangladeshi origin who is particularly socialised in the Pakistani community was also interviewed. In terms of area of residence, the vast majority of interviewees lived in inner-city Bradford. Their educational achievements and their social class were varied. I deliberately excluded 'social class' from the core variables of the research, as to reach an understanding of its emic definition would probably have implied a new doctoral research-topic—at present there is no study on emic perceptions of social class amongst British Pakistanis.

Some white people were included in the sample in order to provide some terms of comparison in understanding and some alternatively generated information about the research context. Among these was a high-school focus group composed of white pupils, and some white members of the police force interviewed because they had important insight about the 2001 riots.

The final organisation of the sampling strategy is consequently based on three groups:
- unmarried, over 16 and under 28 years of age (see Appendix One);

- married or divorced (see Appendix Two); and
- practitioners (see Appendix Three).

2.10 Breaking the Taboo through Methodology: Criminology, Minority Perspectives and Anthropology

The studies analysed here show that the field of crime in the Pakistani diaspora has produced a varied body of literature. These studies include and analyse variables such as gender, age, identities, religion, settlement and economic and political constraints. They tend, however, to focus more on the problems than on the possible solutions. In this respect, there seems to be a tendency to pathologisation, especially as far as male youth are concerned.

This is consistent with initial criticism voiced by potential research participants during the pilot stage of my fieldwork:

- the Bradford Pakistani community is over-researched, and researchers either are not accurate—tailoring the writing-up of their findings to suit their own purposes—or the results of their research are never disseminated amongst the interested sample subjects;
- different researchers tend to speak with the same people (the so-called 'community leaders') over and over again, and some strata of the community are neglected (especially women);
- research tends to focus on tragic or problematic situations; the positives are overlooked, as not lending themselves to sensationalisation.

Given the emic standpoint of this book, the ethical grounds for the research were set according to the suggestions given by the informants. The aim is to move beyond the previous studies mentioned and to look at agency and local influences as a resource, not simply as a problem.

Studying the specifics of a minority ethnic group does not necessarily follow from the will to play the role of informants for social-control agencies (cf. Sharma et al. 1996). Instead, it follows from reviewing the literature above and the need to include more minority ethnic perspectives in this field. This does not seek to be an invitation to contribute to indirect government rule based on sociological analysis, but rather to highlight how in this field the inclusion of minority ethnic groups has been neglected.

The issue about the supposed sensationalism of most Bradford-based research seemed to me resolved by the original idea behind the book: that together with the emic approach I wanted to focus on the agency of the community, and therefore my strategies implied a belief that the study population had the potential for a positive assertiveness about its own future.

If we consider social reality as made up by individuals, their choices based on certain value-systems, their practices and their thoughts as they engage practically with the world and the structures they have built, we will need a wide and extensive knowledge of all these entities forming that very social reality. Therefore, rather than only one aspect of the community under study being considered as crucial to understanding that community, multiple parts of that unique social world will be factored in to the progress of the research. This is why I have used many verbatim quotes from the interviews as to keep the insiders' analysis of their social world as close as possible to what they actually expressed. The lived experiences of the actors in the social world of the research have been tested iteratively, in order for them to inform the subsequent steps of the research. The taboo on studying crime and a minority ethnic group was broken in conjunction with them.

3

BRADFORD AS A CASE STUDY

Like a child is a community
Newborn, an infant in its mother's arms;
All unaware of Self . . .
But when with energy it falls upon
The world's great labours, stable then becomes
This new-won consciousness; it raises up
A thousand images, and casts them down;
So it createth its own history . . .
(Iqbal, *The Mysteries of Selflessness*, quoted in Werbner 1980)

In the previous chapter we discussed how both ethnic resources and networks and ecology inform agency relevant to the social actors. Local history is one of the important aspects that may contribute to the production of relevant knowledge, and here we will review some of that history, together with other political and cultural factors, that are believed to be crucial for the understanding of the definition of Bradford Pakistanis as a community.

The city of Bradford is home to the largest Pakistani population outside of London, and is widely referred to, satirically, as 'Bradistan' (McLoughlin 2006b). As a post-industrial city with economic problems and a high percentage of South Asian inhabitants, Bradford has been a centre of attention for debates on citizenship, race and class, and violent disorders.

This chapter will draw on the existing literature and on the author's findings collected in previous fieldwork (January–August 2002, see Bolognani 2002), and follow the history of the city and of its intersection with the Pakistani community since the early 1960s. The processes of settlement, survival through economic disadvantage and the emergence of political awareness will also be discussed. The account of the last 15 years of violent episodes will draw upon the most significant studies about the riots[18] in order to emphasise how deprivation, racialism and politics may have influenced urban tensions, outsiders' perceptions, and the lives of the communities who inhabit Bradford. In addition, the connection between the locality and the ethnic resources and networks available to Bradford Pakistanis will be highlighted in a bid to make sense of the fluidity and homogeneity of the community, as also of its being rooted within and not disenfranchised from its locality. Although the author is very conscious of the number of different provenances, castes and religious sects that may lead some to think that there is no justification for the use of a singular term to describe the community, it will be argued that an exclusive history, a broad cultural reference and the outsiders' unnuanced representation is mirrored in the interviewees' own use of the singular 'community' rather than the plural 'communities'.

This chapter will therefore explore the consistency and at the same time the heterogeneity of the Bradford Pakistani community, providing a description of the main cultural and social elements that will be factors in the social-control analysis of the following chapters. At the same time the analysis will show how at the present juncture in Bradford adaptation is leading to some major internal changes. Throughout the chapter a particular focus will be placed on family, its 'moral economy' and the social specificity of *biraderi*.

3.1 A 'BrAsian' City

To newcomers, Bradford is generally described as ruled by Pakistanis:

> First thing I was told when I moved here, my uncle he said to me: 'Whatever you do, don't upset a Pakistani.' I went: 'Why?' He said to me: 'They tend to be really violent here.' I said: 'Why?' 'Because there're so many of them. They think they can do anything they want, kick off with a Bengali, with an English or whatever because they know all they need to do is to phone a few numbers and all their friends and family come to help. They have all the connections because they know all of them come from the same place [in Pakistan] ... If you do [upset a Pakistani], run. Don't stay there because in five minutes you'll have 50 of them.' (Chilli, Bengali university student from Northampton, quoted in Bolognani 2002)

In reality, Pakistanis constitute no more than 19 per cent of the nearly 500,000 inhabitants (2001 census), but the clustering is such that the inner city appears to visitors as mainly Asian[19]. Stressing the idea that the city is not Bradford any more but rather 'Bradistan', may contribute to worsening the relations between communities: the African/Caribbean community, for instance, apparently feels neglected because of the prospect that Pakistani lobbying deprives them of the attention they seek for their own problems (Singh 2002:62; Harrison and Phillips 2005:196). However, the prominence of the 'Asian' aspect is a reflection of the impact that South Asian Muslims have had on this Northern town. However, Bradford is also rich in descendants of various other nationalities: Indians, Bangladeshis, Italians, Poles, Ukrainians, Chinese, Germans, Afghanis, South Americans and Irish (Mawby and Batta 1980:34; Siddique 1993:18; Singh 2002:17). Most of them were drawn to Bradford by the prospect of work in the textile industry.

The first study of Bradford Pakistani men was published by Dhaya in 1974. The objects of the study were mainly related to residential patterns and community history since the 1960s (McLoughlin 2006b). Some of his observations concerned support based on *biraderi*[20], widespread suspicion about white people, the reasons for clustering and the lingering myth of return to the homeland (Bolognani 2007b).

In 1964, when Dahya started his research, the Pakistani population in Bradford was estimated at 12,000: 5,400 Mirpuris, 3,000 Chachchis, 1,800 Western Punjabis, 300 Pathans, 1,000 from various parts of Western Pakistan and 1,500 Sylhetis (Dhaya: 1974). In the 1961 census, only 3,457 Pakistanis[21], 1,512 Indians and 984 African/Caribbeans were recorded. By 1970 the Pakistani population in Bradford was already estimated as 21,000 (ibid).

The 1991 Census registered the Bradford population of South Asian descent as 65,450 (14 per cent of the city's total population). 48,900 of them were regarded as Pakistani/Kashmiri. As such, Bradford held the second-largest urban concentration of Pakistanis in Britain. The latest data (Phillips:2001) show that in only a decade the Asian population has grown to 94,520; importantly, 73,900 of them are Pakistani/Kashmiri.

Table 3.1 Asian population in Bradford, 1961–2001

	1961 census	1964 figures (Dahya 1974)	1970 figures (Dahya 1974)	1981 census (Macey 2001)	1991 census (Philips 2001)	2001 census (Philips 2001)
No. of Asians	3,457	12,000	21,000	46,720	65,450	94,520
Percentage of Asians	1.1%	...	...	10.6%	14%	19%
No. of Pakistanis/ Kashmiris	...	5,400	...	34,116	48,900	73,900

As far as single nationalities are concerned, Bangladeshis (mainly Sylhetis) compose the smallest significant, identifiable sub-group within the Asian community (around 4,000 in 1991) and are distributed in the city in a pattern very similar to the Pakistani one, i.e. they tend to cluster according to provenance. Nevertheless, there is no area where Bangladeshis are present in a percentage higher than five per cent (Phillips 2001:2).

Punjabi Hindus and Sikhs, or Gujarati Hindus, have a very different location from Muslims in the geography of the town. These relatively small communities who once lived side by side with the Muslims, or even shared accommodation, are now moving to suburbs or to more heterogeneous areas (Ouseley 2001:9; Singh 2002:25). Ethnic clustering, self- or forced segregation are some of the themes that will recur in this book when arguments about the alleged insularity of Bradford Pakistanis will be put forward.

3.2 Ethnic Disadvantage

One of the wealthiest parts of the country when the textile industry was at its peak, Bradford had become by the time of the present research amongst the most deprived (*Neighbourhood Statistics* 2001); TUC research had suggested that Asian unemployment in Bradford was the worst in the country (Singh 2002:168). More than 80 per cent of Pakistanis lived in areas defined as affected by multiple deprivation[22], against 45 per cent of Sikhs (Phillips 2001:3).

Businesses were suffering from this bad image, and were considerably affected by crime (Bradford Chamber of Commerce and Industry 2003). Social conflict in the former industrial centre was high due to several factors, such as racial tension, widespread economic disadvantage, drugs and criminal groups (WYP 2003:14–15, 17); the Pakistani population were often blamed by some of the local white working-class for violence, crime (Webster 1995:11), political corruption and periodic riots (Amin 2003:461). For some, the perpetuation of Asian models of living had also affected the already precarious situation brought about by the textile crisis of the 1970s (Webster 1995). Other commentators had focused their social analysis of the context on supposed Pakistani undervaluing of education, different attitudes to consumption, marriages with partners sent from Pakistan and gender issues (Macey 2001).

The 1991 census had revealed that the unemployment rate among Asian and African/Caribbean youth in Bradford was amongst the worst in the country, with one out of three young people from minority ethnic groups out of work.

In education Bradford schools were apparently amongst the poorest performers in the nation, in terms of structural inadequacy, quality of teaching and truancy (Ouseley 2001:13, Singh 2002:172), factors that in Chapter Eight will be mentioned as one of the reasons why formal education is not regarded as a useful means of crime prevention.

Together with residential segregation, there was also a phenomenon of school clustering, and the situation in non-white schools was generally supposed to be the worst. In the educational sector many issues of multiculturalism were under challenge—amongst others, language problems, different festivities and a lack of staff recruitment from ethnic minorities. More than 30 per cent of primary-school pupils spoke English as a second, third or even fourth language (Singh 2001). The survival of the use of the original languages may be partly due to the fact that for a long time 60 per cent of the marriages each year in the Asian community were transcontinental (Darr and Morrell 1988)[23] and therefore at least one member of the family would speak his/her mother tongue with the children; children frequently only played with peers of the same cultural background, and consequently tended not to speak English; most of their afternoons since the age of six were spent in mosques where the Quran was not taught in English.

In 2001 Muslim pupils attended school in only seven of the 30 Bradford wards (Lewis 2001); the 13 Asian councillors (out of 90 for the city as a whole) had been elected from these same wards. Some 19 First Schools, eight Middle Schools and three Upper Schools were attended by 90 per cent of all the Muslim students (ibid). National statistics for examinations taken by 15- and 16-year-olds indicated that while Indian children out-achieved white pupils—54 per cent gaining five or more GCSEs at Grade A–C, against 47 per cent for whites in 1998—the figures for Pakistani and Bangladeshi pupils were 29 and 33 per cent respectively. This will be reflected in their occupational patterns (ibid:1).

While clustering and general disadvantage have characterised the history of the Bradford Pakistani community, it is important to highlight that economic and wider resistance strategies to general disadvantage have intertwined with ethnic resources and networks and changed throughout the history of the settlement.

3.3 The Migration History

In Bradford there is a pattern of South Asian male migration found to be more or less similar by the present writer in all the households encountered, as well as by other anthropologists (Werbner 1980).

Typically, a male member of the family would have been given a voucher to go to Britain and work in the textile industry. Men from the Mirpur region were prioritised in the distribution of such vouchers as compensation, agreed by the Pakistani government, for the loss of land as a result of the construction of Mangla Dam (for a deeper analysis of the consequences of the dam, see Kalra 2000: 65).

Once settled, an individual would attract relatives or friends over, organising their journey and providing accommodation on their arrival. Through these processes financial remittances to the family or village increased, and when the original voucher had had to be topped up with family help, this was the occasion to reciprocate efforts. The migration system has been described as 'chain migration' (Ballard 1990:222; Shaw 1994:39; Ilahi and Jafarey 1999:1). Chain migration is 'the processes by which prospective immigrants learned of opportunities, were provided with passage money, and had initial accommodation and employment arranged through previous immigrants' (Macdonald and Macdonald 1962:435). Such processes help explain why the Asian communities of Bradford are so homogenous in provenance: migration was based mainly on personal relations, on which were built mutual help and support. Some informants recalled their fathers' experiences like this:

> After Second World War there was a lack of men in this country. England had a massive wool industry and needed cheap labour. Our grandparents came here to help them. (Sharukh, quoted in Bolognani 2002)

> My grandfather fought in the Second World War [and stayed on in the UK]. Then, my father came over, and the rest. Bradford was famous for its mills. He wanted to make money and go back. Then he realised he could earn 15 or 20 times what he got in Pakistan [and stayed]. (Sadiq, quoted in Bolognani 2002)

> My dad comes from Azad Kashmir, Pakistan, and came here in the fifties. He worked in Scotland and in the Midlands. . . . He came through an agency, British people sponsoring British interests. . . . He brought a few relatives when he got established. In the sixties, my mum came. (Amjad, quoted in Bolognani 2002)

These stories sometimes carry a romantic attachment, as they seem built on the heroic motives of men leaving the homeland for an economic but somehow epic adventure (Werbner 1980). This romantic and idealised view is constantly debated whenever inter-generational clashes and differences come under scrutiny (see Chapter Five).

Nevertheless, the idea of a pioneer generation in Britain and the aura around what has been described as the 'community of suffering' (Werbner 1980) carries consequences in the definition of an alleged generational gap today, a recurrent topic in the present research interviews (cf. Chapter Five):

> I think generally [elders] tend to think that our youth today they're out of hand because they don't have jobs. That is one of the most popular reasons. They haven't got jobs, they're bored, they want to cause troubles, that [is] why they do it. And they don't look upon [the younger generation] too greatly, the elder generation. They seem to think that if we had the hardship that they had in their times, then we'd be more . . . sort of responsible, more thoughtful in what we do, but we are only reckless and thoughtless because we have more freedom, we've got more facilities available to us than they ever had in those times. I remember my father used to tell me he used to survive on five pounds a week, that was his wage. And I could never survive on five pounds a day, never mind a week. But you see the times have changed and they strongly believe that because the times have changed we have been given—what's the word—more freedom and more, more flexibility. (Zaara, shop assistant and special constable, in her early twenties)

The first waves of the migration could not build on any chain. Men at the time used to link up casually and move in together regardless of caste or provenance in order to minimise their expenses. It seems that the very first Indo-Pakistanis arriving in Bradford were a group of sailors who made their way from Hull in 1941 and rented rooms from Polish families (Dhaya 1970; 1974). Today it is still possible to see traces of the once large Polish community in the area between Manchester Road and Little Horton Lane: their Catholic church, the working men's club and a delicatessen.

Slowly the Polish relocated and the Pakistanis pooled together enough money to buy their first houses. Bradford was still a textile capital, they were working long hours and did not waste their earnings. Importantly, their traditional informal system of interest-free money-lending helped to make possible their start on the property ladder (Siddique 1993).

With the purchase of the first houses, an institution of mythical connotations was born: the 'bachelors' house'[24]. The era of these overcrowded basic houses is recalled by the first migrants as the golden era of their migration: the only rule seemed to be camaraderie. In the accounts of the people who lived in a bachelors' house there are extraordinary episodes of generosity; if a new arrival did not find a job straight away, he was maintained by the rest of the group even for up to a year; if a member of the family died in Pakistan, the men of the house would raise the money to send the relative home. These times might be seen as when these men were happiest, when they maintained their traditional values and beliefs, apparently unspoilt by the materialism of Western life, another recurrent theme in the fieldwork on which this thesis is based (see for example Chapter Five).

The living conditions in such accommodation, however, were very poor: the eldest or the ones who had been in England for longer had their own beds, while others would share one (the so called 'warm bed') with whoever was on a different shift; however, many slept on the floor or on two chairs put together (Siddique 1993:20).

The heterogeneity of provenance to be found in bachelors' houses did not last long; different contingencies modified the orientation of migrants of different origins in different ways. For instance, Sikhs who had fled Pakistan after the bloody events post-Partition (Ballard 1990:226; Singh 2002:24), decided to make England their new home, and before any other ethnic group called their families over (Mawby and Batta 1980:36). The same thing happened with the Punjabis expelled from East Africa. With women and children in place, bachelors' houses became unsuitable, although they survived for some time within the Pakistani community. Some observers have seen earlier family reunion of other Asian peoples as one of the reasons behind better economic achievements and integration patterns when compared with Bradford Mirpuris (cf. Singh 2001).

With the arrival of families, the organisation of the immigrants' areas changed considerably: *halal* meat shops, garment retailers, specialised green grocers and especially mosques and madrassas started flourishing. The first proper mosque (men originally prayed in a room in a house) was opened in 1959; in 1969 there were six mosques in Bradford, growing to 17 in 1979, and by 1989 there were 34 (McLoughlin 1998c).

Although accurate data have not been produced, probably due to problems of self-ascription, it is commonly known that most of the Pakistanis were from a relatively small and deprived district of Azad Kashmir called Mirpur, and this group is still the majority (McLoughlin 2006b). Other migrants were from Campbellpur district, in the Attock region. People from Attock, called Chachchis, are popularly seen as a sub-caste of Pathans. Pathans, who are not very numerous in Bradford, come from the North West Frontier, near Afganistan. The Punjabis of Bradford are mainly from Lyallpur (Faisalabad), Rawalpindi and Gujar Khan; only a few are from urban areas. There is also a small community from Pakistani Gujarat (Mawby and Batta 1980:36). These different ethnic origins still seem to play some role in social interactions and stereotypes circulating in Bradford (cf. Chapter Six).

Anthropologists have argued that the rural origin of the migrant population has contributed to shaping chain migration and subsequent settlement. Ballard (2001), for instance, argues that the typical family organisation of the Pakistani rural areas is characterised by an active solidarity that guarantees better performance by an individual in a foreign land because of reciprocal moral and financial support. Furthermore, in the rural areas the common mentality suggests relying only on your own people and being suspicious of strangers. Trying to avoid borrowing money outside the family, living in a sober way and not relying on anyone but relatives seem parts of the rural Pakistani, and especially Mirpuri, culture

Direct sources and relevant literature (Dhaya 1970; Anwar 1979) agree in depicting the first years of life in England as suffused with nostalgia for the homeland: men were hoping to return to their land and families as soon as they had built up some capital to invest. England appeared as a land of sacrifice, where no rest or pleasure should be allowed to undermine the achievement for which the family in Pakistan had sent a man abroad. On the other hand, there were attempts to integrate; for instance, Siddique (1993:25) describes Pakistani men who eschewed traditional Muslim clothing in favour of jacket and tie, and socialised with British women.

Contacts with the relatives were kept constant through letters and pictures. Shaw (1988) argued that a difference in attitude came about when in 1962 a rumour spread that the United Kingdom wanted to restrict immigration laws. Apparently, Pakistani travel agents took advantage of the rumour to encourage more men to leave. Young children seven–nine years of age joined a father or an uncle and, sometimes, by claiming to be older, apparently entered the textile mills. Overall, however, children were systematically enrolled in local schools as education was generally seen as a good investment (Siddique 1993:21). The Pakistani migrants felt that they had to make the most of the final years of relatively easy immigration, and as a result some women followed their male family members. Some men who had attempted to return saw their business projects fail and came back to England The majority thought it better to stay, fearing that if they were not successful in Pakistan, they might have not be able to enter Britain again. One informant described her father's experience in this way:

> My dad borrowed the money off my mother's side. My mum's dad had given him the land because he didn't want him to take his daughter away. . . . After two years he went back. He realised the money wasn't enough and came back again. Eventually my mum came over. Then I was born and they were trapped. . . . My mum always says, 'He brought me here saying we'd only stay for a few years.' (Shazia, quoted in Bolognani 2002)

Understanding the family structure may help to highlight some dynamics of discourses about family-based crime prevention discussed in Chapter Seven. The main question to be answered is whether traditional kin groups may be able successfully to translate their cultural/moral capital in a way adequate to a current British urban environment.

Families' settlement in Bradford only occurred in a second phase of migration. Unlike many other migrant populations, the Mirpuris started their relocating adventure as involving only men. Furthermore, while nowadays part of female migration from other Asian countries and from South America is stimulated by a need in the private-care sector for female workers (Williams 2001:486), in 1960s UK there was not a high demand for women in that sector, while the textile industry still required a cheap workforce. More than anything else, because the honour (*izzat*) of women in Mirpur is a priority—it affects the reputation of the entire extended family (Afshar 1989:214)—sending a woman abroad to work in promiscuous environments would have been putting the whole of the family's honour in jeopardy. It has also been suggested that some families did not wish to encourage women to join their husbands in order to help persuade the latter to return (Saifullah-Khan 1974). As families were concerned about the physical and moral safety of their women (see also Chapter Four), and the living conditions of the up-to-then transient men were not appropriate and comfortable for women, Mirpuri women did not come to England straight away. They also arrived much later than some other spouses, for example Sikhs, who joined their husbands with the intention of settling and staying after the traumas of Partition (Singh 2001). Saifullah-Khan (1974) again reports informants' tales of Mirpuri women sent to England once gossip reached villages that men were seeing English women and spending their money on them. At this point *biraderis* (extended family) sent their wives abroad (*vilayat*) to remind them of their obligations.

Once the women arrived, the bachelors' houses changed into family homes. Properties were rented and bought around the mills where the men had temporarily settled. Families started transforming the alien environment into something more familiar.

Informants in a previous study by the present author (Bolognani 2002) state that as the banks were reluctant to start mortgage procedures with Pakistanis, and Islam discouraged the immigrants from dealing with money lenders unless on an interest-free basis, they chose to pool money together and start buying the cheapest houses around the mills where they worked. As previous migrants or white people were moving out of inner-city areas (Singh 2002), they were able to buy houses close to each other and establish a setting in some respect similar to the villages back home. In rural Kashmir, families belonging to the same *biraderi* live in houses attached to each other. As well as being a way to maximise collaboration and defence, such a building strategy allows the women to move freely among related households. This ethnic clustering became a crucial infrastructural system when the recession pushed the workers out of the mills.

3.4 Ethnic Resources and Networks: the Peculiarities of the *Biraderi* System

Anthropologists have argued that the scale and the success of the Mirpuris migration can be satisfactorily explained only by taking into consideration their traditional family structure (Saifullah-Khan 1974; Ballard 2001). In fact, external circumstances such as the distribution of vouchers after the construction of the Mangla Dam would have not been successfully taken advantage of, had there not been a supportive network sustaining the migrant. For example, the family cooperated in pooling extra money together for contingencies, in looking after the wife and the children of the migrant and in guarding properties.

The importance of the Kashmiri family system imported into Britain has been considered as paramount also for the development of entrepreneurship (Metcalf et al.1996; Ballard 2001), for the urban segregation of communities (Alder, Cater et al. 1981; Phillips 2001; Singh 2003) and for choices about education and careers (Shaikh and Kelly 1989; McLoughlin 1998a; Shaw 2000). In this book it will emerge how many Bradford Pakistanis themselves see it as important at the level of both the problems of and the solutions to crime.

Analysis of the various elements that compose cultural capital in the Bradford Pakistani community will underlie the basis for the evaluation of whether there is a form of such capital that may prove successful in the economy of crime prevention. Values such as internal solidarity and rules of reciprocity appear to be consistent with the definition of cultural capital by Bourdieu as 'symbols, ideas and preferences as they have been consciously or unconsciously transmitted and accumulated in order to inform individual actions' (1986:245).

> The family was important for many reasons: for chain migration, for finding jobs, for buying the house—kameti[25], no-interest loan. Family is finishing now. Also, the family had a role in education: people compare their children's careers. In all this marriage, family play a very important role, as without it people would have struggled to get married. (Umar, civil servant in his 50s)

In these instances, cultural capital has proved profitable (Bourdieu 1986:241), as it has been converted into 'economic capital' (ibid).

Kinship amongst Bradford Pakistanis is thoroughly constructed on the *biraderi* structure, as it is in rural Punjab, Azad Kashmir and the Attock District, where most families come from. The definition of *biraderi* has been considered a complicated matter and is still controversial; a digression that explains its role, in practical terms, seems to be necessary, as the term is considered to be very flexible. According to Anwar (1979), *biraderi* derives from the Persian word *baradr*, brother, and indicates a group of men who recognise descent from a common ancestor. Rather than a static and rigid unit, however, *biraderi* should be seen as a system of alliance, as often it includes men who join because of specific merit towards a family or special friendship. In *biraderi* inclusion, blood relations are ideal, but not crucial. Wardak, quoting Wakil (1979), synthesises the combination of kinship and affinity in *biraderi* in this way: '[*biraderi*] is generally an endogamous group of individuals who *consider* themselves related to each other . . . ' (my emphasis). Relations considered as if based on blood ties, but not so in reality, have been called '*biraderi* of recognition' (Saifullah-Khan 1974:44), 'of participation' (ibid:230) or 'effective *biraderi*' (Wardak 2000); these however are invented terms not used by non-scholars. In theory, the *biraderi* should not cross caste, but 'esogamic'[26] marriages do occasionally take place in Pakistan and are increasing in Britain (Shaw 2000).

Loyalty and attachment to *biraderi* are considered to be particularly crucial values in the Mirpuri moral economy. Non-Kashmiri groups in Bradford claim that lobbies formed by 'MPs' (a derogatory nickname for Mirpuris) take over most of the enterprises and severely restrict opportunities for others (Bolognani 2002); and such clan attachment plays a major role in the outsiders' characterisation of the Mirpuris as backward (McLoughlin 1998a:97). Sometimes the loyalty within the *biraderi* is sarcastically described as Mafia (see Chapter Six), as again exemplified by the novelist Yunis Alam:

> This was a kin thing, a fucking *biraderi* thing, an OUR mother-fucking thing that I wanted no part of. We were worse than the fucking Mafia when it came to those troublesome family matters. . . . One thing that got me was how all these people were the same. Either they were relatives, or people who lived in the same village in Pakistan. Most of all, there was this caste thing going off, and that was what really got me thinking. (Alam 1998:92)

As well as being the main network of help and support, the *biraderi* is also a controlling unit; an informant described the influence that *biraderi* controls and its 'politics' had on his family in this way:

> Sadiq: 'I don't like living in Manningham, there's too much Pakistani politics.'
> MB: 'What did you mean by Pakistani politics?'
> Sadiq: 'My sister was restricted. She went to upper school and then she didn't do anything else because of relatives saying, 'She shouldn't do this, she shouldn't do that' . . . A lot depends on the elder members of the family. The majority of my relatives live around me.' (quoted in Bolognani 2002)

Social studies acknowledging *biraderi* (Saifullah-Khan 1974; Anwar 1979; Werbner 1989; Chaudhary 1999; Shaw 2000; Akhtar 2003), and direct ob-

servation conducted by the author in the Pakistani community of Bradford in 2002 and in the Mirpur district in 2003, contributed to creating the following list of features of the *biraderi* system:
- subjects' use of the term *biraderi* recalls other expressions descriptive of family cohesiveness;
- although shallowly translated into English as 'extended family', *biraderi* can include non-blood-related individuals included on an honorary basis because of special deeds, out of friendship, or because they come from the same area and have shared the same experiences abroad;
- *biraderi* is often influenced by caste, in spite of the egalitarian tenets of Islam;
- it has a normative and controlling role, regulating information and communication;
- it has recognised hierarchies within it;
- branches of *biraderi* separated by migration tend to interrelate and influence each other's decisions;
- it is the main context of *vartan bhanji*[27]
- its members perform *lena dena* (reciprocal taking/giving); and
- it maximises the flow of goods and services.

This complexity and dynamism of *biraderi* very clearly embodies the close relationship between Bradford Pakistanis' cultural and social capital. Not only is *biraderi* the ensemble of relationships, but it also seems to be the vessel for specific cultural symbols, norms and ideas:

> Social capital is the aggregate of the actual or potential resources which are linked to possession of a durable network of more or less institutionalised relationships of mutual acquaintance and recognition—or, in other words, to membership of a group—which provides each of its members with the backing of the collectivity-owned capital. (Bourdieu 1986:248–9)

Another feature of the meaning of *biraderi* is its dependence on context. It can in fact from time to time refer to national provenance (or *quom*, Chaudhary 1999:11), village provenance (or *sharika*, ibid:13), caste subdivision (or *goot*, ibid:13), family tree (or *khandan*, ibid:14) or nuclear family (or *ghar*, ibid:15).

Biraderi appears therefore to be a very broad concept which in terms of social capital is not clearly definable in terms simply of strong/weak ties

(Granovetter 1973) or bonding/bridging social capital (Putnam, 2001:22; Woolcock 2001:13–14).

Granovetter defines strong ties as the closest relationships that one has (i.e. family and friends) and weak ties as the ones that link the individual to the outer world (1973:1378). Woolcock defines bonding social capital in a similar way to strong ties and bridging social capital as that encompassing 'more distant ties of like persons, such as loose friendships and workmates' (2001:14). In more detail:

> Some forms of social capital are, by choice or necessity, inward looking and tend to reinforce exclusive identities and homogenous groups. Examples of bonding social capital include ethnic fraternal organizations, church-based women's reading groups, and fashionable country clubs. Other networks are outward looking and encompass people across diverse social cleavages. Examples of bridging social capital include the civil rights movement, many youth service groups, and ecumenical religious organizations. (Putnam, 2001: 22)

'Inward-looking' to describe bonding social capital sounds negative, and indeed Putnam privileges bridging capital (Field 2003:36); bonding may in fact be the mode of gangs, satanic sects, etc.

The specificity of *biraderi* is that strong and weak ties or bonding and bridging fail to be easily distinguishable. *Biraderi* may imply either term of the dichotomy at different times and in different contexts. However, positive and negative perceptions coexist, as they do for social capital. This may be even more apparent when analysed as part of a historical continuum.

Kinship-based networks had a paramount importance in the first stages of migration, when without such unconditional support it would have been impossible to buy houses or start enterprises. The role of such networks nowadays, however, will appear throughout this book as being quite controversial (cf. Chapter Five), and may be referred to by the derogatory term '*biraderism*'. Currently, the link between relationships, networks and traditional cultural capital may not be as consistent as it used to be. For this reason, although Bourdieu's definition of cultural capital seems to describe some aspect of *biraderi*, Putnam's broader and more pragmatic definition of social capital may be more apt. However, this definition of Putnam's refers to any kind of interrelation between individual and individual, or between the individual and a community (Field 2003:34–6, 65) and it is always described as a positive feature (Boggs 2001:287). *Biraderi*, as has been pointed out about social capital (Bankston and Zhou 2002:286), may be failed by definitions that do not consider it as a process rather than as quantifiable content more appropriate to cultural capital (or 'cultural stuff', Barth 1969). For this reason, and in order to avoid value-laden definitions such as Putnam's, the term preferred in this book will be 'ethnic resources and networks'.

3.5 'From Textile Mills to Taxi Ranks' (Kalra 2000)

By the 1970s, textile mills and related industries, such as engineering, were in difficulties. The textile industry had coped, in spite of obsolete machinery, partly because of the cheap labour provided by South Asian workers (Mawby and Batta 1980:33; Siddique 1993:20; Amin 2003:461).

Migrants who were making their way to England after exhausting interviews in migration offices in Pakistan would no longer be given category-A visas[28].

By the 1970s, however, many Asian families had settled down. The working men who had been made redundant acknowledged the benefits of the welfare state, and some of them were able to build realistic expectations out of the education available to their children. In this context, most of the families decided to stay instead of returning to their homeland. In earlier studies rare cases have been reported to the present writer of people trying their fortune back in Pakistan (Bolognani 2007d).

Investment in neither Mirpur or Bradford was rewarded straight away. In Pakistan, lack of infrastructure to support ambitious businesses, bureaucracy and complicated family dynamics apparently undermined the success of courageous entrepreneurial attempts. In England, poor economic conditions meant tight competition between Asians and whites for jobs, accommodation and other kinds of resources (Mawby and Batta 1980:33; Singh 2002:169).

In 1959 Pakistanis in Bradford owned only five enterprises: two food stores (with a butcher's attached) and three cafes. In 1966 there were 133 businesses owned by Pakistanis: 51 food stores and 16 cafés; by 1970 there were 260, amongst which were 15 private clubs and two bakeries (Dhaya 1974). In 1978 Pakistanis owned 600 businesses (35 per cent of which were in Manningham) (Aldrich et al. 1981).

Some data collected in 1982 show that in Britain 18 per cent of Asian men were self-employed, against only 14 per cent of whites (Modood:1996). This proportion is similar to Bradford's, and shows that entrepreneurship is a likely outcome for Asian minorities. Instead of being a consequence of investing capital already held, the aetiology of Asian entrepreneurship is much more complex (see Chapter Five).

While between the 1970s and 1980s the demographic growth of the

Asian population naturally required more and more specific shops, recession did not hold back their economic development. Entrepreneurship was in fact a solution to what has been called 'blocked upward mobility' (Aldrich et al.1981). Furthermore, during recession the Pakistani community was able to rely on resources that were not available to the white community: they took frequent advantage of traditional interest-free credit options within the community—i.e. *kameti*, a system of credit rotation especially used by women (Shaw 2000; Werbner 2001). While English shops were closing down, Asian shops were being opened. Asian entrepreneurship was not only a symptom of assertiveness but seems to have been generated primarily by resistance to adversity. In businesses, mostly run by families, worker flexibility and total commitment guaranteed better outcomes and durability compared to the then unstable condition of the British labour market.

The success of businesses in those years depended on the need for a focused market able to provide for the specific needs of the Asian community. The differentiation of the market kept the competition between English and Asian enterprises to a minimum for a long time, and has also been seen as a factor enhancing segregation in the city (Aldrich et al.1981).

One evident change, as in other former textile cities in the North, was what has been captured in the phrase 'from textile mills to taxi ranks' (Kalra 2000). Pakistani-owned taxis are significant indicators of the economic history of the community. This is a very convenient occupation for men who still appreciate the value of tradition by performing all the duties of visiting family and friends, or who periodically return to Pakistan for several weeks, as private-hire companies can be flexible (Bolognani 2002). Sometimes the taxi licence is shared by relatives, so the same car can be on the road for more than one shift, driven by more than one person. Taxi drivers seem to represent a substantial part of the 'Asian economic niche' (see Chapter Five). At the same time, however, due to their mobile lives and relatively unsanctioned freedom, they appeared during the research as the occupational category more likely to be treated as a folk-devil (cf. Chapter Five).

Perhaps the most famous Asian business sector in Bradford, however, is the catering industry; Bradford is often referred to as the UK's 'capital of curry'. Importantly, attached to this industry are related activities such as specialised butchers and food-import companies. However, this is only one of the industries that have flourished in Bradford as a result of Asian entrepreneurship. Recently, a new regeneration plan for the city has been based on the 'BrAsian' (McLoughlin 2006b) identity of Bradford: a museum of spices and a public hall called 'Casa Mela'[29], which it is hoped will be the centre of the renewed city centre. The identity of Bradford, it seems, is now permanently bound to its strengthening Asian component

3.6 Assertiveness, Self-defence and Political Struggles in the 1980s

While the Asian communities in Bradford were struggling to survive following the economic recession of the 1970s, the early 1980s saw the British National Party widely campaigning in West Yorkshire. The National Front opened the 'Yorkshire Campaign to Stop Immigration', and racial attacks and violent episodes increased. Asians were being blamed for the bad economic situation (Amin 2003:461) and some of them felt compelled to find alternative ways to resist and to defend their community.

In 1981 the police arrested twelve teenagers (later to become known as the 'Bradford Twelve') who were putting together home-made bombs, apparently for the purposes of self-defence (Murphy 1982; Singh 2002:27; McLoughlin 2006b). At the same time the Asian community found itself once again cohesive, in spite of internal differences; they built a strong lobby to persuade the City Council to provide *halal* meat in schools (Siddique 1993:162, Singh 2002:27).

Between 1982 and 1984, Bradford was on the front pages of national newspapers through the so-called 'Honeyford affair'. Honeyford was the headmaster of the Drummond Middle School in Manningham, one of the areas with the highest concentration of Muslims. Honeyford published a series of articles against the multicultural position of the City Council. In an article which appeared in the *Times Education Supplement*, he accused the Pakistani population, according to Siddique's (1993:168) and Kureishi's (1996) reconstruction, of having a genetically hereditary lack of democratic knowledge. If these racist views were not enough, some crucial passages from the *Salisbury Review* were translated into Urdu in the *Yorkshire Post* (Singh 2002:35), and they had such publicity in the Muslim community that many of the families felt as if they had been challenged in their *izzat*. Subsequently, an alliance between Muslim families, the Labour left and socialists compelled Ray Honeyford to retire.

The Honeyford affair has been regarded by some interested in the political history of Bradford as a turning point for the participation of the Asian community in public democratic life. Mirpuris in particular, who successfully mobilised against Honeyford, realised their capacity to apply pressure even without involving other Asian groups. The Council for Mosques opened in 1981 and quickly gained recognition in the city by participating in a variety of political campaigns; its members took part in the first attempts to free Lumb Lane from prostitution by organising petitions (Sid-

dique 1993:119).
3.7 The Rushdie Affair and Vigilantism
After the awakening of political awareness during the Honeyford affair, there was another event which marked a turning point in the way the Pakistani community perceived itself in the city—the Rushdie affair.

In January 1989 a group of Pakistani men publicly burnt a copy of *The Satanic Verses* (Samad 1992; Siddique 1993; Lewis 2002; Singh 2002; Herbert 2003). The local branch of W.H. Smith was forced to remove the book from its shelves, and even today Bradford University library only gives access to a copy after the completion of a form; the subject is still considered sensitive.

The promoter of the public outcry was the Council of Mosques, the same institution that had coordinated the upheaval against Honeyford and had been commonly perceived (Lewis 2002; Singh 2002:41) as a major example of good will in Bradford race-relations matters.

The absence of a blasphemy law covering the Muslim faith became the focal point of the protest (Herbert 2003), and heated debates in the city lasted until they were absorbed in 1990 by issues surrounding the war in Iraq. In this tense atmosphere, somewhat like that following 11 September 2001, Bradford Muslims became victims of physical attacks and prejudice (Samad 1992). It seems that the popularity of and the reliance on the Council of Mosques grew sharply. While the few Asian councillors were perceived as too diplomatic, the Pakistani community saw in the Council their principal defendant. Samad argues that in this way a pseudo-religious revival started. In fact, religion was in some sense a political issue and a means of cohesion, as the number of people regularly attending mosques did not undergo any change:

> The Youth were resorting to Islamic idioms and metaphors to express their discontent against society which refused to accept them on an equal footing. Symbolically this was epitomised by their exclusion from the Yorkshire Cricket Club, despite being excellent cricketers who were born and bred in Bradford. (Samad 1992:516)

Samad also reports that some young people lobbied the Council of Mosques—willing to build bridges with the younger generation—not only to condemn the war on Iraq, but also to support Saddam Hussein. It was clear that none of these positions were seen favourably by the majority in the city, and political success on these matters naturally was impossible.

In addition to the pseudo-religious revival, Herbert (2003) has pointed out how important it is to see the Rushdie affair in the Mirpuri cultural context. Herbert argues that Bradford Muslims, given what is considered by many as worship of an almost deified Prophet, were particularly affected by the 'lampooning' of his person in the book.

While the Honeyford affair was a political matter relating to multiculturalism and citizenship, the Rushdie affair and its extension for some participants into the support of Saddam Hussein became a stimulant for religious radicalisation.

One informant synthesised this process in these words: 'It is a logical step to become radical as a Muslim in the West' (Amjad, quoted in Bolognani 2002).

One of the main manifestations of public action based on or at least articulated through religion was the violent eight-week struggle in 1995 against prostitution in Manningham, followed in the summer by the riots (Bolognani 2007c).

The 1995 riots were the climax of tensions which had been building up since the elections in the spring. The electoral campaign in the Asian areas was characterised by contests imported from Kashmir. Even the younger generation became involved, and groups of young men organised noisy public manifestations in the streets shouting 'Jat' or 'Bains', according to whether they were supporting the candidate of one caste[30] or the other (Vine 1997). In Pakistan, this is the way electoral campaigns are conducted (Samad 1992), but it may have contributed to creating a climate of unease in the city.

At the same time, a group of residents, including whites, started patrolling the streets in order to prevent prostitution; soon a religious group had monopolised the campaign. The clamour for action led to other men joining the campaign, and it was soon transformed into something else, as described by Bradford-born novelist Alam:

> Manningham [is] a pretty quiet part of town, compared to what it used to be a few years before. The locals, mostly fanatical Muslims (words from the press, not me) set up little petrol squads which chased out prostitutes and dealers ... And when I say chased, that's just what I mean: ran them out, with bats, petrol bombs and God knows what else. (Alam 2002: 123)

The action lasted eight weeks. As the campaign had started by referring to the necessity of changing Manningham into an area more compatible with

Islamic values and customs, the religious idiom was taken over by those who had joined later and resorted to violence. Many older men, although taken aback by such action, struggled to condemn the degeneration of the campaign because of its Islamic connotations. After rediscovering their Muslim identity through the Rushdie affair, the younger generation were trying it out as a powerful cohesion device, as a source of pride and satisfaction (Macey 1999a, 1999b).

The riots took place on 9–11 June 1995. Around 300 young British Pakistanis attacked the 'Cop Shop' in Toller Lane and non-Muslim shops, looting and getting hold of petrol bombs. At the end of the riots, the action was reconstructed (Allen 1996; Singh 2002:43) and the starting-point was traced to a rumour about police attacking a Pakistani woman and her child and the running-over of a Pakistani man. Further investigation (Allen 1996; Macey 1999a, b) showed that the police had only intervened to suspend a street football-match that had appeared to be becoming violent. When the police were insulted as a response to their intervention, the tense atmosphere and the prejudice which had built up in the preceding few months exacerbated the situation. Rumours circulated, stirring up a protest not addressed at any specific target. Some Pakistani women tried to mediate in the streets (with the experience gained in the guerrilla action against prostitutes) between the men who were ready to riot and the police, but unsuccessfully. There is a belief nowadays in Bradford that the police tend to disregard much ambiguous behaviour by Pakistanis, because they have experienced how easily a riot can start even from an innocent police intervention, but this is countered by perceptions of 'over-policing' and complaints about discriminatory stop-and-search (see Chapter Eight).

Subsequent interpretations noted the lack of preparation of the police and the bias of the City Council (Taj 1996). The Conservative government refused to invest money in a public inquiry, and Bradford itself only produced documents which which presented inconsistent accounts and ended up being published separately (Taj 1996; Macey 1999a; Singh 2002:46).

3.8 The Climax of Tension: 2001

Between 1995 and 2001 Bradford's smaller police stations were attacked a couple of times, and periodically small groups of young Pakistanis confronted the police. The national press had overlooked such incidents and the outburst of the 2001 riots surprised British public opinion. Bradfordians, however, had foreseen the escalation of violence, and some were in a way prepared for it. In spring 2001, a commission chaired by Sir Herman Ouseley had started working on the report that was only launched after the riots in July.

The Bradford riots had been preceded by a series of events in northern England that had put the police on the alert (see disorders in Lidget Green, Bradford, Leeds, Burnley, Accrington and Oldham (Macey 2002; Bagguley and Hussain 2003b). On 7 July 2001, after a public Anti-Nazi League rally against the British National Party (BNP), who had threatened to march on Bradford but had been banned by the local authorities, the worst riots on English soil in 20 years took place (Macey: 2002). The rioting went on for two days in the Manningham area[31] and cost Bradford City Council £23 million and the police £10 million (ibid).

These riots seem to differ from the past as there was no clear collective political agenda behind them, and they included organised looting and stealing (see Khalil's words quoted below). The political claim, implied, but not articulated with the same force as in the previous 1980 and 1995 episodes, was that the police should have defended the territory from the BNP and the National Front (NF):

> [The rioters] were really pissed off with the police because the police took their [BNP's] side rather than ours, rather than moving them out, they moved us out . . . these were outsiders, they should have got rid of them first, they shouldn't have allowed them to come[32]. (Jamal, student in his early twenties)

A clash between the young men and the police materialised in the absence of the real target, the BNP/NF. The Pakistani community, however, seemed to be united in its condemnation: most of the elders condemned the events, and it is said that many denounced the young people who had taken part in it (Macey 2002) when pictures of more than 150 rioters (or alleged rioters) were published (Bagguley and Hussain 2003b). However, a feeling of double standards in terms of sentencing prevailed, and in 2005 it was more popular amongst Bradford Pakistanis to observe a feeling of indulgence towards the rioters; the 2001 riots seemed to gain a more rounded political status after their occurrence. Had it not been for the harsh sentencing, the condemnation of the actions of a few young men might have lasted longer. The majority went to prison, and the harsh sentences they served were widely criticised:

> These young lads only wanted to go looting . . . but what about these football hooligans? How come they aren't in for three–four years? (Amir, quoted in Bolognani 2002)

The harsh sentencing was perceived as discriminatory against minority ethnic groups (Kalra 2003); as a result, on coming out of prison the young men were not ostracised by the community and some were even praised:

> My sister was just telling me that one of her friends, her brother, just got released from prison, not because of the riots, but because of something else, and on the same day there was this other boy who'd been released because of the riots, and their family, they ordered a limousine and they had like quite a lot of music, and happiness that he'd come out of prison. But they made a big show about it! [laughs] It was this idealising way, that you took part in a racial thing . . . fighting for your own territory. (Fatima, student, 19 years old)

In 1995 the lack of policing in areas inhabited mostly by Pakistanis, and the perception of police racism, were some of the causes of the riots. Locally, the institution of the Minority Police Liaison Committee guaranteed a better exchange between minority ethnic groups and the police. Nationally, the publication of the MacPherson Report (1999), with its recognition of 'institutional racism', dictated new guidelines and focused public attention on the police. The recognition of minority ethnic groups and their needs became paramount. The 2001 riots seem to have been organised on a different premise. Most of the community were not behind the young men who participated in the violence. Collective rights were not part of the discourses used by most of the rioters when speaking about their experiences:

> Jamal (student in his early twenties): 'The people I know who were in the riots, they said "we were just having a laugh" . . . their intentions was to get past the police, go into town, break into shops, get all the design clothes for themselves, keep them or sell them, this is all they wanted to do.'
> MB: 'You imply there was no link with the threat of the BNP?'
> Jamal: 'That was an excuse. The first guy who got slashed by the BNP[33] lives around here and I was chatting with him yesterday and the guy who has come out from prison was there as well, it was the three of us. Basically he said . . . the riots was because of the BNP and the BNP shouldn't have been there . . . so it was a bit of both . . . a laugh and the BNP.'

Causation may not be adequately explained in terms of a response to a pattern of social exclusion and discrimination linked to racist governmental practices, but rather in those of a multiplicity of local factors (such as long-term cultural, educational and material deprivation), and of grievances with local police accumulated over a number of years (Bolognani 2007c).

Numerous racist attacks against Asians took place after the riots, in a punitive reaction to the 7 July disorders.

Between 2001 and 2002 Bradford was in the limelight when major political changes were occurring, both in Europe and at a global level. While the debate about the civic loyalty of Muslims was developing in Britain following the riots, the world was struck by the 11 September atrocity ('9/11'). In spring 2002, in France, Le Pen, the Front National candidate took second place after Chirac in the national elections, increasing the fears of fascism that had stirred the riots in northern England eight months earlier.

3.9 Local and Global: Bradford Post-9/11

Bradford in 2001 was struggling to counter the national stereotypes about the city, which seemed to be perceived as mainly related to its Pakistani community. At the same time, a series of problems connected with crime had served only to reinforce the general perception of a 'degeneration' of inner-city life.

In 2002 Bradford had been given the name 'Capital of Heroin' (Apaxton 2002). Although there are no data on the ethnicity of the criminals involved in the drug trade, Asian residential areas are widely affected by the phenomenon (ibid; *Careers Bradford* 2002:3). Drugs are a major problem, and the police have adopted a zero-tolerance strategy to break the dealership business (West Yorkshire Police 2004). In 2001 and 2003 the Bradford Chamber of Commerce and Industry conducted an independent crime survey among its members, as well as responding to the one distributed by the British Chamber (BCCI); the results show that all five priorities outlined by the respondents in order to improve their business included crime control and the fight against deprivation (BCCI 2003).

Although in Bradford there is little official evidence of a significant Pakistani share in the drug-related business or in drug consumption, the city seems to have been victim of a moral panic that regards Pakistanis as the main agents of trafficking and selling (Webster 1996; Macey 2002). Emphasis on the alleged self-segregation of communities (Phillips 2001), their 'otherness' (Alexander 2004) and the international climate of suspicion affecting Muslims (Grillo 2004) have all contributed to a moral panic about British Pakistanis in general and Bradford Pakistanis in particular.

As we have seen in this chapter, since the 1980s, with the Bradford Twelve episode, the Honeyford and Rushdie affairs, then the 1995 disturbances and the 2001 riots, the Pakistani community in Bradford has presented an image of assertiveness. But, at the same time, forms of unconventional protest have contributed to the racially-motivated moral panic present in the city (Samad 1992; Herbert 2003). Various cases of violence have taken place in the last 20 years which have been viewed as political acts or as self-defence (Mawby and Batta 1980:18). Asian vigilantism was a turning point in territorialisation, and in the process of acquiring a local identity (Webster 1999:549, 551; Alexander 2000:4), but has been misread as a change in the reliability of law-abiding Asians (Alexander 200:8, 128; Kundnani 2002). The visibility of territorialism, and the 'spectacularisation' of particular events like the public disturbances, have given a bad image to the Pakistani community (Webster 1997).

It is the intent of this book to investigate to what extent the crime issue is affecting the Bradford Pakistani community, and how it is tackled by all generations in terms of prevention, social sanctions and the reintegration of criminals. This reflection may benefit from a contextualisation into the diasporic history of the community, as the level of general integration may also be measured in terms of patterns of deviance, as Alam sarcastically states:

> I'd come across ignorant racists in my time and the ones on the drugs scene sounded no different. For these people, pakis took their jobs, their women, their shops, their homes, and now, pakis were in on their criminal activities. Us pakis, we had this habit of taking one liberty after another... Fucking losers couldn't even work out why they were so shit at what they did. (Alam 2002:70)

3.10 A Community caught between *Biraderi* and the *Umma*?

This chapter has described how *biraderi* is a central and probably unique feature of the Pakistani communities in Bradford, and the historical development of their settlement can be only fully understood by acknowledging the role of *biraderi* in it. For the scope of this book, however, it was important to highlight how a traditional structure such as *biraderi* may strengthen the internal relational proximity that has been considered by some as a crucial variable of informal social control (Braithwaithe 1989:14; Burnside and Baker 1994:19, 21; Wardak 2000:16; Hope 2001:430). Such internal proximity may be considered both an asset and a liability, and in Chapter Five it will emerge that there is an increasing number of individuals who would refer to '*biraderi*sm' as a negative phenomenon. During the research stronger ties were often perceived as potentially causing fragmentation, and weak ties as more advantageous for individuals. Virtual ties such as the one of the global Muslim nation, the *Umma*, also played an important referential role in discourses encountered during the fieldwork.

By comparing the 2002 findings (Bolognani 2007d) and the present ones, it was possible to see a consistent use of the word 'community' as the signifier of an ethnic and religious group. Although this term was rather fluid and could significantly change depending on context, by for example referring to regional parochialisms, it is important to confirm that a Bradford Pakistani distinctiveness was recognised, in terms of culture, symbols, religion and modes of interaction. In spite of the internal fragmentation of diasporic groups, it has already been observed by other commentators that 'community' may not be an imagined construct necessarily conveying ideas of homogeneity. Back, for example, argues that:

> Ideas about 'community' are understood to consist of a series of organising principles (community discourses) that are interrelated and mutually reinforcing (a semantic system). . . . I view the notion of 'community' or 'local style' as the product of competing social definitions, not homogenous, and composed of a variety of community discourses and although I accept that in some contexts particular definitions—or versions—of community predominate, all community discourse should be treated as having equal significance. (1996:29, 30)

Werbner illustrates a similar standpoint through a British Pakistani example:

> Community had become, in effect, a kind of argument through practice: an argument of images between those different knots of friends with their different lifestyles, consumption patterns and visions of what their community should be like, by comparison to other communities, seen from a particular vantage point.
>
> Community was nevertheless constituted as practice by the traces of localised discourses and interactions taking place in a myriad of public events: at weddings and funerals, fund-raising drives, mosque elections, factional struggles, public protests, religious festivals, national and religious celebrations and ceremonies, as well as in multi-cultural or multi-racial or multi-religious forums and arenas created by the state and local state. (1996:70)

And Saifullah-Khan, one of the most thorough authors writing on Bradford Pakistanis, argues that:

> Contact with non-Pakistanis who tend to classify minorities according to nationality, colour or some notion of 'Race' influences the self-perception of the individual concerned, particularly when and if the connotations are derogatory. This external definition, and the accompanying behaviour influence the development of a minority. . . . The external definition of the majority is indicated in the persistent use of such terminology as 'The Pakistani Community' in the society at large, in the media and, most significantly in the field of community relations. (1976b:104)

During the Bradford fieldwork, the strong sense of community, and the frequency with which it was referred to, contributed to understanding how Bradford Pakistanis earned the name of 'urban villagers' (Saifullah-Khan 1976a) in the 1970s. Today, they may be called 'global villagers', an exception in the 'isolated, anomic, acted out segmented roles of urban men and women' (Bell 1976:292), but at the same time increasingly literate, with discourses of international brotherhood and sisterhood, of universality and maximum 'bridging'. They have preserved certain characters of distinct ethnic resources and networks, 'trust, norms, networks that can improve the efficiency of society by facilitating coordinated actions' (Putnam 1993:167), and have characterised the survival at first of a *Gemeinschaft* in a *Gesellschaft* (ibid:114), but it would too simplistic to see them as essentially inclined to situate themselves in a global 'Ummatic' setting, when their relationship to Bradford, its history and how it overlaps with their family heritage is one of the most fundamental qualities of their civic engagement (see Chapters Five, Eight and Nine).

4

CRIMINOLOGICAL DISCOURSES: LABELLING

'Deviance is in the eye of the beholder' (Simmons 1969:4).

In Chapter One it was argued that social constructionism may be of relevance to the study of crime amongst minority ethnic groups, insofar as it unveils their structures, belief systems and means of social control.

The major challenge for studies that break the taboo of studying crime and culture together is therefore to reach the inner mechanisms of the process of constructing deviance and social control, and thus to combine culture, structure and agency.

The idea of crime as social construction seems to have become paramount in criminology (Wilson and Herrnstein 1985:21–2; Muncie 1996:9–10; Eadie and Morley 1999:438). Furthermore, the connection between crime (especially as a violation of moral codes) and cultures is an issue common to many criminologists' writings (Muncie 1996:13), whether discussed from a cultural, ideological, historical or political point of view. Malinowski affirmed as early as 1926 (cf. Chapter One) that as customs are the primary instrument of social control, even occasional detachment from customs produces a tendency to criminality. In this view, perceived deviance gains its existence through detachment from a community's standards, a concept similar to anomie.

In 1963, Becker outlined 'labelling theory', which made crime a relative concept. According to Becker, an act is criminal when it is labelled as such by society (Braithwaite 1989:2). Becker's theory has more to do with hegemonic discourses than with culture: powerful groups invent the rules whose infraction means deviance.

While academia has accepted crime as a construction, it has been reluctant to include culture in the study of crime (Philips and Bowling 2003:270, 272). Outside academia, instead, the racialisation of crime (that is to say the alleged link between a specific group and some criminal activities) has been much more explored. Often, it has been argued, media investigation of such links has had counter-productive results for race relations (Miller 2001:1), reviving the belief that some cultures may be more violent than others (Curtis 1975:115). Werbner (2004:898), for instance, has exposed the situation of a 'South Asian morality' under scrutiny by the public gaze of White Britons. Webster has denounced the construction of a 'British Asian criminality' (1997) and Alexander (2004:535) has recorded a widespread public concern towards an 'Asian disfunctionality'. This moral panic has particularly affected external representations of Bradford and its Asian community since 2001, when the riots took place and the attacks on the Twin Towers spread the fear of 'home-grown terrorists' (Sengupta 2005).

Instead of reviewing external views on crime in the community, which might provide a statistical analysis and a survey of methods and techniques, this chapter will analyse the internal points of view. Unveiling the major preoccupations according to the community rather than to outsiders will contribute to the understanding of how practical concerns, cultural and religious beliefs and moral dilemmas play a part in the construction of the idea of crime, and consequently what strategies are adopted by the community itself to debate and understand them.

The chapter opens with an evaluation of the positions taken on a supposed Bradford Pakistani pathology with respect to crime. Informants denounced the moral panic about their community stirred up by biased media attention, while that community, it was said, was facing the same problems as any other. Ethnic specificity, however, was to be found in a distinctive way of facing the same problems and defining criminal activities. A classification of priorities in the fight against crime emerged in terms of crime's perceived long-term effects on the structure of the community, and drugs were considered to be the greatest present problem.

By comparing the main concerns expressed by the media (i.e. terrorism, and racial tension culminating in rioting) and those expressed by the community, this research will generate the first data-based evidence of the criminological and labelling discourses circulating in the Bradford Pakistani community, and their connections with more familiar national concerns.

4.1 Crime in the Community: an Endemic Problem?

In starting to investigate the existence of community-based criminology, it was important to delineate a definition of 'community' which responded to what the term meant to the research participants. The fluidity of the term, or *apna log* (our people), has already been discussed in the previous chapter. It is important to recall here that a strong Bradford Pakistani distinctiveness was recognised in terms of culture, symbols, religion and modes of interaction, both by insiders and outsiders, but at the same time coexisting subcultures, religious differences or ethnic provenances constituted important variables in the heterogeneity of discourses.

Once the existence of such constructions of the community was verified, it was possible to investigate whether Bradford Pakistanis also believed that their relations to crime, whether as victims or perpetrators, had some specificities as compared to other groups in the city.

Throughout the research, participants claimed that in their view crime in the community had risen exponentially over the previous few years (usually it was said in the previous ten years). Most of the sample lived in areas with high levels of clustering, and this may be a reason why when they spoke of crime they mainly referred to deeds committed by members of the community, and only in a few cases by outsiders (either people coming from different cities or whites, Afro-Caribbeans and gipsies from Bradford).

The transmission of the Channel 4 documentary *Edge of the City*[34], however, had a considerable impact on the interviewees, a majority of whom saw it as a biased account of some of the district's problems and one that damaged the reputation of the Pakistani community. They had felt overexposed as a group by the actions of a few individuals when, it was argued, similar things were happening in all communities. The reaction of the community towards the documentary had become so strong that a young film maker was researching the topic in order to make a 'counter-documentary', including an analysis of the same problems affecting white Bradfordians.

In the course of fieldwork the research itself was often challenged, as most interviewees found that such a study on crime might create a pathological view of their community, while they believed that the whole of society was under the same strains. However, once the aim of the research was clarified, participants usually pointed out that some degree of specificity existed:

> I personally don't think it's a problem with a particular community. I believe there's a problem with the society at large; the only difference is that certain communities have decided to deal with it differently.
> (Imran, teacher in his early thirties)

Although the whole society had to face the same problems, then, the Paki-

thing to put up with had started trickling into the popular understanding:

> They [the parents] will be worried because it's their kids at the end of the day, but the thing is, right, you know when there's something happening in the community and is happening regularly like a routine sets ... (Adam, community worker in his late twenties)

> The kids ... I suppose ... it's all they know ... they're very street-wise in the sense that they know what is going on around them and I think they accept that sort of life. (Bashir, student, 19 years old)

> But I think [by] the elder generation ... they are looked down upon ... but they [the older generation] don't say it, because of this 'we're gonna die soon, it really doesn't matter'. You know the sense of hopelessness ... it does exist, quite a lot. (Fatima, student, 19 years old)

The ones who were able to compare today's situation with that obtaining during their adolescence seemed pessimistic:

> I'm not joking but virtually every second family ... it's accepted. It's become a social construction thing now, where it's accepted as an ideal. (Amir, unemployed, in his mid-thirties)

> MB: 'And what about these shootings that happened, do you think people are scared of walking around?'
> Jamil (entrepreneur in his mid-thirties): 'No, this is normal! Seriously ...'
> Adam (community worker in his late twenties): 'He's right ... you see, something happens, a couple of days later ...'
> Jamil: 'It dies out!'

However, the diffused sense of hopelessness and frustration was accompanied by a unanimous agreement on the one key source of the general criminal threat to the life of the community:

> When we were growing up there wasn't so much drugs around, and there wasn't so much violence ... and we, I'm not saying we were angels, because as teenagers you do good and bad, you misbehave and I think we misbehaved as well, but the difference is proliferation of drugs. (Zameer, community worker in his early thirties)

The causes of the recent proliferation of deviant behaviours, therefore, were not to be looked for in a Pakistani endemic pathology, but in the universal problem of drugs.

4.3 Many Problems, One Name: Drugs in the Community

As we have begun to indicate, one of the findings consistent with other published information (Apaxton 2002; West Yorkshire Police 2004) was that the main problem affecting the community was considered to be drugs. Although there is only a limited amount of research on the drug problem amongst Asians in the Bradford district, it is consistent in reporting that Asians are under-represented among users (Webster 1996:11; Pearson and Patel 1998:17). In spite of these data, drugs were cited by the respondents as their main concern, confirming the discrepancy between external perceptions informing policy outputs and insiders' concerns.

Drugs were seen as the trigger for almost all other criminal activities, from prostitution to gun crime, but also, and more importantly, as destabilising for the core of the community. Drug-related offences, in fact, were seen to jeopardise the stability of families and produce role models and lifestyles consistent with neither the Muslim ethos nor the binding collective social values of Pakistani tradition (cf. Chapter Five).

Although drugs were part of those problems considered by the research participants to affect all Bradford communities, there seemed to be a popular understanding that the drug market nowadays was mainly in the hands of men of Pakistani origin. One teenage girl expressed the view that asylum seekers from Iraq were playing a major part in the local drug market at the moment, but this view was not been expressed by anybody else or backed up by any evidence. The popular understanding was instead that the drug market had been taken over from men of African/Caribbean origin by men of Pakistani origin.

> Twenty years ago when I was growing up, you had the Afro Caribbean community, quite a large community in Bradford. And they were into a lot of the drug-dealing, prostitution and stuff like that. Now we've sort of taken over from them, while the Afro Caribbean community have sort of moved on, and we're doing that kind of stuff, although if you look at it from our community, it is frowned upon, that kind of behaviour, if you look at our background, our religion . . . you know, that's the last thing we should be doing, selling drugs and pimping. (Zameer, community worker in his early thirties)

Tahir (teacher in his early forties): 'When I'm travelling in a taxi I talk with taxi drivers, and they tell you. Some of them are very hurt that the community is into this, some of them are very proud that all the drug business is ours now, and we're taking over. I've heard this! "We have taken over from the Afro Caribbean, and there was a big fight", and whether it is bravado or this person is involved, God knows, but you'd hear "we have taken over", but obviously this person's criminal, that's why he's very happy with his achievements.
MB: 'They wouldn't tell me these things . . .'
Tahir: 'Yes, but because I'm mischievous myself and I try to find out information, I'm saying "what's happening with this fight" and the lingo would suggest that I want information "what's going on here" and also they think maybe I'm Pakistani, I'd approve this, or maybe [I would] feel happy, a part of the gang maybe [laughs].'

> The black community are currently kicked out from Bradford because the Pakistani community, the drug-dealing Pakistani community, is too strong. (Abdul, social worker in his early forties)

4.4 Drug-dealing, Drug-taking and the Chain of Criminal Activities

While during the interviews the older generations did not clearly distinguish between drug-taking and drug-dealing, the younger the respondents were, the more they were able to provide detailed information on the drug market.

Drug-dealing, according to all the young respondents, was in some sense spread more widely than drug-taking, as some people would take up the former as a business venture or as a way to gain quick cash but would not take part in its consumption:

> I used to believe that they had to take drugs to sell them on, but there is somebody, some sort of disgustingly selfish people, who look after their own body but won't think twice about destroying someone else's body. There will be people who take drugs and sell them but then I also know people who are very clean-cut, the only thing they take from the drugs is the profit they make by selling them on. (Zaara, shop assistant and special constable in her early twenties)

Participation in the drug business was described as not necessarily a lifetime activity. It was possible, it was said, that some individuals would agree to sporadic drug deals (cf. also Webster 1997:78) or even a one-off job when needing to pay a debt or to invest in a business venture. The demand for such jobs was such that one could easily move in and out the drug-dealing circle, unless caught:

> There were two Pathans, they were brothers and one of the brothers said to the other, if you bring the heroin back you can pay the mortgage off and you'll have a big life. And the police followed them from UK to Pakistan and chased them and they caught them in Manchester airport. . . . They used to work and everything, and they got into this one drug thing and nobody knew until they got caught. (Adam, community worker in his late twenties)

Such mobility across the boundaries of criminal activity (some people being defined by Webster as 'go-betweens', see Chapter Six) was, albeit disagreeable, not a major source of stigma for the ones who were known to have participated in illegal activities for a limited period with a view to investing such revenue into a 'kosher business' (Kamran, interview with author). Those who did this tended to benefit the community in some way, for example through donations to mosques (Amir, interview with author). As discussed above, the higher grade of stigma appeared to be based on the relation between a criminal activity and the stability of the community: the most serious offence was that perceived as undermining the community. Drug addicts and those living off the drug business, therefore, were the cause of the most serious preoccupations expressed in the course of the research. Informants tended to believe that drug-taking would rarely be a sporadic activity, but would often become an addiction, in contrast with the only relevant research evidence existing that register high rates of recreational use (Pearson and Patel 1998:17).

Because of health and behavioural effects known to be produced in the addicted, class-A drugs were linked to the potential breakdown of families, the core of the community structure (see Chapter Three). More surprisingly, when addiction was discussed, dependence on prescription drugs appeared to be a major concern, especially as far as women were concerned (data consistent with Pearson and Patel 1998:14–15). Practitioners recorded a rise in depression and consequently a growth in the chance of abuse of the medicines prescribed (see below). Individuals who abused prescription drugs were often said to having sunk into depression or 'stress' due to family problems. Sometimes even the consumption of cannabis was linked to family problems, although amongst young men its consumption had often started as a recreational activity:

MB: 'What do you mean by stress then?'
Bano (student, 18 years old): 'A lot of Asian families I think . . . what happens in families nowadays, maybe when . . . I've got a mate, a really, really good mate, and he's a guy and his sister ran away from home and he smokes weed like on a daily basis, like he has two, three cigarettes a day of weed, and I was asking "why do you smoke?" and he says, "it just releases me, it's like if I didn't smoke it and I came to school, I'd be like a miserable git, so when I smoke weed I feel so happy, it just releases the tensions." The sister, she liked this guy and she ran away from home. She's gone back now but it's like . . . we call it *izzat*. Basically it's bad name, like if it goes out in the community, it'll be really bad name. That's why a lot of guys smoke it because they can't take the pressure, they just want to get everything off their shoulders and that's the main reason why guys smoke weed. . . . [My dad] started smoking weed when he was about 15 and now he's about 40 something.'
MB: 'Was your dad born here?'
Bano: 'No, my dad was born in Pakistan. He came here when he was about ten. He's been here most of his life and he smokes weed, so . . . but he's so addicted to it he can't leave it and that's why he's so ill, because when he leaves it he gets so ill. Because when my granddad had a stroke he fell into depression and now he hasn't really been able to get out of it.'

Many people who would smoke cannabis would not drink alcohol, as their popular understanding of the Quran, orally transmitted by older friends or family members, mentioned alcohol but not cannabis (cf. Pearson and Patel 1998:15). Recent research on addictions in Asian communities in the Midlands found that among Muslim drinkers, the majority tended to indulge in 'binge drinking' (Orford et al. 2004:27), and even in Bradford it was rare to hear of occasional drinkers amongst Muslims, as those who broke the Quranic law were, according to interviewees, more likely to be 'binge drinkers' or alcoholics. Men consuming alcohol or drugs were perceived as more likely to commit other offences, including domestic violence. Although it was not one of the most commonly mentioned issues in the research, domestic violence was a serious concern for practitioners, who were said to see a high proportion of these episodes in the Pakistani community:

> Obviously [domestic violence] is not only [based on] one factor, is a combination of factors, and majority of my clients, I can say with cer-

tainty, they are either dealing drugs (I am just focusing on the Asian community, because I work with Asian clients), or taking drugs, and all kinds of frauds. I've got clients whose husbands are doing benefit frauds, or clients whose husbands who are known pimps in Bradford. (Alina, community worker in her late thirties)

Domestic violence was therefore again something connected with the use of drugs. Nevertheless, according to some respondents, it was part of the troubles present in the community even in the pre-drugs era.

During the research, honour crimes such as killings or mutilations were very rarely talked about, but sexual behaviours not conforming to Islamic laws that prescribe abstinence before marriage were seen as connected with deviant behaviour. In particular an imam who was routinely called to help families whose children were taking drugs (see Chapter Seven) was convinced that it was through sexual encounters that young people would start breaking the Islamic law and then experiment with alcohol and drugs. At other times, through the consumption of drugs and alcohol, young people would agree to have sex and therefore, in his opinion, it was difficult to separate sexuality from drugs. Again, if drugs were connected to promiscuity, it was obvious that they were threatening the core structure of the community.

Amongst the crimes mentioned most often as a cause of deep concern there was gun crime, stemming, according to the respondents, from drug-related activities. This may have been due to the location of a big part of the interviews and participant observation on the Leeds Road area, where in 12 months there had been a few shootings, some not reported by the press but known to the participants:

I myself went to an MP . . . and I said 'OK it's gun crime but has anyone tackled why they are using the guns, getting to the point why?' . . . I even said to this MP, one of those kids will get killed, that [drugs] is what it gets down [to] . . . and what happens? Three weeks later someone's killed and I could say that to him, it happened because the community won't tackle the problem, they don't get to the core of the problem. Ok, it's gun crime, but what's related to gun crime? (Adam, community worker in his late twenties)

Ahmed (student, 16 years old): 'I don't know if they [my parents] are scared, but there was like that shooting on Leeds Road, a couple of minutes from our houses.'

Maria (student, 16 years old): 'But it's not like we go out and they shoot us, they don't just shoot you . . .'
Aqdus (student, 16 years old): 'It's their enemies . . .'
Maria: 'If you've got a problem with someone they"ll sort it out that way.'

In January 2005 a video was publicly presented by Age Concern about safety in the Asian community of Barkerend Road (parallel to Leeds Road). In the video, a Muslim woman complained that the area was affected by burglaries, car theft and fights, all related to the drug business. On top of that, a new concern was emerging: some of the more established drug dealers had taken the law into their own hands, and, with the excuse of helping acquaintances to sort out their grievances, they managed a system of revenge that was growing in popularity. The fear expressed in the video was that this would soon become a vicious circle of violence.

4.5 'Poisoning the Community'

While most of the press attention and moral panic about Bradford and its Pakistani community involved fear of terrorism and rioting, these were topics rarely discussed by the respondents, unless openly asked to. Terrorism and rioting were considered extraordinary episodes that would not necessarily erode the core of the community, although there was awareness of the effects of terrorism-related Islamophobia and the strain on their reputation produced by past riots. Behaviours seen as having long-term destabilising consequences, instead, were of greater concern. This was evident in conversations with shopkeepers on White Abbey Lane (where the 2001 riots started) and Leeds Road (once defined by the *Telegraph and Argus* as 'the Bronx' and now commonly referred to as such). The former group were optimistic about the development of their businesses and were surprised that I mentioned the riots as a symptom of a general disadvantage of the area; they considered it an isolated episode that had nothing to do with the community, but rather with reaction to an isolated event: the threat of the BNP marching on Bradford. By comparison the latter group, in spite of enjoying a renaissance in Leeds Road, where many new shops had opened and the house prices had risen considerably, tended to have deeper concerns about the future of their areas[35] These, according to some parents, ranged from anti-social behaviour to drug-dealing:

> Anti-social behaviour impacts on the community because we are living in the community, it impacts on me! . . . . we're Pakistani, yeah, and

if you grow up in an area where there's quite a lot of your extended family there, you're very inter-linked, aren't you? One's doing it, potentially the other one's doing it, the third's doing it, the cousin's doing it, the nephew's doing it... they find it quite difficult to manage that... where... a son's going off the rails, and another son's going off the rails and they all seem to get off the rails, they're all hanging around in gangs, they're not doing anything constructive... they're not going to school, they're not learning... they might not be selling drugs, but it may go on to that kind of behaviour and they're finding it very difficult. (Zameer, community worker in his early thirties)

One respondent defined the long-term process of negative change with the evocative expression 'poisoning the community':

They've poisoned the community. And you know, when you do well in the community, everyone wants a piece of that. If you've got a nice car outside your house, the next person will buy a nice car as well. If you buy nice clothes, [the] next person wants to wear it. This is what I'm talking about. They're like sheep, they can't think for themselves. The thing is they can't think for themselves because they don't understand they're poisoning the community, their own family. Because they're all following their way. (Abdul, social worker in his early forties)

Another seemed to express a similar concept with a religious metaphor:

So for example the teachings of Prophet Mohammed... for example, he says that if you keep company with a blacksmith you'll smell like a blacksmith afterwards. So you haven't done anything, you just kept company with him, but his type of job is very dirty, very smelly and if you keep company with him you'll smell like him after a while. But if you keep company with someone who sells perfumes you'll smell like him afterwards, so we do believe that changing the atmosphere and the company makes a big difference. (Imran, teacher in his early thirties)

The idea that modernity in its various forms is the cause of the 'erosion of communities', especially when supposedly 'rootless urban anonymity' destroys 'social bonds of culture and tradition', is an increasingly popular discourse (Pearson 1999:401). Here, however, the poisoning took both this moral form (degeneration of customs) and a more practical one (undermining businesses):

> Jamil (entrepreneur in his mid thirties): 'Business wise we have been affected ... because a lot of people have [been] driven away from this area, so people ... you know, we used to get a lot of the clientele from outside, to come to the area to buy. Now we don't get much of that.'
> MB: 'And is that because of the reputation of the area?'
> Jamil: 'Exactly. ... They [drug dealers] aren't benefiting the community, they're making it worse because to be honest with you, if somebody hangs around, 16–17 years old, doing nothing and being better off than anybody else, they'll want to do the same thing as him. That's why they don't go and work for somebody. They don't wanna work hard labour, they want it the easy way.'

> If they [criminals] had actually stopped and thought about it, they looked back at it, they'd see how much impact it has on people who're stealing ... they might steal from, let's say, a supermarket, and they might steal for years and years and years, what it comes down to at the end, it comes down to the taxpayers, that loss ... even your local community such as in the riots when in my area ... our taxes have been high. I couldn't actually get a credit card for two years because I lived in that area of Bradford. It was just my postcode that stopped me from getting a credit card. And I actually found this out when I spoke to someone about it 'cos I kept being refused. And I talked to someone and [they] said, "It must be your postcode" and I asked "Why does that matter?" They went, "If there've been a lot of troubles in that area, if that area's black-listed for some reason or the other and it's not a potential area where we can get profit from that area, so ... things like that they have an impact. (Zaara, shop assistant and special constable in her early twenties)

The poisoning of the community was a practical and moral term also linked to 'community breakdown' (see Chapter Five). Participants normally referred to a time when the community was very cohesive and the crime rate low, while at present the situation was the opposite. Sometimes, however, there were different positions on whether the breakdown was an effect of drugs and their string of deviant behaviours, or whether these had been generated by it:

Akbar (retired shop owner, aged 70): 'Everybody now is [a] family man. Before they live[d] with 15, 20 people, not just by [oneself], it was too different [a] position [from what it is] now. Everybody [now is a] family man, the children are born, children grown, that is a problem, growing. When they grow it is problem, it is not all the time [the] same position . . . everybody think of himself, [they are] not in the same position [to] help one another.'
Amir: 'I think because before they were only single males from different families, and then some brought the wives over, then they got their own families and the second generation, third generation, their families have got so big that they can only help themselves.'

If I'm out for myself, who cares if I affect another 15 people . . . at last I have succeeded and this is the mentality we've been bred into. This is the mentality my father has been bred into, and this is the mentality the kids are growing into. (Imran, teacher in his early thirties)

The idea of poisoning and contamination can help in understanding the managing of the classification of crime within the community.

Douglas argues that 'Society reward[s] conformity and repulse[s] attack' (ibid:115) and ideas of purity and non-purity maintain the social structure (ibid:132). Pollution, according to Douglas, is linked to feelings of threat, of a perceived danger, that leads to frustration as society members recognise their inability, in practice, to punish disorder: 'when moral indignation is not reinforced by practical sanctions, pollution beliefs can provide a deterrent to wrongdoers' (ibid:134). In the case of pollution by drugs in the Pakistani community, the lack of practical sanctions obviously does not refer to the lack of a legal system with proscriptions on drug-dealing and drug-taking, but to the widespread feeling of frustration that despite the law, there is not much that can be done about it (cf. Chapter Seven).

4.6 Purity and Contamination: *Haram, Halal* and *Makkru*

Amongst the behaviours threatening to 'poison the community', drug-related issues were mentioned most often. The strings of their consequences were also considered as jeopardising community life. Moral fervour and ideas of order, of purity and non-purity[36] in the community, seemed to be underpinned by both a religious and a cultural discourse, with blurred boundaries typical of the 'religion vs Culture' debate (see Chapter Five). Religious terms used to describe wrong-doing were *haram* for the deeds (i.e. 'drinking is *haram*') and the profit they brought (i.e. '*haram* money through drug-dealing') and *hrami* (also translated as 'bastard') for the subjects involved in *haram* activities (i.e. 'don't speak to that guy, he's *hrami*'). These religious terms seemed to bear a cultural connotation when they were used to increase negative labelling by quantifying their impact on the community networks:

> You know, a lot of businesses in Bradford, the ones who were really successful, when they came first over, they're the ones who brought the stuff over first and everything. I can quickly mention companies and names . . . because you know my mum, my family, you go to Mirpur and everybody knows everybody, it's a community where they know everything and it's like . . . my mum tells me stories that so and so, how they have done it. And we say *halal* or we say *haram*. *Halal* is when you're eating from your plate and you're sharing, and people do *haram* when they've got so much but they don't share from the same plate. (Adam, community worker in his late twenties)

And again:

> If you feed *haram* to your family, it will grow *haram*. (Adam)

In Islamic jurisprudence, *haram* is translated as 'unlawful' or 'forbidden'; *halal* is its opposite, while *makkru* is the area in-between, where what is accepted but not encouraged lies. The most known side of this part of Islamic jurisprudence is related to food: alcohol is *haram*, meat butchered according to the Islamic way is *halal*; in the absence of *halal* meat, any meat but pork may be consumed, as in that circumstance it would only be *makkru*. During fieldwork this terminology was much more widely deployed, as from Adam's example above.

The definition of *haram* in fact seemed to include the potential of a contamination consistent with pollution discourses mentioned above: money earned through criminal or non-Muslim activities (e.g. selling alcohol) was seen as creating negative contamination. For any act of contamination, however, there seemed to be an act of purification, though this would not necessarily happen without controversy. Some respondents, for instance, were aware of a higher form of money-laundering, or money purification, that some drug dealers seemed to exert. Through donating part of their *haram* earnings to mosques or charity, the rest of the capital was by some believed to turn into *halal*, as it had gone though purification. Henceforth:

Amir (unemployed, in his mid thirties): 'It is the case we have to have . . . and then the drug dealer in the community or the businessman will say "well, I'll donate so much" . . .'
Mahima (student in her late twenties): 'You're not allowed to accept that money because that money has killed and ruined families . . .'
MB: 'Is it *haram* money?'
Mahima: 'It doesn't belong anywhere.'
Amir: 'The number of mosques that are run with *haram* money . . . [sighs]'

Pakistani people believe that religion and business are one, unlike the Pathans, so the Pathans see nothing wrong in drug-dealing. OK, they see it as "we're breaking the law, but we're not breaking Islamic law", you know what I mean? But they do, because it isn't *halal*, it's *haram*.
(Jamal, student in his early twenties)

Many respondents of Mirpuri origin held the belief (not corroborated by Pathan research participants) that Pathans would make allowances for themselves in doing *haram* as they were living in a non-Muslim country, and therefore they survived by taking advantages of the corruption of the land. A similar view, described with the concept of *ghanimal*[37], was said to be circulating in groups such as Hizb-ut-Tahrir, and referred to the idea of war booty, in the case of drug-dealing in exploiting *kuffars* (infidels). One fifth of the war booty is supposed to 'belong to Allah' and therefore may be used for activities related to *zakkat*.[38]

Other comments about living in a *kafir* land (*kafir* is the singular of *kuffar*), although completely detached from war metaphors, were reflected in comments about living as good Muslims in such an environment. Shaheen, whose two 15-year-old nephews had been sponsored by a local mosque to go to India and become a Quran *hafiz*[39], believed that being away from any *haram* manifestation (from bad television programmes to drugs) was the only feasible way to pursue a *karim* (blessed) life.

Some allowances for *haram* activities appeared to be made in an instance that seems to be consistent with the concept of *makkru*. For example, a rumour circulated in Bradford that a religious figure was willing to make *taweez* (amulets, see Chapter Seven) for the success of businesses, in spite of their selling alcohol.

The extreme view on the *haram/halal* dichotomy was represented by Faisal, a young listener to a Sunrise Radio talk show at the end of February

2005, who called the programme to complain about the views represented on air that tended to blame the parents for young Asians going astray. Faisal instead said that in a country where Muslims could hardly avoid *haram* substances hidden in food colourants etc. or were not bothered by eating *halal* meat, let alone by drinking alcohol, these forms of intoxication could not help but develop bad behavioural patterns. The effectiveness of prayers would also be jeopardised by the presence of *haram* in the body. This view, however, never emerged during fieldwork. Research participants were instead concerned with a broader concept of *haram/halal* and pollution, strictly linked to the preservation and well-being of the social structure. Social structure, however, was considered positive only in its broadest connotation; inward-looking networks were in fact considered negative in the crime-prevention economy (see Chapter Five).

4.7 Crime as a Threat to Community Stability

This chapter has explored the main concerns about criminal activities from the Bradford Pakistani point of view, and therefore its process of labelling. In the focus groups the initial brainstorming led to the acknowledgement of drugs (including smoking), rape, gun crime, street gangs, unprotected sex (given the danger of contracting AIDS), kidnap/abduction, joy-riding, mugging/stealing, racial abuse and drinking as their parents' concerns. Burglaries in some areas were also described as a serious problem, and practitioners added domestic violence to the list. Everywhere, however, the greatest preoccupation emerged as drugs. Some were aware of what was considered a massive threat to the preservation of the community: the involvement of women in criminal activities, or their struggle to cope with families where drugs had been taken up by the men of the family. In conversations, drugs were described as the source of a chain of deviant behaviours, including all those mentioned in the focus groups, plus burglaries and domestic violence. Furthermore, drug addiction and the emulation of the dealers' life-style were considered as major causes of family and community breakdown, the 'emptying-out of social structures, of the institutions of socio-economic and cultural regulation' (Collison 1999:437) experienced by other urban communities.

The Pakistani community was therefore confirmed as an important element in the study of deviance, for three reasons:
• the effect on the community as the main factor in assessing the seriousness of crimes;
• the diffused panic about the 'erosion of community' (see Chapter Five);

- the community's distinctiveness in dealing with crime (see Chapter Seven)

A widespread perception of the necessity for the self-preservation and stability of both families and the community recurs in other Bradford-based research on Pakistanis (Harrison and Phillips 2005:173, 175), and here emerged from interviews across the sample groups:

> [Parents] are afraid they [their sons] might just walk out of the house. This is what they're afraid of. (Jamil, entrepreneur in his late thirties)

> MB: 'I heard stories about families not really caring about their children dealing, but starting getting worried when they take it . . .'
> Zaara (shop assistant and special constable in her early twenties): '[Because] it's gonna affect the balance of the family. Especially if it's girls.'

Although community was an endangered element, and its stability was at stake, that very community was seen by many as the potential solution to the present problems:

> The first-generation community is looking for stability; the second generation has lost its identity . . . how do we bring it back? Identity is brought back by belonging to something, whether it's a football club, or it's an association, by belonging to an association you need to have something in common . . . You have to start initially to bring that stability back, some of these after-schools mosques or Sunday schools, or after school hours, I'd encourage anybody to send their child to go and learn the language of their mothers and fathers. (Iqbal, entrepreneur in his late fifties)

The vision that the community is at the centre of the threat but will also provide the solutions to the problems was corroborated by a narrative of what in the analysis was called 'putting things back in the community'. By reinvesting in one's community, both economically and personally, many research participants believed that the drift towards bad role-models could be fought:

> So I joined the Public Services course and learnt everything from there and decided, 'yes, I want to go in' . . . for many reasons, such as putting back something in the community I grew up in, it sounds such

a cliché . . . I'm sorry, but giving something back to the community you've lived in and helping someone, if you help one person it might be a minor difference to someone else. (Zaara, shop assistant and special constable in her early twenties)

I was kicked out of my school because I was always in fights with other girls and boys. I decide I would do something for people like me, people who didn't get anything out of school. I decided to take up youth work, although I'd been offered a job at the Inland Revenue and I would've been paid more. (Ameena, community worker in her early twenties)

'Putting things back' appeared often as a criterion for addressing positive and negative role models: passivity towards the community was generally considered as much of a sin as being involved in illegal activities. A respondent, in spite of his being very devout, accused some religious groups like *Tableegh Jamaat* (see chapters Five and Seven) of neglecting the community by employing their energies outside it:

That's the other extreme, they don't work, they become very lazy, they give nothing back positively in the community. (Imran, teacher in his mid-thirties)

On the other hand, many interviewees defined 'putting things back in the community' as a strategy to win if not consensus at least non-opposition from their area:

Some drug dealers sponsor good things in the community, they're saviour with one hand and instigator with the other. (Kamran, community worker in his early thirties)

Exceptions aside, the narrative of 'putting things back in the community' seemed to identify a commonly shared moral value in the circulation of positive norms, models and economic capital. This seemed to suggest the positive connotation given to horizontal ties, a theme that will be dealt with in Chapter Five.

Overall, the construction of a pathological Bradford Pakistani community was strongly challenged, although very serious concerns about its future emerged. The solutions, however, were according to many lying within the community itself. In the plenary session of a conference organised by a grassroots organisation, one Pakistani man working for a local institution criticised the organisers, arguing that they were letting people leave the conference with a very damaging idea about the Pakistani community, thus contributing to diffusing the views that external commentators had created about Bradford. Instead of focusing on drug abuse, mental illness and forced marriage, he suggested the conference should have been about the potential of the Pakistani community which, according to him, happened to have more resources than other communities to fight these problems. As an example, he mentioned the role that the extended family could play in helping children to avoid drugs and to find employment (see Chapter Seven). The community resources and networks (see Chapter Five) were described as essential to articulate discourses around crime, the same principles on which national-level community crime-prevention strategies are based (Burnside and Baker 1994:19).

For some research participants the level of toleration of illegal activities would be affected by the potential for positive side-effects in the community (i.e. when drug dealers invested in charity or created legal employment)—a typical case of differential association. So, if somebody seemed to be carrying out illegal activities, but keeping the welfare of the community in sight, some may forgive such 'short-cuts', as it seemed had happened at some stage during the settlement process. This notion may be related to the concept of *khidmat*, or service to the community (cf. Werbner 1997:238). See also 'putting things back in the community', in Chapter Five).

5

CRIMINOLOGICAL DISCOURSES: AETIOLOGIES OF CRIME

The old generation was nothing else but work, work, work, and then take the money back home and that's it. But the new generation they're not bothered by work, they're getting money, they live. (Jamil, entrepreneur in his late thirties)

Many accounts of the lives of Pakistanis in Britain have pointed to deprivation as the main factor leading to general disadvantage and to social problems (Singh 2001:8; Bagguley and Hussain 2003c:1; Jan-Khan 2003:33). Criminological studies that have tried to dispel the myth of some 'racial' pathologies have in fact drawn attention to specific structural constraints affecting certain groups. Consequentially, it may seem that a group, although not criminogenic *per se*, could be criminogenic by virtue of the specific structural disadvantages affecting it, producing similar effects: an essential deviance (Tatum 2000:xi, 5). So far the tendency has seemed to be to research the community as a *pathological* context where economic struggle victimises the community. Some authors, on the other hand, have tried to balance this view by saying that focusing only on economic variables may be the equivalent of attaching to the community a passive character (Ballard 1992, quoted in Chapter One). Others have highlighted a series of questions that cannot necessarily be answered only by deprivationism, i.e. why some men of South Asian heritage are academically under-achievers and others over-achievers (Modood 2004:95). In these studies, however, there is little space for emic accounts, that is to say an approach that links evidence into the coherent complexity of a specific context, and consequently leads to the acknowledgement of agency.

Moved by the need to combine knowledge of agency, this chapter will consider the variables, both environmental and cultural, that may share in the attribution of blame, as far as crime is concerned, on the part of the study population. By environmental (or structural) factors we mean all those elements that are not internalised in the community or the individuals, but are objective, existent variables that have to be accounted for in social life. Environmental or structural factors mentioned during the research were economic recession, discrimination, deprivation, demography and education, but their role as causative factors in crime was seen by the research participants as only a partial one.

Overall, in fact, research respondents across the generations seemed to perceive the rise in crime in terms of establishing a link between some environmental factors, on the one hand, and specific ethnic resources and networks on the other, in particular when referring to family structure and traditional sets of values. This is not in contradiction with the claim made in Chapter Four that crime was not seen by participants as endemic to Bradford Pakistani cultures; the interaction of certain ethnic elements with the environment, however, was indeed considered as problematic. Respondents described the interaction between the environment and their ethnic resources and networks according to four discourses; these will be denominated here as: 'out of place' culture; the erosion of ethnic networks; *biraderism*; and fatalism. However, insiders' views on the structural variables that appear constantly in policy-related reports (see for example Ouseley 2001) need to be investigated in order to understand the link between environment and agency.

5.1 The Asian Economic Niche

The long-term economic or social consequences for the lives of Pakistani communities in Britain (Kalra 2000) of the conversion from textile mills to catering and taxi ranks (see Chapter Three) has not yet been fully investigated. Some authors have described ethnic entrepreneurship as saving minorities from the harshest backlashes of the 1970s recession and of the industrial crisis (Ballard 1990:224; Basu 1998:314–15, 323; Singh 2001:9), and some have referred to this stream of analysis as 'ethnicity as a resource' (Modood 2004:88).

According to many research participants, some choices made by the pioneers of ethnic entrepreneurship led to some fundamental changes to family life and consequently to the community.

One of the most popular views in this respect will be mentioned with regard to bad parenting. Local politician Iqbal offered a sort of *mea culpa* by saying that fathers who worked on multiple shifts day and night or unsociable hours in take-aways or taxi ranks had unavoidably neglected their children, who grew up without guidance. Community worker Kamran said that when the ones who were supposed to be role models were out working day and night, their sons could only find guidance among their peers, and that was when everything went wrong in the community. Kamran also believed that the drug problem within the Pakistani community was something that had come about no more than ten years earlier. Many others, on the other hand, were ready to point to an involvement with drugs much older than that, and whose origins were connected to the new 'Asian economic niche'. They believed in fact that although the nature of that involvement was different at this earlier time ('it wasn't a life-style like it is now', Kamran, interview with the author), many of the older generations had been involved in the drug business as a sporadic activity in order to pay a mortgage, open a shop or start a restaurant (cf. also Pearson and Patel 1998:220):

> Amir (unemployed, in his mid-thirties): '99 per cent, 99 per cent of Asian businesses are from drug money, or . . .'
> MB: 'I will have to write this, are you sure you want to say it?'
> Amir: 'I'm serious . . . or on crime-related money, that's a fact. The only business I know that hasn't built up on it in the whole of Bradford it's my dad's business and it closed down because we couldn't survive.'
> MB: 'What's your perception, Mahima?'
> Mahima (student in her late twenties): 'I'm sure the majority is drug money.'
> MB: 'But the drug business came along quite recently . . .'
> Mahima: 'You can go back 20 years and you can look at one of the biggest companies around . . . can I mention people's names?'
> MB: 'Yes, but I'll delete the name in the transcription.'
> Mahima: 'OK, like [. . .] for example. We all know that his wife went to jail because she was bringing drugs over from Pakistan to start the business here. She got caught, but a lot of them . . .'
> Amir: 'All gold shops are [built on drug money] as well . . .'

According to some, the new professions that came with the 'Asian economic niche' gave an ideal flexibility to the search for bigger illicit profits; for example, many believed that the drug business had flourished in taxi-driving, due to the mobility implicit in the job. Hence many research participants refused to introduce the author to taxi drivers, who often appeared as the 'folk devils' of Bradford. Again, certain timetables typical of the catering business were seen as ideal in providing a suitable alibi to present to parents (see also 'double life' in Chapter Six):

> They [the parents] will worry, but now it's come to a stage where lads will say to mum and dad 'I'm going to work, I'm working in a restaurant or a take-away somewhere' and they'll be out dealing, rather than working in a restaurant from five till three in the morning and get £15, 20 . . . if you look at the small-time dealers they can make a couple of hundred quid in a night, but then if you look at top-end dealers, who are heroine dealers, you know . . . they can make . . . what? Sell a kilo of heroin for 90 grand and they get it for a third and they sell it 90. (Jamal, student in his early twenties)

Many respondents said that whenever people did not withdraw from the drug business after the alleged 'one-off' paid off the costs of a mortgage or a shop, drug-related fights or arson attacks between drug-dealing clans led to a vicious circle, where crime started feeding more and more criminal activities. This was not only a case of 'poisoning the community' (cf. Chapter Four) by creating bad role models, but also the cause of more practical effects such as the discouragement of investment in the areas affected:

> You were destroying your own community because, you know . . . if people are gonna give investments to the Asians, it's not gonna happen, is it? (Zameer, community worker in his early thirties)

So, if a certain area missed development opportunities as investors were discouraged to put money where there were so many troubles, the area would get more and more impoverished.

5.2 Deprivation, Discrimination and Unemployment

The concept of poverty or deprivation was described in this way:

> When someone's poor it means there aren't enough jobs, not skills enough, the education attendance is poor. (Kamran, community worker in his early thirties)

Shamim, who had been a health visitor and community worker for 20 years, recounted that when she started her home visits in the Pakistani community she would see families living below the bread-line. Although she no longer saw episodes of malnutrition, she still had to deal with overcrowded houses, poor health and a lack of sensible attitudes to health, and with gender discrimination or even domestic violence—all related, in her opinion, to ignorance and lack of education. The view of those respondents employed within the social services or grass-roots organisations tended to be that it was too early to celebrate a success in the fight against deprivation, although something had been achieved. Where social disadvantage was still present, they would expect criminal behaviours to develop, although dictated not by economic necessity but by lack of education or even 'greed'.

Lack of education and opportunities were generally classified under deprivation, and the frustration about it appeared in the following words of a woman whose job was to organise training in equal opportunities. In her view, the attention of politics and the media was erroneously focused on issues that were not those mainly affecting youth:

> Across the board is discontent. I think for a lot of young people, for not being able to access jobs, career opportunities, schooling, they see the discontent in the way they are treated and they are not heard. You know, with me when people say, 'Oh this Asian youth are so aggressive and so loud', but when you go to a white council estate, what do you see? White aggressive youth, it doesn't matter what colour they are, and I think it's time that people stop seeing them as colour, as black and white, but see them as kids and young people. When we did our last conference we had the media ringing up, 'We want to interview you, we know you do stuff on forced marriage and we want to speak with a young person' and this was like national media, but I said I'm sorry, but I'm not interested, this is not the only thing we work on. We do drugs, culture, truancy, substance misuse, we're doing it on issues that affect all young people and there is a bit on forced marriage, that's it.' (Ayesha, community worker in her early forties)

Sometimes deprivation was seen as an act of denial of resources, which should be a right (to education, health, etc.), by either the government or the council:

> The most common problem in Horton Grange is poverty. When someone is poor it means there are not enough jobs, not skills enough, the education attendance is poor. There are two or three schools in the area, but there's one teacher and one or two support workers for 30, 40 students (it's because the government spends all the money on war). (Kamran, community worker in his early thirties)

Some, however, still saw the general lack of job opportunities as the cause of some young people turning to crime:

> MB: 'So do you think people turn to drugs because they don't have any other opportunities?'
> Jamal (student in his early twenties): There's no other way out. I know a guy with a PhD who's dealing because he can't get a job. He's got a PhD and his friend has got a master in philosophy or something and none of them can find a job, so they're dealing in drugs. That's what it's come to. I've got a cousin of mine who's got a master in chemistry and he can't find a job.'
> MB: 'Why do you think they aren't as law-abiding as the first generation . . . is it because of unemployment?'
> Jamal: 'Exactly, there's no industry around here, the mills are closed, so . . .'

Men in their thirties, however, would refer to the 'laziness' of the younger men in comparison to their experience, and entrepreneur Jamil complained he struggled to find people to employ in his local shop:

> It's hard at the moment, nobody wants to come into this trade, nobody wants to work now. (Jamil, entrepreneur in his late thirties)

> It's not the case about making a quick fix, nobody wants to struggle now, nobody wants to say, 'I've got to get up at four o'clock in the morning, go to the factory and walk there and come back at five in the afternoon' . . . [rather] 'son, forget that, just get a couple of kilos of heroin, go and sell it on the corner, come around in a nice Porsche . . . it's accepted unfortunately. (Amir, unemployed in his mid-thirties)

Drug dealer Azad, twenty-three years old, admitted that after working hard in a local greengrocer's for six years he wanted to 'chill out a bit' with a different life-style. On the other hand, some believed that laziness was not a character feature of drug dealers:

> MB: 'Other people would argue that if they really wanted a job they'd have it, but they're lazy.'
> Jamal (student in his early twenties): 'You know, drug dealers work hard for the money. It's not easy dealing with drugs.'

Although institutional racism (MacPherson 1999:5, 20–35) did appear in the interviews, mentioned by those who had familiarised themselves with this terminology and theory through jobs such as probation officer and development and social worker, many more thought that the notion was insufficient to justify the rise in criminal activities in the community:

> There's a lot . . . there's still a lot of stigma about racism and it does exist, there's no doubt about that, but . . . it's up to you . . . my belief is, if I didn't get into a job that was the dream job I wanted, and even if I did believe and had solid proofs it was due to racism, I wouldn't turn to crime, I'd just go back and do something else until I knew that maybe there'll be a chance to get this job in the future and tackle this racism head on if I can, and I'll do it, but going into crime . . . You're not starving. You're choosing to be a criminal, it's not out of desperation. If for example . . . in Britain there's no reason why anyone should be a criminal, unless for very extreme reasons. For example if you . . . someone was in Iraq at the moment with all the situation going on now, someone was stealing, and you can't . . . and you say to them, 'Why have you stolen?' 'It's because I need food'. You can justify it. Not saying it's right, but you can justify why they've done it, you can sense a logic in that, but here you have every single benefit that you can possibly think of. (Zaara, shop assistant and special constable in her early twenties)

> It's there, but you've got to make an effort and you've got to challenge it and things don't change without people doing something. You as a person, you as a community are not gonna change unless there's an effort made. So you can't blame all your problems on everybody else! You've got to take some responsibility! . . . You know, humans have a choice between making right or wrong. (Zameer, community worker in his early thirties)

These views seemed to reflect a mentality that has been described in this way:

> We as a group are striving and struggling to achieve higher status and prosperity, respectability, in this land where the dice is loaded against us but success is achievable, and you have to play your part. (Modood 2004:100)

Some thought that mentioning racism was the 'survival of the survival argument':

> [Some] people say, 'You know we're in an alien environment, we've got to survive and survival is the highest priority, so can we really condemn?' (Abdul, social worker in his early forties)

Hussain and Fozia, a married couple in their late twenties, had been looking for jobs for some time when they were interviewed. They did not believe in institutional racism, but Hussain was convinced that many employers had a problem in taking him on because of his beard and his Islamic tunic, a style he had slowly developed after abandoning the peers who had apparently introduced him to light drugs. This was one of the many cases encountered during research where Islamophobia was mentioned as one of the causes of frustration and discontent amongst the Pakistani youth. Islamophobia was mentioned more times than racism as a form of prejudice and discrimination. On the other hand, Hussain and Fozia, who were also first cousins, said that they could rely on two sources for surviving: their extended family (cf. Mawby and Bhatta 1980:26; Wardak 2000:72; Harrison and Phillips 2005:181) and the welfare system. They did not perceive discrimination at a state level and praised the welfare state, as many other informants did, although some worried that 'signing on' would become a habit for many young men who had never seen their fathers working and therefore did not have a positive role model in this respect.

5.3 'The Lure of Big Things': Strain Theory

If many participants agreed that in Bradford criminals did not become so out of necessity, thanks to the welfare state, on the other hand many could see a cause of an economic kind behind the rise in crime:

> I think a lot of it has to do with easy money. I think it's when the kids, they've got this head set, it's easy money, fast cars, fast life, and they'll be the heroes ... and for others it'll be more putting food on the table, keeping the family together, because the responsibility of some young men who are forced to take for themselves, you know, as ... you'll grow up, get married, take responsibility of your parents, your family, and you'll provide. Very, very big responsibility. (Ayesha, community worker in her early forties)

> It's like families from generations that they say 'Don't do it' and then

their kids are revolting against them, you know, they want to make money really fast because they've seen their family poverty and they don't want to be in that, so to get money really fast, this is what people have done. (Abdul, social worker in his early forties)

Some called it poverty, although they were not speaking of being below the bread-line, but of a relative deprivation:

Young people commit crime because of poverty; if they like a pair of trainers and they can't afford it, they'll use any means to get it. But they don't have to do that for food or accommodation, the parents provide for that. . . . They also say, 'I'm not gonna screw up with a degree and still [be] driving a cab'. (Kamran, community worker in his early thirties)

Young people tended to describe scenarios where other young people would be influenced by 'the lure of big things' and aspired to a life-style that either for lack of education or alleged 'laziness' was precluded for them:

I think is the lure of big things, money, cars, nice clothes, status, recognition. I think it's the lure of those things why people do illegal things because then they become recognised . . . in the community, [you] become highly respected, if you've got money you've got clout. (Abdul, social worker in his early forties)

Discourses of relative deprivation and lack of opportunities to reach the goals that consumerist society promotes seemed to be compatible with Merton's strain theory (1938): individuals frustrated by the impossibility of achieving what they aspire to—society's 'must-haves—are likely to by-pass orthodox ways and resort even to criminal activities through a process labelled 'innovation' (Braithwaite 1989:31; Eadie and Morley 1999; Tatum 2000:5)

Older people, instead, tended to assume a more judgemental position labelling this attitude 'greed' (Abdul, interview with author):

My reasoning for that is this came about because the whole mentality, whether it was Asian mentality, whether the indigenous-population mentality was actually changed during the Thatcher era, because the greed factor came in. Prior to that I remember as a child, you know, we didn't have that greed factor. It was just... we got by, OK. But the greed factor came in where I noticed... priority wasn't given to the thinkers, the teachers, the people who do the very important jobs like electricians, plumbers, engineers, and plus they were not paid accordingly to what accountants' pay was. And that's when things changed and accountants decided how many nurses should be working in this department instead of the person who was in charge of the nursing staff. So that's when the change came about and affected everybody, not just the Asian community. (Iqbal, entrepreneur and politician in his late fifties)

5.4 Demography and Education

So far the discussion on the Asian economic niche and on opportunity theory has seemed to focus mainly on the experiences of young men[40]. The attention given by the community to them will be more thoroughly discussed in Chapter Seven, when taking masculinity into consideration. Here the analysis will be limited to demographics as one of the alleged causes of the rise in crime:

> MB: 'What changed from when people came here to open honest businesses, and now...'
> Akbar (retired, in his early seventies): 'Most of families, Indian and Pakistani, they don't have children at that time. Because not lot of family.'
> Amir (unemployed, in his mid thirties): 'What he is trying to say is that in the 1960s if the children were growing up, there would've been something going on! [laugh]'

Many respondents believed that taking risks was a sort of rite of passage for young men in any society, and therefore the demographic indicators specific to the Pakistani community would automatically mean a proportionally higher rate of crime. This was consistent with the literature on youth and crime (Collison 1999:434). Social worker Abdul called it youth's 'sense of invincibility', and younger respondents agreed with this view:

> I think people grow out of it, don't they? The younger ones, they just want to have fun, a bit of a laugh, then they grow out of it. (Aqdus, student aged 16)
>
> I think amongst crimes like car thefts and ... things like that, they

happen amongst teenagers. One of the reasons for that is they're bored, there isn't enough to do in that community... I've not come across that, I've met people who were stealing, especially when I was young, but I never come across someone doing it just to feed themselves, to put something on their table.... they should just realise that teenagers... it's not good to do crime, but they want to have fun. (Ali, artist in his late twenties)

This may be one of the reasons why some families may be lenient with their sons:

> We [parents] know it's *haram*, but we say, 'He's only young, he's only enjoying himself.' (Sheikh Ahmed Ali, 'Muslim Youth')

If youth are more prone to commit crime as a characteristic of their age, which they will grow out of, the educational system where they are supposed to spend a substantial part of their lives was bound to be scrutinised in its roles and duties in controlling potential deviants:

> And I think are schools which are failing all kids in Britain and that's why if you do a careful study of the statements we hear, we expect prisons to bring up our children, we have a solution: schools, and if not, they go to prison and we expect the prisons they're now doing their job. (Tahir, teacher, in his late thirties)

These views were consistent with much of the literature on the educational achievement of young Muslims living locally in inner-city areas (McLoughlin 1998c:222, Singh 2001:11) and with other research data highlighting the fact that many parents would consider sending their children to Islamic schools because of the lack of trust in the educational system (Khanum 2000:131).

Some even thought that inner-city schools might become oppositional to the home upbringing (see Chapter Eight):

> Eight hours the child spends in schools, you know the filth they teach you. Eight hours the child spends in these schools, they're attacking these imams in every direction, they're working that this child somehow becomes a *kafir*, if he doesn't become a *kafir* he accepts and embraces the ways... they work on the child for eight hours a day. (Sheikh Ahmed Ali, 'Muslim Youth')

interview with Umar, he explained that the educational system for Asian pupils that one might think it was a strategy set up cians to block the social ladder to minorities and guarantee in the capitalist society. He added that it once had been the white working class (Irish and Polish people), but now it was easier to rely on what he defined as 'the global underdogs': Muslims. Others, instead, argued that Muslims in Bradford happened to have a more business-oriented mentality than an education-oriented one:

> You see, with the Sikh community, their daughters, their sons, they all work, they're in a community where they all work, they get education and everything. Our community is following that but they're a bit . . . lack in mind . . . they don't thrive in education, they thrive in their own businesses, you see the take-aways, the restaurants, and when the father opens a restaurant, take-aways, taxi stands and places like that, the extended family goes in there and works in there and they won't pursue a career in education and they find it more difficult because they follow their parents. (Adam, community worker in his late twenties)

More often, both pupils and practitioners lamented an institutional racism within the system that discriminated against Pakistanis, who were believed to be less likely than students from other ethnic groups to rate education highly as an aspiration (cf. Modood 2004:93):

> I hated school, I think schools for me just didn't work, I think if I was left to my own devices I would have learnt more myself, because there was always this attitude, 'She's an Asian girl, she'll get married at 15, so what's the point?' Teachers used to tell us all the time, even the Asian teachers. (Ayesha, community worker in her early forties)

5.5 The Interplay of Ethnic Resources and Networks: the 'Out of Place Culture'

So far we have analysed how the environment was seen by many research participants as contributing to the rise of crime in the community. This chapter will now turn to how some ethnic resources and networks (cf. Chapter Three) were seen as interacting with environmental agents in producing crime in the community. Family will be the first theme to be analysed in this respect, as its function in regulating behaviour in society has not only been a popular feature of recent New Labour policies (Knight 2006) but also a popular subject of criminological work on the causes of crime (cf. Hirschi 1971:95; Wardak 2000:167, 178). In this research, two aspects of family life seemed to be very important in discussions on the attribution of blame: the Culture transmitted by the parents (discussed in this section), and the forms of relations and reciprocity embedded in such culture (discussed later on in the chapter).

What will be called here 'Culture' refers to the traditional customs that young informants perceived as passed on, consciously or unconsciously, by their parents[41]. For older research participants, Culture was an unspecified but very clearly perceived set of values and behaviours, differing both from Islamic practice (see the 'religion vs. Culture debate' below) and from white people's traditions.

In the course of the research many young respondents argued that such Culture either was obsolete or was inappropriate for dealing with the problems of urban Britain:

> I don't have high regard for the first generation, I think they're really stuck in their old ways and they haven't really moved with the time, they really haven't and they don't want to either. . . . Part of the problems the youth are facing [is that] the first generation, their parents, they're not moving, they aren't willing to compromise, not willing to change, not willing to look at the same circumstance from a different reality, they're stuck. (Imran, teacher in his early thirties)

This was also the argument of the Muslim chaplain at Armley prison, who disagreed with the notion of bad parenting put forward by some interviewees and preferred to describe it as parenting 'inadequate to the environment'. This definition seemed to include the lack of knowledge about the problems affecting youth, as exemplified through other data:

> MB: 'Do you think in general parents know what goes on exactly as far as drugs are concerned, and drug crimes and other things?'
>
> Aqdus (student, 16 years old). 'They don't know how harm ['harmful'?] they can really be.'
> Maria (student, 16 years old) 'Like if somebody gets addicted . . . they wouldn't know . . . we see it from the streets, but they wouldn't know.'

The 'inappropriateness' of family-transmitted beliefs, priorities, aspirations, however, seemed to be a particularly popular subject when inter-generational communication was discussed. Some informants described how the family is supposed to take up the burden of any problem affecting any of its members, and children brought up in this context should see members of their families (normally uncles and aunts) as confidants. Yet, some problems could not be told even to the more sympathetic relatives, and in those cases, young people would feel lost. The thoughts of a teenager who does not know whom to turn to when facing a problem was described by Fatima who, by her own definition, used to live 'a life at odds with Islam', until she went on *Umra*:

> Before, when I was 16, I was really confused. I had this Pakistani traditional values to be held at home, outside I used to be a different person. So I did not know how to deal with my problems because I could not turn to my parents because I know what they would say, I couldn't turn to my grandparents, because I know what they would say, and I wouldn't have liked to hear what they wanted to say. But I still knew, even if I turned to my friends they wouldn't tell me something that is correct as well, so I could only trust the one thing, which is my religion, my Islam . . . (Fatima, student, 19 years old)

The respondents emphasised the inadequacy of culture in relating to the environment. Some informants seemed to perceive that crime would have been manageable and preventable had the individuals been able to draw from on and well-defined norms that at the moment seemed to be lacking in the community[42]. Others, like Fatima, seemed to think that a certain tradition within Islam could provide families with aspirations and values that would be a very efficient crime-prevention strategy.

However some could see a resource in culture. This was not related to its 'contents' or practices (the 'cultural stuff', Barth 1969) but rather to its form and articulation, the ethnic networks. The loosening of community ties was considered by some as one of the causes of the recent crime rate.

5.6 The Erosion of Ethnic Networks: the Generation Gap[43], Vertical and Horizontal Ties, and *Khidmat*

According to the above quotes, culture seemed to be the domain of community elders, who were failing to adapt it to present-day necessities[44]. At the same time, many preferred to criticise the elders for lacking rapport with the younger generation rather than for failing to adapt their culture to the environment:

> The parents don't have that interaction with their child (Maria, student, 16 years old)

> Parents, obviously there's a communication problem, that's why the problem has risen in the first place. (Iqbal, entrepreneur and politician in his late fifties)

Commentators—both outsiders (Webster 1996:11, 1997:67, Archer 2001:82; Kundnani 2002) and insiders (Imtiaz 2002:11; Malik 2004)—have viewed the 'generation gap' as one of the main problems of some ethnic minority youth, impacting on their sense of identity and belonging.

'Gap' in the context of this research means the distance between members of different generations (when they do not spend time together, or scarcely interact), and the differences separating the two (when they do not share the same expectations, values and sometimes language). In this research such a view was widely shared across sample groups, and the issue was believed to have very practical consequences that went far beyond the more abstract questions of identity and heritage that ethnicity scholars usually draw upon. The gap between a stereotypically law-abiding first generation and one that does anything 'hardly by the books' (Jamal, interview with author) meant that there may be a real obstacle in fully developing parents' potential as agents of crime prevention (see Chapter Eight).

In general, older people considered their generation as hard-working and the younger generations as spoiled and lazy.

However, one respondent tried to challenge such absolute comments:

> The first generation in them days were worse than the second generation now. When it comes to drugs and stuff, plenty of people from the first generation they did it.... Majority of the first generation was good and minority of the first generation was bad. Second generation seems as the other way round. The majority of the second generation is socially excluded or whatever you want to put it and there's a minority who does everything by the system, go to school, get GCSEs, do A-levels, go to uni, get into debt, get a degree and work the rest of your life to pay uni fees off. That's the system. Then you have people who're out of the system, don't bother with GCSEs, don't bother with A-levels, leave school at 16, get a job, work for a couple of years, buy a car . . . got a car, what shall I do? I'm driving around anyway,

so I might as well sell drugs while I'm driving'. (Jamal, student in his early twenties)

Some respondents narrated episodes from their childhood when visitors from Pakistan would come hiding drugs for personal use in their clothes. The view that drug consumption was not extraordinary amongst the older generation is backed by other Bradford-based research (Pearson and Patel 1998:213, 218). Some, however, argued that drug-smuggling beyond personal use had happened as well (ibid: 220). Amir, 35, unemployed, in conversation with his father Akbar, seemed convinced that the community had always had contacts with the drug trade, but for the elders this was a side business linked to survival or economic development (see above), while for the younger generation it had become a life-style (see Chapter Six). Still, once the myth of the 'perfect' first generation was dispelled, the model survived of the older generation as 'grafters' and the younger as 'screwed up' (Kamran, interview with author). The difference seemed to be in the context in which even illegal activities were put by the older generation: the community (see also Chapter Four):

> I think that the current generation they're lacking or are deficient in the knowledge that reliance, dependence on each other, discipline and sacrifice of the individuality, what it means it gives you protection, it gives you security means that your needs are much better met and we all have needs. We have emotional, psychological needs. (Abdul, social worker in his early forties)

The generation gap seemed to indicate a loss for young people who missed out on a system that provided 'reliance, dependence, discipline'. While during fieldwork strong criticism of an obsolete culture emerged from some, the loosening of traditional community ties was regretted by others. Iqbal criticised the transformation in the nature of support networks by placing attention within the family:

> Why should they [young people] need them, mothers and fathers? I was talking to somebody from India . . . and I put the question to him and I said 'What about these relationships?' and he said 'Every relationship is based on need . . . and when you have the welfare state, what does a wife need you for, as a husband? What does the husband need a wife for?' I mean [laughs] there is plenty of restaurants and take-aways and launderettes and vice versa, and the welfare state is

there. Same with the child, what does he need the mother and father for? As soon as he's 16, 17 does he need the mother and father? There's no need for that, he's independent. The welfare state itself creates a problem . . . I mean, it solves a lot of problems, but it creates a lot of problems as well . . . I'm not saying that we should do without welfare state, because I believe in welfare state, but it does create that problem, somehow, because we have to put that structure back in . . . how do we put it back in, I don't know. (Iqbal, entrepreneur and politician in his late fifties)

According to Iqbal, unless young people felt part of a system, they would not abide by any rule apart from their own interest.

In Bradford, it seemed that there had been a general weakening of these ties. Fatima, although only 19, was able to compare the situation of today to the supportive networks of her father's accounts:

So say for example in a community there should be this sense of trust the sense that we can go and talk to each other about it . . . when it comes to these problems and these matters [talking about young women taking drugs and running away from home], basically, we leave your own family to deal with it, there is no sense of help to each other, so I think that is a great loss within the community. Because in the past, my dad, you know, when they used to have a problem and stuff? they all used to get together and deal with it, you know, in the correct way, but nowadays . . . (Fatima, student, 19 years old)

One statement by the oldest respondent in the research, however, seemed to cast light on the process of the weakening of the wider community-networks, not by blaming external factors such as Western socialisation (see below) but by simply acknowledging what naturally happened in the course of settlement:

Akbar (retired, in his early seventies): 'Because everybody now is family man. Before they live with 15, 20 people, not just by myself, too different position now. Everybody family man, the children are born, children grown, that is a problem, growing. When they grow it is problem, it is not all the time same position.'

Amir (unemployed, in his mid-thirties): 'I think [he means] because before they were only single males from different families, and then some brought the wives over, then they got their own families and the second generation, third generation, their families have got so big that they can only help themselves.'

It almost seemed that due to growing family concerns less priority was given to the well-being of the collective sphere. Or, without making a causal correlation, fewer people in practice adhered to the ideology of 'putting things back into the community'. Wider horizontal ties were therefore weakened, as was the vertical generational hierarchy that gives a sense of belonging and duty to the community (*khidmat*). The family's inward cohesiveness, instead, seemed to resist more successfully than the community's. However, some research participants argued that this was the result of 'keeping up appearances' in spite of multiple threats to the family system and that sometimes striving for such preservation may be counter-productive for the community at large (see *biraderism* below).

5.7 The Risks of Excessive Bonding and *Biraderism*

Whilst rapport was considered a very positive feature, and individuals' and families' interactions with the rest of the community for the common good were generally considered crucial (see again the concept of *khidmat*), the particularisation of bonding within one's *biraderi* was believed to have many negative effects[45]. Akbar's description of a society that would work for one's family rather than for the wider common good could be seen as the first step towards complacency about deviance. When the good name of the family was at stake the struggle to protect it, and therefore the denial of the problem, was believed to have repercussions on the rest of the community.

According to Akbar, parents were bound to keep quiet in the face of their children's misdeeds as they were under threat of their leaving home:

> If anybody has the problem and they put pressure too much on children, now they will [have] lost the children because they leave the home. If you have a problem with children you better keep quiet.
> (Akbar, retired, in his early seventies)

Even worse, some respondents thought that some parents had transformed the traditional struggle over different *biraderis*' competition for status into something that belonged to a culture[46] where different 'clans' measured themselves in this way:

MB: 'Parents must be worried for what is going on . . . what do you think they think the solution is?'
Zaara (shop assistant and special constable in her early twenties): 'You see, they're proud. They're proud of the fact, like I said earlier. 'My son's a drug dealer, nobody will touch me because . . . they won't start with me, that's it . . . my son's gonna go and sort them out.'

MB: 'But don't the parents question their kids when they see their kids not working and buying big cars?'
Jamil (entrepreneur in hi s early thirties) '[Laughs] No, they don't care: they have a nice car outside!'

Even parents who may not encourage criminal activities were considered complacent when withdrawing from the responsibility of delivering appropriate guidance or at least checking on their children's networks and behaviours. This attitude was often linked to the alleged habit of some young dealers to 'treat' the parents to jewellery, plane tickets to Pakistan and even cars, in order to have them turn a blind eye to their illegal activities:

I know a guy on our street and he deals in heroin and his family and friends are not bothered, he says, 'Here you are, mum, five grand, you go and do yourself shopping.' To the dad 'Here you are, twenty grand, go and buy yourself a car', his sister 'take a couple of grand go and buy some jewellery and clothes.' They aren't bothered, money is money for them. (Jamal, student in his early twenties)

Who's the one who turned a blind eye when his son had a £40,000 [car] outside his house and he knew that his son didn't work? Who's the one who didn't question his son when he put £1,000 on the table when he knows that he doesn't work? (Sheikh Ahmed Ali, from the tape 'Muslim Youth')

Funny thing is, these days I see fathers, five-times-a-day people with beards, the prayer beads and the tickets to paradise, knowing damn well what their sons are up to and not doing a thing about it. Matter of fact, as long as the sons bring in a few hundred notes every week to go towards the mansions in Pakistan, or the upkeep of the family four-wheel-drive, there's no problem. (Alam 2002:150)

The reasons behind parents turning a blind eye were described as being either keen on a series of 'treats' or motivated by the preservation of the family *izzat*:

> The Asian community is a very tight community so . . . if anybody else in the community finds out it just looks bad on them, so that's why they don't want anybody else to find out. (...) They've got this . . . *izzat*, like that, so . . . when they do[find out] . . . rather than dealing with it they just push it away. (Ali, artist in his late twenties)

> Because my experience is that the elders aren't addressing the issues, they're only waffling basically to protect the honour of the family. (Alina, community worker in her late thirties)

The Muslim chaplain of Armley prison recounted some cases where young men had been protected by their parents until they were arrested and their names published in newspapers. Then, in order to protect their standing in the biraderi, parents had not accepted them back in their home. Some thought that parents had a further reason to conceal their children's misdeeds: apart from the threat to the whole family's *izzat* there seemed to be a tendency to blame the parents before blaming anything or anyone else:

> If you imagine a situation where somebody's taken to prison I think the neighbours will start blaming the parents, they'll say, you know, perhaps 'If he'd been brought up in the right way he wouldn't have done such a crime', but then I think, they'll start talking and they'd actually start blaming the parents 'so and so's son' . . . you know, they won't even mention the person's name, you know, they wouldn't say my name, you know, they'd say the parent's name, 'so and so's son'; they actually put more blame onto the parents [laughs]. (Yousef, student, 16 years old)

> If you've just come out of jail people will say 'so and so's son', they'll never mention your name, they'll always mention your father's name. 'So and so's son has come out of jail, he went in for drugs. (Jamal, student in his early twenties)

Some participants, therefore, seemed to perceive a parallel decline of wider community-relations alongside the growth of a negative exclusivism in family ties. Criminology has debated whether relational proximity, the closeness of a group, may be considered an advantage for reciprocal social control. In fact some studies have emphasised the deterrent role of shame in front of close acquaintances (Goffman 1968:43, 49; Burnside and Baker 1994:21), while others have shown how close relations tend to be more forgiving (Erickson 1977:6, 8; Braithwaite 1989:87). The perceptions reported in this section seem to be consistent with the latter criminological hypothesis. The situation was explained by an account of the exclusive bonding inside the family or extended family that was detrimental to society, both for its protection of the criminals and its causal link to the diminishing of interrelations with the wider community:

> There are a lot of people from Mirpur and a lot of people from Attock, they're Chachch . . . from Campbellpur area. Quite a large community both of them. I know, a lot of people from Mirpur won't mix, wouldn't intermarry outside their *biraderis* . . . it's true . . . they marry in the family, they keep it very close-knit, and what you find is that when people are so insular and keep themselves to themselves, their mentality doesn't change, and their behaviour within their family structure, their *biraderis* or whatever you wanna call it, their clan, it stays very sort . . . within themselves, and the same with the Chachch community, they're very sort of insular as well, they very rarely marry out, even though things are changing slightly . . . (Zameer, community worker in his early thirties)

5. 8 Competing Sources: Culture, Islam and the West

So far, three different discourses on blame attribution have been discussed: first, 'out of place' culture, second, the erosion of ethnic networks, and third, excessive bonding or *biraderism*. What has not yet been described is what generates different positions, and whether these produce alternative choices that may be presented to individuals once they feel let down by their community in its cultural or social forms. An example of a strategy to find an alternative has already been presented in the person of Fatima, who described her frustration at being unable to seek help either from elders (with inadequate knowledge) or from the community (deprived of its collective focus). Fatima's choice of an alternative source of guidance and support had been religion. Her adherence to a form of 'de-culturised' or 're-culturised' Islam (cf. McLoughlin 2006a) made her a supporter of the first discourse.

The 'religion versus Culture' debate has recently been the focus of many discussions on Islamic revivalism (Cesari 2004:54). Although Muslim and non-Muslim scholars (El-Zein 1977:240; McLoughlin 1998a:106,

2006a; Ramadan 2004:9) have talked about the natural adaptation of Islam through local identities and environmental circumstances, revivalist discourses tend to refer to an orthodox Islam in opposition to its mediation through any cultural capital alien to the Arabic matrix (Cesari 2004:153; Ramadan 2004: 6). In the research data, whenever the word 'culture' was presented, it seemed to have a negative connotation, for example:

> Most families are uneducated or too cultural. . . . What parents still do is tell the children, the male, the boys [against the Islamic principle of equal inheritance amongst brothers and sisters], that when they die they will inherit all their money, all their wealth, this is through their house, their car, their properties, their businesses, the money in the bank, everything . . . nothing to the daughters . . . This has an effect on the education, or on crime as well, because I think that once the sons become street wise at the age of 16, because they're out of school, if they're gonna inherit their parents' wealth or live off their parents throughout their life, they're gonna play truant as well and miss their classes, and that's where crime starts. (Mahima, student in her late thirties)

> From your parents you find that you get culture and from the mosque you get religion. . . . so what you find is that religion is just mixed with different cultures to make one, and I think that this is where the mistakes are because what's wrong in culture they say it's wrong in religion, but in a lot of cases it isn't. So that's why when I see people studying Islam and stuff, they study it and then they realise that they made a big mistake here, mixing the two, they're very different and they should separate them. (Ali, artist in his late twenties)

The opposition seen between culture and religion further undermined the role of culture [47] in maintaining stability and sustaining progress in the community (So widely discussed that it may be formally labelled 'religion vs Culture debate'). Often culture represented the rural and uneducated background where most of the migration pioneers in the 1960s came from:

> Because a lot of the Asian community in Bradford are from Mirpur and they aren't educated, they lack the parental skills to build a relation with their children and they raise their children to place their beliefs on culture rather than religion, when the sons do commit crime, the Asian males of community commit crime, it is not looked down

[on] as bad . . . (Mahima, herself of Mirpuri heritage, student in her late twenties)

Young people tended not only to claim that Culture might be co-responsible for crime in the community, when in the name of 'reputation' illegal activities were hidden instead of being dealt with, but also that it was an obstacle for the development of 'true' Islam:

> [Traditional culture] is more [about] giving Islam in a secular way, it's just personalised in your own home, it's praying your *salat*—your obligatory prayers—and respecting your elders, it's just picking certain things that are taught, and that doesn't equip you with problems that you will face in the wider society. As Muslims we should accept Islam in its totality so we shouldn't be nit-picking, so you're going to find at home somebody who is totally different, but when you're outside in the wider society, if you've got drugs problems, girlfriend-boyfriend problems, society problems, free-mixing problems, you know, all this type of different problems, we aren't gonna see them, we aren't gonna see Islam dealing with these problems because our institutions like *madrassas* or these mosques are little study circles that . . . they haven't taught, they haven't equipped us with the true Islamic ideas to deal with those problems because it's been given in a very secular way. (Fatima, student, 19 years old)

An attempt to go back to 'the original Islam' has been adopted by movements and associations of young people—for example Young Muslims UK or the Muslim Women Forum and Islamic Society of Britain (cf. McLoughlin 2006a)—in Bradford and is the cause of most of the changes in the practice of Islam locally. For example, in 2002 the Muslim Women Forum was promoting the creation of areas for women in the local mosques, as only a minority of buildings provide this facility. One of the changes in the perceptions of Islam by the younger generations is that while for a large part of the older generation Islam becomes important during life-cycle rituals (McLoughlin 1998a:99), for an increasing part of the younger generation, who read the Quran in translation, religion is apparently an integral part of their lives and has a constant bearing on daily life. For these individuals religion becomes a public matter and is practised through strict dietary rules and political demands (for *halal* meat in student refectories, for example).

'Supporters' of both Islam and the revival of *khidmat* as a solution, however, often seemed to have to fight the same 'demon': Western culture.

Participants who prioritised Islam as their main point of reference tended to criticise those who relied on culture. Those who privileged the system provided by the traditional community networks as a supportive system for the common good tended to accuse certain interpretations of Islam as being too exclusive and as unconcerned with the community at large[48]. Both positions, however, seemed to fear a vision of life emanating from their present environment:

> Fatima (student, 19 years old): 'Ideas like freedom and individualism, that . . . is where Islam or religion . . . basically doesn't start to play that major role . . .'
> MB: 'So you think Western culture actually prevents the Pakistani youth from being close to religion, Islam?'
> Fatima: 'Yeah.'
> MB: 'And where do you think the young Pakistanis have picked up Western culture?'
> Fatima: 'I think . . . firstly they get these ideas from obviously the people they've grown up with and the way society pushes certain things, say for example freedom and individualism . . .'
> MB: 'And you think this detachment from religion or otherwise this kind of proximity with Western culture is giving the Pakistani community some problems?'
> Fatima: 'I think it's giving problems to the Pakistani Muslim community because you find that the way they would idealise the ideas of freedom and idealism . . . it's not handed out on a plate, "this is freedom, this is individualism", is covered up with so many attractions so many illusions that the youth have been given, so it is through the role models, like the media industry, you know, the pop stars and rock stars, whatever, this kind of mentality of Bollywood, even, so the way they take in this culture or these ideas of freedom and individualism is a very disillusioned way . . . they think they'll get this freedom and, you know, get what they want out of it and you understand the way this affects the Muslim community or the Pakistani community is in a negative way, so now you've seen that the parents have taught them in one way and they're going in another way, which is away from their parents' culture and the way parents think. So this creates quite a lot of family problems in itself because the parents aren't willing to accept their values and nor the children to accept their parents' values . . . we're still humans at the end of the day, there will be problems, but equipping the youth, taking their disgusting Western ideas out of

them, you know the idea of freedom, that they're free to do whatever they like, this is all . . .'

Let me just tell you an incident. There was trouble in a street and the police contacted the mosque. I don't know how it happened, there was [a] representative of the mosque, [a] police person and there were youth, so the police said to the mosque chairperson, 'You need to look after your lot', and what the response from the mosque chairperson was—I found it amazing—'This is not our lot. This is your lot. It comes from your schooling system, from your system, from your society, it's not my lot, it's your lot. My lot is me, my age group. We came, we never went into crime, so don't tell me this is my lot, this is your lot. You've done this.' So it was very interesting, I just happened to hear. Do you understand 'It's not my lot, it's your lot', because 'This is the product of this system, I haven't agreed to this system.' (Tahir, teacher in his late thirties)

The position of anathematising 'the West', on the other hand, was heavily criticised by the majority as a 'cop out' (Zameer, interview with author):

That is . . . total nonsense in my opinion. If it's all down to the Western culture, then the West don't believe in honour killings, which the Eastern culture believes in, so they've found their roots and said the Western made them into gangsters, so when they came to the Eastern culture side, and they decided to do . . . my sister ran away with so and so, I believe this deserves to be called honour killing, that's also like a gangster act as well . . . so it's not the Eastern, it's not the Western, it's what they believe in. (Zaara, shop assistant and special constable in her early twenties)

Even more interestingly perhaps, some supporters of the discourse of 'out of place' culture believed that Western knowledge would be positive in helping their community to deal with crime problems:

In the communities where I work (mainly white and black) where they have centres where there are print-outs of places where you can have . . . drugs [treatments] . . . HIV projects and stuff, they're doing that in their own community day in day out. That's why I've worked in that community, I've learnt so much from the white community it's unbelievable. If I was in the Asian community . . . nobody's there to put these protocols forward for me to learn all this. (Adam, community worker in his late twenties)

A further group of individuals who do not believe that any of these sources (Islam, culture or the West) have anything to do with crime can be represented by Akbar, whose point of view will be described in the conclusions as 'fatalism':

MB: 'When your children were growing up were you worried that they would lose their tradition or religion?'
Akbar (retired, in his early seventies): 'I really not, I don't think that, because the children are like lottery ticket, you don't know what will be their position when they grow. If it growing right OK, if not, not. It's a free country, otherwise if I worry if they grow what they do and I take them to my country and grow there, I don't know what they can do there. . . . All over the world something is wrong. In one country one thing is good, another country another thing is bad, you can't decide, but I think England is better.'

5.9 Conclusion: Theories of Community Criminologies

This chapter has compared the different discourses that combine environmental factors with cultural and social aspects in the search for attribution of blame for crime.

Commentaries reproduced here showed how although there seems to be a link between criminal activities and environmental factors, on the other hand participants were reluctant to consider the latter as the main causes of crime. They acknowledged, instead, a greater role for group and individual agency, 'behavioural strategies' (Mamadouh 1999:400) and moral beliefs.

Some participants tended to see a combination of structural and cultural factors as the most accurate aetiology of crime in the community. Others seemed to refer to discourses of Islamic revivalism, like Imran, a teacher in his early thirties. Similar attitudes in other studies (Tatum 2002:16) have been described as a 'postcolonial theory of crime violence and minority youth', which like other post-colonial theories accounts not only for structural constraints, but also for responses to oppression coming from the oppressed and their support systems (for example religion)[49]. Modood (2004:99) has located the agency—the resistance to oppressive, society-wide socio-economic forces—to the management of the ethnic capital emerging from the agents' combination of their cultural and social capitals[50]. Ethnic resources and networks appear to be more common explanations of the rise of crime in the community, recording a significant switch from 1980s deprivationist positions (see Aldrich et al. 1981) to more 'cultural' ones.

The first position (1) referred to culture (see Table 5.2 below). Participants who supported this view argued that norms inherited by parents in Bradford were insufficient for helping young people to deal with the risk of deviance. This group was formed mainly by young people, and was divided into two. The first sub-group (1a) claimed that adopting a set of norms which claimed universality (such as Islam) instead of the particularity of the Pakistani ethnic resources would be a solution. The second sub-group (1b) believed that enhancing parents' awareness about specific risks through Western knowledge would be sufficient.

The second position (2) referred to a very wide sense of ethnic networks. Those sharing this standpoint pointed to the erosion of the organisation of the community and the dynamics of passing values on, rather than to the content of what was passed on. This group was formed mainly by older people or individuals who had a very good relationship with the elders. In this discourse both Western individualism (2a) and certain religious traditions (2b) that neglected community concerns (such as Tableegh Jamaat) were blamed.

The third position (3) referred to a particular, and denigrated, aspect of culture: *biraderism*. Almost all the interviewees agreed that this was a very popular trend in the community. Those who would put their *biraderi* before anything else, even at the cost of turning a blind eye to illegal activities, were the focus of blame in this discourse.

A fourth position (4) of those resigned to fate (*kismat*) was also identifiable. However, the reticence of these respondents raises doubt as to whether their standpoint may have been dictated by their attempt to avoid attributing blame to any specific set of values or behaviours.

These discourses are summarised in the following table:

Table 5.2 Theories of Community Criminologies

(1) 'Out of Place' Culture Focus: Culture Attribution of blame: immobility of cultural capital Supporters: 1a) believers of the religion vs. Culture argument (Islam as positive solution) 1b) most young people and practitioners ('Western knowledge can help')	(2) **Erosion of ethnic networks** Focus: interrelations, from intergenerational to intracommunal, *khidmat* Attribution of blame: erosion of wider than *biraderi* intracommunal ties and dismissal of the 'common good' Supporters: 2a) critics of some aspect of Western individualism; 2b) critics of exclusive religious groups such as Tableegh Jamaat.
(3) *Biraderism* Focus: *biraderi* Attribution of blame: excessive intra familial bonding Supporters: almost all interviewees who look down on 'cultural Muslims'; the West does not impact on this discourse.	(4) Fatalism Focus: *kismat* Attribution of blame: none, resigned to fate Supporters: individuals who do not believe Culture, Islam or the West have anything to do with crime

These typologies do not always exclude one another, as proven by reactions against *biraderism* that were shared across supporters of different theories.

These different discourses seem to add an important element to what will be discussed here as the core of community criminologies: the threat to the community itself. This element is the consideration of a split between *biraderism* and community, where families appear to be no longer necessarily functional to the stability of the community, but where the exclusiveness of intra-familial bonding may jeopardise collectivity. Families' strong ties ('a combination of the amount of time, intimacy and reciprocal services', Granovetter 1973:1361) once perceived as being the pillar of internal cohesion may now be an agent of fragmentation wherever the particular interest of a family is in conflict with the community's common good:

> Community, I don't think they're united, so it doesn't really make a difference, it takes a big thing to happen to remark their presence, which is negative sometimes. Then personally i don't feel that a lot

of community activites take place or a lot of discussion takes place . . . You're already a small community and if you differ because of religious sectarianism, language, ethnicity, geographical orientation, then obviously your voice will be difficult to . . . you're not Mirpuri, Chachchis . . . (Tahir, teacher in his late thirties)

6

CRIMINOLOGICAL DISCOURSES: GENDER AND DEVIANCE

> There was a time when every Muslim child was a gem... Every child that a Muslim mother gave birth to was unique because behind the making of these children there were mothers and fathers even greater. The only concern of a mother was to preserve the child from the fire of hell. But now things have changed and in the last 15, 20 years things have changed drastically. Muslim mothers are giving birth to drug pushers, Muslim mothers are now giving birth to drug takers; Muslim mothers are now giving birth to smugglers; Muslim mothers are now giving birth to car thieves and children who would still the shoes of the worshippers. Muslim mothers are now giving birth to stealers, shooters, killers, and we have fallen so low that Muslim mothers are now giving birth to children who are living on the dirty earnings of bad women. Muslim mothers are now giving birth to daughters who are walking hand in hand with a kafir without nikkah. Muslim mothers are now giving birth to daughters who roam in around the streets with the latest GTI without hijjab, purdah, with the latest glasses. This is what Muslim mothers are now giving birth to.
> (Sheikh Ahmed Ali, *Muslim Youth*)

The previous chapter analysed competing discourses in the community in order to shed some light on the processes of attribution of blame for the rise in crime. This chapter will provide a description of the groups and the areas at risk. If the views in the preceding chapter implied that an erosion of ethnic resources and networks was impending for many young people, widespread internal and external moral panic about young men seemed to reveal that they were more at risk of crime than young women (Webster

1997:65; Kundnani 2002; Alexander 2004; Burdsey 2004:764). However, while the existing literature on deviance in the Pakistani diaspora refers mainly to men (Alexander 2000; 2004; Goodey 2001; Wardak 2000) and to crime, broader notions of female deviance have been overlooked. Most academic research on and media attention to Pakistani women has focused instead on forced marriages, violence and veiling (Werbner 2005; Shaw 2006). In a sense, female seclusion and what is generally perceived as oppression can be considered part of Pakistani male deviance from a British norm. Women's status and male deviance, therefore, are coupled through a differentially gendered field of social relations. The present chapter aims at analysing the perceptions of female deviance in the Pakistani diaspora and to link them to wider considerations about the imposed role of passivity attached to Pakistani women, both by their own community and by state legislators. The chapter will analyse the data relevant to the correlation between gender, competing cultural capitals, and deviance.

We have so far mentioned an allegedly demographic explanation of the relation between Pakistani men and crime, but ignored the interaction between cultures and masculinity that has been considered by other writers as an essential point in the creation of subcultures (see among others Goodey 2001:434). In this context we will highlight the way in which some young Pakistani male sub-cultures are not considered to be deviant per se, but are described as 'grey areas' between good and evil, where young men are more likely to be lured into criminal activities. In certain descriptions it will emerge that sub-cultures may be a product of environmental and cultural interaction. This may be one of the reasons why the concerns surrounding young women and crime produce a different kind of moral panic, based on more 'cultural' notions such as gender roles in the community. As far as men are concerned, competing resources and networks seem to co-exist in their choices as to how to relate to the local social environment (see for example the notion of vigilantism in Webster 1997).

6.1 Pathologising Young Men: Subcultural Studies in the British Pakistani Context

Traditionally (see Chapter Three) men in the Pakistani community of Bradford are considered the main breadwinners. This expectation is considered to be an essential part of their gender, and they may thus be considered the economic pillar of their families. In spite of this, many young men nowadays are considered a liability, as destabilising agents for their families and the whole community.

The extent of the state of wariness surrounding young men is reflected in a series of conversations on their characters recorded in the field and through a literature review of Bradford-based research. These views go from the brief theorisation of three categories of young men by Umar, a research participant, to the academic work written by Bradford-born Atif Imtiaz, and echo in the work on Bradford of such white academics as Webster (1997).

Views emerging during the present research were very similar to Imtiaz's model analysed in Chapter Two, although tending to emphasise that categories were very fluid and could only delineate a potential towards either deviance or adherence to norms. In particular, one respondent, an occasional editorialist for a local newspaper, combined the categorisation of youth with a historical and gendered perspective. Umar believed in fact that 20 years ago there was 'only one type of Pakistanis', now there were three categories: 1, educated middle-class; 2, religious, ranging from liberal to fanatical; and 3, those described as street yobs or criminals and *lafanga*, who wore chains round their wrist and chest and spoke 'like Afro-Caribbeans'). The term *lafanga* was explained to me as follows:

> *Lafanga* is somebody who's not pursuing an education, just messing about; it's not a term for someone who's a drug dealer. There's not like a certain word for someone who deals and stuff like that. *Lafanga* is someone who's lazy and just messing about. (Adam, community worker in his late twenties)

> *Lafanga* I'd say it's someone who's always around the streets, you know, not taking care of anything, they say *lafanga* . . . (Jamil, entrepreneur in his early thirties)

For Umar, *lafangas* were also those young men who took advantage of the 2001 riots to go looting. *Lafangas'* lifestyle was also blamed for the bad stereotypes outside the community:

> You see some of the youngsters and their behaviour's very disrespectful, you know, and it's very . . . and sometimes the way they'd park up in cars . . . they might not do anything wrong, but it's just what they portray to people . . . and particularly to the white community, the sense I get is that they're quite wary of Asian kids, Asian teenagers and youngsters, you know, when there are three or four in car, they may not be doing anything wrong, but it's just that . . . maybe it's sometimes the thing that we portray . . . (Zameer, community worker

in his early thirties)

Lafangas, otherwise described as 'screwed up' or 'lazy', became the folk devils of the community. Although only Umar presented a full classification of youth sub-cultures, almost all interviewees spoke about an equivalent of his category 3. According to Umar, 9/11 had been a catalyst for the proliferation of category 2, but category 3 was the one 'to be worried about' and was the result of bad schools (see Chapter Eight) and lack of discipline at home (see Chapter Seven). The proof of the latter would be in the comparison between female and male siblings: the girl would always be 'better', as she would be more likely to have grown up disciplined. Girls would be respectful, do housework, and even be explicitly told 'not to behave like boys'. The boys, instead, would become *ladla* (favourite), and the parents would not check what they did with their money. Most of the responsibility would be on the mothers (cf. Chapter Seven), as the fathers would be too busy with work (cf. Chapter Five) and would only intervene if something major happened. According to Umar, children socialised in a family with strict norms would end up in category 1, where it was required to be either 'in' or 'out', and there was no chance of leading a 'double life'. The idea of ricocheting from 'in' and 'out' and of living a double life has been expressed also by Webster (1997), as discussed in Chapter Two.

It may be interesting given the purposes of this chapter to compare the existing literature on male sub-cultures in British Pakistani diaspora[51] with the research data (see Table 6.1 below). These analyses tend to overlap in their acknowledgement of different dynamics in combining diverse sets of resources and networks, while sometimes disagreeing in their identification. The first striking difference is that only in Umar's labelling is there a 'good' sub-group of eligible role-models (category 1). Members of such a subgroup would disenfranchise themselves from any specific set of resources and networks in order to pursue a perceived universal 'common good'. Although in Imtiaz's classification 'coconuts'[52] are seen as law-abiding, that very label suggests a derogatory view; this category is not perceived as a good role-model, because of its perceived detachment from its own community. In Wardak's and Webster's studies there is reference to a positive, trouble-free 'public propriety' as 'appropriateness, seemliness, decency, conformity with good manners, conformity with convention of language and behaviour' (Cohen 1979:124, quoted in Webster 1997:74). However, this propriety is adherence to family tradition, and is not independently forged by young men. In Wardak's Edinburgh study the positioning in a cultural vacuum, a sort of neutral or somehow universal framework, that was positive for Umar is seen as negative, as this is the attitude of those rebelling against everything and which therefore may undermine community stability. While in Bradford-based accounts the combination of different sets of resources and networks is seen as negative (see next section), Wardak does not seem to register a negative view in his sample with regard to this process. Imtiaz's and Umar's emic views, together with Webster's etic account, depict a negative picture of individuals or groups that try to combine cultural capitals.

Table 6.1: Comparison of British Pakistani Male Sub-cultural Models

	Adherence to Traditional Resources and Networks	Combination of Resources and Networks	Adherence to Exclusivist Resources and Networks	Reference to Alternative Resources and Networks	No Adherence to any Specific Resources or Networks
Imtiaz (2002)		*Rude Boys* (mix 'religion' and 'culture', capitalise on their difference within mainstream society)	*Extremists* (reject traditional culture, resources and networks in favour of one vision of Islam)	*Coconuts* (adhere to alternative resources and networks, while detaching themselves from traditional ones)	
Umar (present research interviewee)		*Category 3* (mix Asian and Afro-Caribbean culture, lack adherence to norms)	*Category 2* ('religious', 'all the way from liberal to fanatical')		*Category 1* (adhere to the idea of a universal common good above competing sets of resources and networks in the community)

	Adherence to traditional Resources and Networks	Combination of Resources and Networks	Adherence to Exclusivist Resources and Networks	Reference to Alternative Resources and Networks	No Adherence to any Specific Resources or Networks
Webster (1997)	*Conformists* (passive guardians of 'public propriety'; blame youth and may be rewarded by integration within white society); and *Vigilantes* (active guardians of 'public propriety', using improper means for white society's standards)	*Experimenters* (defend what used to be racialised territorialism and is now control over drugs); and *Go-betweens* (occasional criminals)	*Islamists* ('non-cultural' Muslims)		
Wardak (2000)	*Conformists* (full-time followers of social norms: no separation between real and ideal)	*Part-time conformists* (stick to a few 'token' activities to avoid being labelled 'deviant' for family's sake); and *accomodationists* (more like conformists, but allow for some compromise)			*Rebels* (violate and challenge all norms)

6.2 'Double Consciousness' or 'Torn between Two Cultures'?

Negative comments about those who try to juggle different sets of behaviours are easily to predict, as the boundaries between propriety and impropriety (see above) may blur.

In a community where for many it still seems so important to have a widely recognised social standing (see Chapters Five and Seven), it seemed to be natural to question how it was possible for *lafangas* to conduct their alleged life of 'chilling' (Azad and Khalil, interviews with author) without being restricted or sanctioned by their families. A common answer to this question was a criticism of their 'double life':

> MB: 'But the children [who are involved in crime] don't actually get to the point of leaving the house . . .'
> Fatima (student, 19 years old): 'That's right. Because . . . they were still brought up with those values or some values or morals towards their parents, so they're totally different outside the home than they are at home.'
> MB: 'But they'd want to move somewhere else away from the parents?'
> Fatima: 'No, they'd still . . . because for example the values they've been given by their parents when they were small, this idea of being good Pakistani children living with your parents . . . that's the way of tradition, you know, the boy and the girl . . . the children live at home and if they do, when they do get married they can still stay at home if they want, so this view, this concept . . . but the Western values, they still have a dominance in the children's way of life because when they go outside the home, they act upon those Western values.'

Khalil had even planned to go to Pakistan and get married to a cousin chosen by his parents, making them happy and at the same time putting his conscience to rest. In this way he would provide them with a carer for their old age, and through this he would have enjoyed more freedom than now, as what really mattered to his parents, according to him, was the perpetuation of and stability in the *biraderi* (see Chapter 3). In some aspects, therefore, the traditional cultural capital was preserved, but room was made for the individual's choices. According to the models in the table above, Khalil could have been a 'rude boy, an 'experimenter' or a 'part-time conformist'. In Imtiaz's thesis, however, the point was made that labelling in the research ignored women, thus responding to an external hegemonic representation of Muslim women that was not as threatening to wider social order as that of men was.

In the course of the present research, however, some women could have been described as 'rude girls', leading a double life and seriously, albeit not necessarily willingly, threatening the community stability:

> [Some girls start dealing] because I think ... they have these two sets of ... like identities. So when they're at home they have a different identity, when they're outside in the wider society, they act differently. It's the sense that you're free outside in the world but when you come home, you dress in a certain way, you speak in a certain way and them sort of girls that I've described ... basically they haven't got the freedom from home so they leash out their freedom in that way. So you know ... they have that sense of control, so if they've been controlled at home they want control outside. So this is the way they find their control, this is the way they experience their freedom ... (Fatima, student, 19 years old)

Hence, given the freedom, even girls could activate a double-life system.

In Umar's opinion, there may be individuals who move from his category 1 to category 2 and vice-versa, but there were no hopes for category 3 young men, who combine 'Mirpur with LA' (Imtiaz 2001:127); although their parents might cultivate ambitions of seeing them in category 1 (their frustrated aspirational frame; see Chapter Five), they will never get the tools to shift there. One interesting comment made by Umar was that he would estimate that in Bradford only 100 girls would fit into category 3, which was an essentially male group, while many women would comfortably fit into category 2. Double-life regimes, therefore, appeared not as a positive resourceful dynamic to fit into any environment (Gilroy 1993), but rather as a strategy to maintain family stability without missing out on individual desires and aspirations. This regime seemed however easier for males to assume. A reduced freedom of movement for girls, in fact, may push them towards looking for alternative sets of resources and networks as they could not move in and out their family control with the same ease as boys. For this reason they may appear as more prominent agents of change. For instance, a girl who is not allowed enough freedom to lead the double life many men appear to have may be more motivated to fight for radical changes in her family norms that would allow her to have the life style to which she aspires[53]. Young men, on the other hand, may be content to live their freedom in the space created by their double-life regime.

Although the numbers mentioned by Umar are not statistically reliable, his theory of young sub-cultures is interesting for its analysis of the constructions around young men that are talked about in Bradford, and related to criminality. Category 3 was not described as necessarily made up of criminals, but this would be the potential labour-pool for criminal activities. Category 3 seemed to equal other descriptions of youth by many other research participants: lazy, 'hanging-out' and *lafanga*. Hirschi (1971:22) theorised that involvement in conventional activities prevents young people from committing crime for the simple reason that they are too busy. This attitude was shared in many portrayals of 'rude boys'.

6.3 Women and Deviance: Unveiling the Problem [54]

Western feminist criminology has been analysing the question of female deviance since the 1970s, basing its major argument on the finding that criminology had always tended to portray criminal women as pathological or 'double deviant' (Rosenhan 1973; Carlen 1985:2) as they not only were breaking the laws of the state but also (what are believed to be) the laws of nature, which have endowed them with caring attributes. For example, a woman taking part in a murder would automatically be depicted as non-human, a monster, since the nature of a 'normal' woman could not allow the possibility of violent behaviour. Bisi has also argued that the subordinate position given to women in criminology was somehow connected with the belief that women are incapable of acting autonomously (2002:24), unless the crimes committed were connected to their biological nature, for example prostitution and infanticide. In the data collected here, a different sort of double deviance seemed to be part of the common labelling process. While the legal aspects of deviance were rarely discussed when speaking about women[55], the dual aspect of female deviance was more likely to be seen in breaches of female nature and of family honour (Bolognani 2008). Afshar (1989:215; 1994:134) has observed how in West Yorkshire Pakistani women are considered to carry a double moral burden: an individual one, based on conduct thought appropriate to their gender, and a family one, based on their successful maintenance of the family honour (*izzat*[56]). Also, in a sense, women are at the same time appreciated for their 'inherent' caring and 'soft' attitudes, and considered irreparably weakened by them. Women who 'naturally' want to get married are more prone to be misled by unworthy men for whom they have fallen, and 'soft' mothers, valued for their love that knows no boundaries, are incapable of appropriately disciplining their children. Women taking drugs may be seen as victims of a 'polluted' society and bad men, and mothers who do not adequately discipline their sons are

as a group with an endemic problem of depression and mental health. Some women would become addicted to such prescription drugs for life. In some cases, their daughters or other female relatives would get access to them, and start a more dangerous non-prescribed intake. Although no statistical evidence was collected to triangulate community workers' perceptions, depression was a very well-known and often-mentioned problem for almost all research participants (cf. Pearson and Patel 1998). One development worker was convinced that white GPs do not know how to deal with 'Pakistani culture', and see anti-depressants as the only way to help women to lighten their emotional burdens. White GPs were seen as 'illiterate' in complex Pakistani family problems, which, according to this community worker, were the main cause of depression. At the same time, the number of trained Pakistani counsellors is insufficient to be effective in counteracting the spread of such illness.

A general perception by community workers and professionals working with Pakistani women was that British and European institutions were misled in their focus of attention. For example, the debate on the veil and the notion of the helpless passive Muslim woman were not thought of as leading to an increment in assertiveness or awareness among women in need. Even the overwhelming attention given to forced marriages[57] (Werbner 2005:25) seemed to deflect attention from other important issues affecting Pakistani women:

> When we did our last conference we had the media ringing up: 'We want to interview you, we know you do stuff on forced marriage and we want to speak with a young person', and this was like national media, but I said, 'I'm sorry, but I'm not interested – this isn't the only thing we work on. We do drugs, culture, truancy, substance misuse, we're doing it on issues that affect all young people, and there's a bit on forced marriage, that's it.' (Ayesha, in her early forties, member of a grassroots organisation working with young people)

Unconsciously recalling established critiques of orientalist approaches to the study of migrant women of Islamic background (cf. Lutz 1991), interviewees thought there was a common assumption of an inherent disfunctionality in their heritage, and therefore policy-makers' attention was predominantly addressed to issues directly involving family. It could be argued that hegemonic discourses seem to view Pakistani families' socialisation as a hurdle in the way of a functional self (see Bolognani *et al.* work in progress). This pathologising of the family has a long history in the way that British institutions have viewed South Asian women in general (see Parmar 1981; Brah 1996).

From within the Pakistani community itself, however, similar notions of passivity and helplessness emerge, bringing up the question of reciprocal influence of insiders' and outsiders' discourses on women (see Bolognani 2008). In the following conversation, recorded during a focus group, 16-year old girls discuss an imaginary scenario in which a Pakistani girl of their age was found consuming drugs by her family:

> Aqdus (student, 16 years old): '[People would say]: "She's going down the wrong path" and stuff . . .'
> Maria (student, 16 years old): She'd be looked down upon not just by her family, and there'd be so much stigma attached to her, like probably nobody would want to get married to her or nothing, and then . . . that's why girls don't want to do it.'
> Aqdus : I think it'd be difficult for girls to get hold of drugs . . .
> Sundas (student, 16 years old): [Laughs].
> Rhya (student, 16 years old): 'You think that because you don't know how it works . . . you think like "here do you get drugs from?" . . . but someone comes to you and they give it to you. That's all it is. [These girls] probably want to get married as well.'

This narrative seemed to imply that any girl of their age would 'naturally' aspire to get married. However, encounters with bad characters would lead onto the wrong path. The existence of a 'natural' female predisposition for certain choices was a recurrent topic when discussing deviance amongst young people. The difference between the involvement in crime of men and women was explained by a focus group's participant in this way: 'Boys get more attracted to go outside than girls do.'

As in the discussions about parental strategies (see Chapter Seven), with their descriptions of parental roles based on soft, passive and 'domestic' mothers and authoritarian, active and 'public' fathers, this dyadic gender perception strongly affected representations of deviant characters. If the popular conception was that girls 'naturally' aspire to create a home, but may be misled by criminal men, it is evident that a greater threat was posed to the system if they were involved in deviant lifestyles. If women make a home, deviant women may jeopardise a whole extended family. Hence, the moral panic about female involvement in drugs. However, as will be argued in the next chapter, once a woman has 'fallen', her redemption seems quite impossible, and one way to prevent her from contaminating other girls or the family is to evict her. Douglas (1966/2002:2; cf. Chapter Four) has argued that the frustrations of a society that does not know how to prevent or sanction behaviours that may jeopardise its existence are met with outrage, and with discourses of 'pollution'. In a context where women are on the one hand (at least in words) put on a pedestal because of their femininity and on the other considered victims of weaknesses attached to this elevated status, such complex threats may be met by beliefs about pollution (see Chapter Four).

6.5 Women as an Indicator of the Level of Deviance in the Community

In Chapter Seven, family and children's upbringing will emerge, according to research participants, as one of the most important variables in crime-prevention strategies. In Chapter Three family was already mentioned as an economic shock-absorber, providing an informal welfare system in times of hardship. In particular, within the family women seem to play a very important role in the administration of the its 'moral economy'. They also seem to be supposed to contribute in an essential way to the perpetuation of ethnic resources and networks. Women are not only socially constructed as markers of the community in the way they behave or implement traditions of honour and purity, but are also the main transmitters of cultural values to their children (Afshar 1994; Anthias and Yuval-Davis 1996; Archer 2001:97). In particular, women are the main *izzat* carriers. *Izzat*[58] is situationally translated as family 'honour', 'reputation', 'face-saving' and 'prestige':

> Amrit Wilson (1978) reports *Izzat* to be more than honour or self-respect, it is 'sometimes plain male ego. It is a quality basic to emotional life . . . It is essentially male, but it is women's lives and actions which affect it most. A woman can have *izzat*, but it is not her own, it is her husband's or her father's. Her *izzat* is a reflection of the male pride of the family as a whole. [What is more] saving her *izzat* (and through her own *izzat*) is perhaps the greatest responsibility for her parents or guardian.' (Afshar: 1989:214)

How a woman manages her *izzat* can consequently be considered as an indicator of her family's status, their socio-economic position and their moral values. Consequently, whenever crime touches her it could mean that the honour of the family is affected; but according to the research participants it is also a sign of how much crime has spread in the community if it has reached its most protected stratum.

Izzat is a pillar of social life in rural Pakistan. The role played by a family in a community is strictly linked to its reputation (Lutz 1991:129), and reputation may be strictly linked to the concept of reciprocity (Chaudhary 1999:68). The importance of reciprocity, or the diasporic version ('putting things back into the community'), was discussed in Chapter Five. The question of honour is therefore typical of close-knit *Gemeinschaften*[59] and appears to be more the consequence rather than the cause of isolation (ibid). Bradford Pakistani communities, being still very 'face-to-face', seem to continue to be largely regulated by *izzat*. As one interviewee put it:

> What happens in the Asian culture itself, it depends *all* on your family background. It's . . . my opinion, I'm not suggesting . . . but it's my own opinion. It all depends on how your family is, how you've been brought up, how your ancestors . . . it goes back . . . you know, it's the entire family, the way they were. (Jamil, entrepreneur in his early thirties)

Chapter Seven will investigate if *izzat* had an influence on criminal behaviour, in deterrence or in social control.

6.6 Rude Boys' Lifestyles: Appearances, Locations and 'Sharifisation'

Interviewers seemed more comfortable with and more versed in talking about boys 'on the edge', perhaps mirroring Imtiaz's observation of a hegemonic discourse on young Muslim men that has successfully penetrated this community. *Lafanga* or rude boys may not be criminal, but, dangerously, they were living a life that in between switches of behaviours may produce deviance. Some description caused a certain deal of confusion.

Some respondents argued in fact that drug dealers were known to the rest of the community, although the biggest deals happened at night. Even young teenagers were reported to know who the dealers were, and were supposedly seeking some work for a share of the drugs earnings. On the other hand, there seemed to be a spectrum of differences amongst drug dealers – their beliefs, life styles and whether they only dealt or were also consumers – that made their identification more difficult. One of the most surprising examples was told by Bano:

> Bano (student, 18 years old): '. . . you know what a *hafiz* is? When you know the Quran by heart. A lot of Asian boys they're becoming *hafiz*,

I know quite a lot [of them].'
MB: 'Do you think that's going to keep them off [drugs]?'
Bano: 'Not really; it depends. Because I know a guy and he's a *hafiz* and on the side he's a bit of a drug dealer. How does he cope? I asked him that question. I actually get shocked 'cos it's like . . . your religion . . . he's like "I do it for a living", it's like "you can't do it for a living". Living is like a job, working for Morrisons part-time is a job, not dealing in drugs, it's not a job.'
MB: 'Does he take drugs as well?'
Bano: 'No, he doesn't take drugs. He only deals.'
MB: 'So he hasn't got another job . . .'
Bano: 'I think he's got a job, I'm not too sure about the job . . . I think he does [dealing] for pleasure and as they say, one day you're gonna get banged up and that'll be the end . . .'
MB: 'And has he got a beard [and does he dress in the Muslim way]?'
Bano: 'Yes, he has a beard and he wears the traditional dress and all, and it's actually quite shocking because when you look at him you think "aaahhh", and when you hear about anything, you think "aaahhh" . . .'
MB: 'And do people around him know?'
Bano: 'I don't think so, I don't think his family know, but his friends know, because I'm one of his friends and I know, but I always think "you can't do that, that's really bad", but he sees it as a way of living.'

The co-existence of 'rude boys' and of a religious set of resources as described by Bano was not presented in any explicit elaboration of sub-cultures (see Table 6.1), although in Webster's data (1997) there is evidence of 'public impropriety' colluding with certain interpretations of Islam in the category of 'vigilantes'.

If outsiders may be preoccupied by certain traits of the youngest Pakistani generation, reinforced by theories of disaffection towards British society stirred by post-2001 events, many insiders showed similar concerns about the possible ramifications of rude boys' lifestyle in the community; it seemed they were negatively perceived for being perceived as 'cool' by younger and younger boys (see 'poisoning the community', in Chapter Four):

Young men do it because of easy, quick money, and there's also the fashion of the 'bad boy'. (Ameena, community worker in her early twenties)

> Our friend who lives down the road, he's got a degree in . . . I can't remember, something to do with biology, genetics or something, and he can't find jobs and he turned to drug dealing. His younger brother knows, his older brother knows, but his mum and dad will never know. His younger brother's at that age when it's cool if your brother's a drug dealer . . . it's the 'in thing' to be a drug dealer, it's a fashion statement. (Jamal, student in his early twenties)

Recurrent features describing rude boys were big cars and designer clothes, although this may be somewhat deceptive in the case of the Quran *hafiz* with beard and tunic described above.

Class and its relation to crime was rarely mentioned. Whether there existed a belief that middle-class individuals were less likely to commit crime was therefore left unexplored, although comments on the positive relations between education, areas of residence and lawfulness may assume that working-class people were more likely to engage in crime. However, comments seemed to be more concentrated around a quite vague notion of status.

Informants have suggested that 'back home' i.e. in Pakistan) politics and social relations are still very strongly determined by caste. In *vilayat*, however, issues regarding caste as a hierarchical system appeared to be sheepishly avoided, because of Islamic egalitarian teachings, and also because of changes in the perception of zat (caste). One of the processes that can arise from migration is 'Ashrafisation' – the process by which someone adopts a name and a way of life different from the original in order to be more cohesive with a caste, a process which would be similar to the status gained by a person through economic success (Werbner 1989:100).

A similar process seemed to be in action amongst drug dealers. One interviewee interestingly pointed out how drug dealers enjoy all the commodities that originally people assumed were only owned by eminent figures in the community: 'They live a life of *log sharif* (Fatima, interview with author), that is to say of 'respectable people'. This paradox is not due to the fact that drug dealers are treated as respectable people, but to the fact that they are able to share the same façade:

> I do believe that as a result of them becoming more affluent within the community because of the car, the nice house, when they see this is what they were, this is where they are now, nice house, nice car, you know . . . and the community, although it knows that they've done this by these means, i.e. drugs . . . it's *haram* money . . . they know that,

there's a certain eliteness, 'Look, I don't care, I got here, this is what you wanna be anyway.' (Imran, teacher in his early thirties)

This could suggest that the aspirational reference (cf. 'strain theory' in Chapter Five) is similar for any sub-group, but the means of achieving it are different. This may be confusing:

> People who don't deal in drugs, but they've got a top-end car, still dress well, they're labelled as drug dealers. A friend of mine has just spent £17,000 on a car and he's not a drug dealer, but still he's labelled as a drug dealer wherever he goes. (Jamal, student in his early twenties)

Drug dealers therefore seemed to be engaged in a process of 'sharifisation', by developing consumerist patterns and acquiring status indicators that once belonged to *log sharif* such as doctors, lawyers, etc. At the same time, however, the children of *sharif* families were developing the 'bad-boy fashion' (cf. Chapter Six), allegedly causing some confusion in stereotyping as 'bad'. One anecdote shows how this confusion may reflect on outsiders' perceptions. One evening the author was speaking with a lawyer and a former policeman in their BMW, parked on a cliff, eating a take-away, as it is customary with many Asian young men[60]. The two men were dressed in casual designer clothes (a style adopted by some drug dealers). A police van stopped and questioned us, searched the car and caused some tension when one police officer seemed to make inappropriate remarks.

The importance of fashion and consumerism in the rude boys' sub-culture may be a cultural extension of strain theory (see Chapter Five). Collison (1999:432) in fact has described 'unnecessary consumption' as a mean of constructing and enhancing self-identity in front of others. Depending on the opportunities and the means at hand, then, such a process of identity construction can be more or less legal.

> 'I'm a drug dealer, let's see who's got the biggest car, who's got the best car, who spends most on the car, who's got the most jewellery on, who has the best clothes on' – it's one big competition. People who're against it, they look down, but in the drug-dealing community it's a trend: 'I've just bought this car today, I've just spent five grand on a car', 'I've just spent 20 grand on a car' . . . The people I know who were in the riots, they said, 'We were just having a laugh' . . . their intentions was to get past the police, go into town, break into shops,

get all the design clothes for themselves, keep them or sell them, this is all they wanted to do . . . A couple of years back the coppers, the police, were always stopping and searching young Pakistani Asian lads with furry tops on, with trainers and track-suit bottoms thinking, 'These are the guys up to no good', but if you look at it, drug dealers are moving away from that . . . a drug dealer, for example, if he's got a hoodie top on, a track-suit bottom and a pair of trainers you're attracted to think, 'He's dealing in weed', and he's probably driving a Subaru sports car, dealing in skunk, with a four, five grand car . . . fair enough, he's dressed like [not clear], but then if you've got somebody who's driving for example a Range Rover and the guy only dresses smart, he'll be the type of guy you presume he's dealing in top-end drugs such as cocaine and heroin. So there's always a stigma, a label attached. (Jamal, student in his early twenties)

MB: 'Don't you have an idea of people in the area who deal with drugs?'
Fatima (student, 19 years old): 'Yeah, you know for example, if you have like a boy who's like a drug dealer and he's making really good, quite a lot of money from it, and then they do the house [up] really nicely, they've got a nice car and all that, [you'll know] . . .'

When the person next door has got a Porsche or a Ferrari, they say, 'Hang on, if you can get a Porsche or Ferrari we can get something better' . . . and they don't work! They've got a 60,000 car parked outside a 40,000-pounds house. (Adam, community worker in his late twenties)

A certain image has thus begun to make some members of the community feel uncomfortable on the streets:

> It used to be guys hanging around street corners and even if they weren't doing anything wrong, just the walking past them, walking down the street and seeing ten, 15 young lads with hoodie tops on and trainers and stuff, smoking, you'd feel intimidated by them, regardless whether they were being doing something or not. (Jamal, student in his early twenties)

'Keeping them off the streets' – an expression that often was used to describe the need for new youth or sport centres – seemed then to acquire a double meaning: not only would young men have needed a place where they could be involved in activities, but also a place that would attract them and leave the streets more secure (see also Chapter Eight). Streets were widely seen almost as criminogenic: 'hanging out' (as described by older people) and 'chilling' (by rude boys themselves) might in fact lead to criminal activities, either out of boredom or seeing and envying exciting but unaffordable lifestyles:

> When I first came over to Bradford I asked my sister-in-law's brother, where do your guys . . . where's the most popular hang-out place for Muslims? I think you know anyway for white communities, there's your pub, your club, etc. etc., so there's lot to do, but for Muslim communities . . . well, the answer I got when I went around and they showed me around, it's cars! You see a car there, and you see five guys sitting in a car, and some of them even have the portable televisions. Because for them that's their space, this is the space, this is the private space, they don't get that at home. They live at home, maybe someone's married, his wife lives at home, you know . . . maybe a brother, married, the other brother lives at home, the sister lives at home and you've got a two-bedrooms house. And that's what they do, drive around, sitting in cars, cup of coffee. (Imran, teacher in his early thirties)

Snooker centres were widely considered an unhealthy alternative to the streets:

> Imran (teacher in his early thirties): 'Snooker places, but . . . I was recommended not to go there . . . [laughs].'
> MB: 'But there's no alcohol there, is there?'
> Imran: 'No, but unfortunately a lot of drug-dealing in those places . . . takes place in that environment. This is the reason why I was advised not to go. Because when someone's involved in drugs, to be honest, they don't see colours, they don't see loyalty, they just see a customer, benefits. When it comes to drugs there's no boundaries.'
> MB: 'You mean these places are affected by drug-taking as much as drug-dealing?'
> Imran: 'Drug-dealing.'
> MB: 'Not drug-taking?'
> Imran: 'Not drug-taking. There are some places that I don't know of, but I've been told. But the snooker places I've been to they're more

a mixture of whites and Pakistani community. If they're mixed you tend to find there isn't that much of drug-taking in those places. So if . . . predominantly Pakistani area, you find there's something happening there.'

If streets were seen as almost criminogenic, at least they were safer than they had once been for young men of Pakistani heritage, who did not seem to have to face the racist attacks their fathers had to conjure with.

6.7 From Self Defence to Heroes: the Growth of a 'Mafia Mentality'

Some believed that the present sub-culture of rude boys was somehow connected with the era when self-defence had to be organised by young men against the fascists (see Chapter Three):

> I heard that a group of young men I was talking to they said they went to a pub the other night and there's a group of few white men there and said, 'They daren't even start anything'. Once upon a time you walked into a pub one person or two people you get beaten up, but now we're sure that we're safe, they didn't even lift their heads up. So those kinds of ideas have been reinforced that if you're strong, if you can fight back you get respect and I think that's wrong . . . That conflict's been there since I was very young in the seventies . . . (Abdul, social worker in his early forties)

According to Abdul, this attitude that tends to show strength is a survival of a legitimate right, and of a need for self-defence that emerged when Pakistani men rebelled against the myth of the 'white sahib' (*sic*), discovering that if you hit a white person 'their blood had the same colour' (a citation from the book *Hand on the Sun*, a book by Tariq Mehmood, a member of the 'Bradford 12'; see Chapter Three):

> So, once these people found was they were here, this was their home, they had rights and the individuality that they developed at school is very much apparent and they have rights as individuals, and eye for an eye and tooth for a tooth kind of thing, if you brought up with those values, these kids found that, yes, the myth of the invincible white master, the 'sahib', that was shattered amongst kids. (Abdul, social worker in his early forties)

Although interviewees denied that racist attacks were a constant threat in Bradford nowadays, there is some evidence that the problem had survived in some areas in the 1990s:

> Bashir (student, 19 years old): 'When we were growing up in Bradford 3 we were different groups, organised around friendship and the sort of locality . . . like your street . . . I think it had to do with the fact that we were Asians and there was a few white people living close by and they didn't like us for some reasons.'
> MB: 'So was it white groups and Asian groups?'
> Bashir: 'Once they started playing with branches like weapons and then we would start . . . and when we'd go back home for dinner they'd break the boughs in the garden . . . my mum encouraged us in a way to get sort of . . . "If anyone puts you down you've got to teach them a lesson, if someone starts on you, you can't just back away and say, 'I don't wanna fight'." But sometimes they'd come up to us without any reasons, like one time we were just playing football in the field and one jumped [interruption] . . . when I was there it was only between the whites and the Asians because within the Asians, your parents knew each other and you couldn't really get into [a] fight with anyone because the parents would get involved and you'd get into troubles . . . it's not worth it then . . . you just deal with your differences.'

One view was that emancipation from passivity might have led to the formation of groups, which in turn might have escalated into other kinds of mutual help and activities, with a sense of invincibility and competition ascribable to youthfulness and masculinity:

> Currently they think they're invincible, all 18-years-old think they think they can drive at 150 miles a hour on the motorway and nothing's gonna happen to them. At 18 you think like that, until something happens, of course. I just heard at the weekend a 15-years-old stole a car, wanted to impress his girlfriend, and of course he was killed, he had a crash. (Abdul, social worker in his early forties)

> I don't know what goes on with many of these large families; my guess is that . . . they're looking at their children and they think if x can do it, and y can do it . . . (Zameer, community worker in his early thirties)

> Young lads growing up now, you know like gangs . . . ganging up and stuff like that. (Jamil, entrepreneur in his early thirties)

'Gangs', 'gangsters' and 'mafia' were expressions often used to describe groups involved in criminal activities; often (although not necessarily) they were even described as belonging to the same biraderi, but this would enhance the efficacy of the mafia metaphor (around which are written Bradford-based crime novels by Bradford-born author M.Y. Alam).

This seems consistent with the fear of a negative impact from the excessive intra-familial bonding described in Chapter Five. Hence the popularity of mafia scenarios:

> Bano (student, 18 years old): 'My little nine-years-old brother . . . knows all the gangsters in West Bowling, and it's actually quite scary sometimes, because . . .'
> MB: 'What do you mean by gangsters?'
> Bano: 'There's like, you've got like . . . in West Bowling you've got guys who are well, well, well-known, they're really well-known, maybe because they've got really good cars, or maybe because they're drug dealers, or just maybe because they've got older brothers who're really, really famous. I don't know, it's like being in 'pop stars' when you've got the really famous people that you can look up to. That [is] what it's like for youngsters in West Bowling.'

> Strength amongst individuals and groups is feared by any community . . . [The elders] have great contempt, but because they have money you don't know when they're gonna be able to do you a favour, so people again are very pragmatic. (Abdul, social worker in his early forties)

> They're afraid because them people have got that . . . they've got that respect . . . basically they've got the car, the money, nobody can say anything to that because they 've made it up there, whether it's by drugs, whether it's by anything . . . It's like a gang culture, a mob culture . . . they're afraid of that type of people. They're not ostracised, but basically there's a sense of 'We can't tell them off because we might get into troubles ourselves'. (Fatima, student, 19 years old)

> MB: 'Were you saying you know somebody who got arrested? Did the people know he was dealing before he was actually caught?'
> Sarah (student, 17 years old): 'Yes, because they've got that image, haven't they?'
> MB: 'What image?'

Bano (student, 18 years old): 'Like . . . where I live there's this guy and he deals drugs but no one . . . it's not a good thing, but the fact is that everyone's very scared about him and no one ever has the guts to . . . you know...like stand up . . . because he's got so much back-up, so much people . . . even if you say something, you get your head bashed and you know . . . that's like normal.'

Adding to the sub-cultural 'mafia mentality', territorialism was mentioned as one of the concerns informing young men's behaviour. Graffiti used to be sprayed in the Leeds Road area, before a council task-force was called in to remove them. At the time of the research only a small one was still visible, but it used the gangster lingo: '[Name], [Name], [Name], Lower Rushton Mafia'. Protection of the territory was also seen as one of the triggers for 2001 the riots (see Bolognani 2007c).

6.8 Conclusion: Young People and Moral Panic

Studies, including sub-cultural models in the Bradford district (Webster 1997 and Imtiaz 2002), present some overlapping traits and are partially consistent with a similar theorisation made by research participant Umar. They are based on male typology and incorporate to some degree local knowledge and labelling processes. Although only one research participant (Umar) articulated a sub-cultural grand system to apply to Bradford young men, most interviewees mentioned a male youth-culture similar to Umar's category 3 (almost overlapping with Imtiaz's 'rude boys' and Webster's 'go-betweens').

Young men who combined sets of values and behaviours deriving from the family (for example 'cultural Mirpuris'), from television (for example, through R'n'B 'gangsta videos') or from other minority ethnic groups (for example, references to a stereotypical black 'LA culture') were largely considered the folk devils of the Pakistani community of Bradford. Far from being considered agents of a proactive process of combining local and global sets of values and behaviours (multiple consciousness), they were considered 'at risk'. Their 'hanging out' on the streets, their materialist aspirations, their exposure to the deals of the established gangsters and the lack of control exercised by their parents was generally thought as easily pushing them into criminal careers. Additionally, activities such as sitting in cars in back alleyways and 'hanging out' on street corners wearing hoodies were considered behaviours that would project a bad image of the community to outsiders, and were sometimes blamed for the bad reputation that Pakistanis had gained in Bradford.

Although 'mafia mentality' and 'gangster culture' were often mentioned to describe deviant behaviours in the community, the networks and organisations of the allegedly existent gangs were still rather obscure to the informants. One of the reasons for this lack of information may be that some of the dealers' networks were said to be mainly based on their biraderi or their ethnic origin. The knowledge about what were called gangs seemed to be still quite obscure, while generalisation and sub-cultural descriptions of individuals living in the grey area of rude boys were much more readily articulated. Young men as folk devils seemed to be the sub-cultural definition resulting from a moral panic about male youth. However, the anecdotes about the biggest drug dealers and their deeds that interviewees enjoyed recounting ('proper gangsta stuff, I tell ya!', Adam, interview with author) most often concerned men in their forties and fifties. This was somewhat in contradiction to views about the law-abiding older generation and the deviant younger one (cf. Chapter Five), but concerns about young rude boys seemed to be a priority for most of the interviewees.

In the panorama of crime a particular position seemed to be held by women, as described by a young female:

Maria (student, 16 years old): 'I don't know because like the female in the Pakistani culture is like . . . even if . . . a boy was defined as a drug taker he won't be seen as so bad . . . because it'll be seen like "This is just what boys do" . . . like "he'll grow out of it, forget it" . . . but if a girl did it, it'll be just too bad for the girl.'

Evidence from this fieldwork seems to record a dramatic increase in the engagement of young Muslim women of Pakistani descent with criminal activities. Although relevant statistical data are not available and much of the rumours surrounding this topic may be part of informal social control through ubiquitous gossip, a serious concern emerges as far as the position of Pakistani women in contemporary Britain is concerned. It appears that both their community and hegemonic discourses are likely to portray them as passive subjects and deny them agency. Consequently, as regards passivity, the alternately praised and blamed natural attribute of softness is the root of the concern that leads to enclosure. As regards the denial of agency, the alleged universal subjugation of the Muslim woman is likely to be ended only by a de-culturation process. These attitudes translate into two main practices. The first consists of neglecting ad hoc education aimed at understanding problems, for instance, of addiction, in favour of broader notions of protection from the outer world; the second consists of policies

sidered an essential part of crime-prevention strategies (Burnside and Baker 1994:19; Hope 2001:430). Following this criminological interest, this chapter will open with an analysis of the evaluation of social control exercised by families, which in Chapter Five was part of the attribution-of-blame system. However, in the emic analysis of present forms of social control it emerged that great attention was also paid to the system generated by formal institutions. Chapter Eight will therefore be complementary to the present one. These findings will be particularly significant in the conclusion, where the definition of 'community criminology' will have to consider the enmeshing of formal and informal elements in local criminological discourses.

7.1 Social Control through the Family: Prevention for Girls, Retrieval for Boys

In Chapter Five it was argued by some that the family may be problematic in terms of social control, for two reasons: the parents' 'out of place' culture, and the practice of internal exclusive bonding. This section will present a detailed evaluation of both the potential and the alleged inadequacies of many families in dealing with social control.

During the research two main issues were highlighted regarding social control exercised through the family. The first was that many parents would not abdicate their power in contributing to the moral education of their children, but after the latter reached a certain age they would be keen to delegate it to mosques and madrassas. Views criticising this delegation included the following:

> I think the first teachers are your parents, I mean, they actually bring you up in the norms and values that they share ... they're supposed to teach you in the right way. There are certain things that your parents are supposed to do while you're small. They're supposed to teach you right and wrong, the difference between right and wrong and things like 'you shouldn't lie, you should go to the mosque', etcetera, but once the person reach[es] a certain age they'll have their own understanding and they go to the mosque and then it's the duty of the imam of the mosque, the priest of the mosque to teach them norms and values ... (Yousef, student, 16 years old)

The second issue was that family upbringing was gender-biased, and ended up conceding too much freedom to boys (as already discussed in Chapter Six). Social control exercised by families seemed to be mainly about prevention for girls and retrieval for boys, as will be discussed in the next section.

In general, however, evaluation of social control exercised by families tended to focus on one element: *izzat*. While preservation of the family honour (see Chapters Three, Four and Six) would in theory be a trigger for preventing deviance in one's children, many respondents described family social control as functional to the preservation of an honourable façade (see section on gossip and scandal below) rather than the uprooting of deviant behaviour (cf. family exclusivism, Chapter Five). Rather than tackling a problem, things may be 'swept under the carpet':

> Our community ... I don't know what to say, they don't want to open up, they don't want to talk about issues and things, and that word again, *izzat*, because they're scared, and what's happening in their family unit, what their kids are doing and everything, because they don't want other people to know their business. (Adam, community worker in his late twenties)

One imam recounted that when he saw a member of a family he knew pictured in the *Telegraph & Argus* following their arrest for drugs-related offences, he went to visit the family to offer emotional support, but he was called *maulana (maulvi)* 'bastard' on their doorstep and turned away—they despised his acknowledgement of the dishonour that had occurred to their family.

As already discussed in the previous chapters, *izzat* has a special application to women, and perhaps for this reason respondents registered different articulations of social control for boys and girls (Bolognani 2008).

In Chapter Six we saw how women involved in drugs are likely to be considered victims of men, of contact with outer society or of their own weak and soft nature. As Bisi puts it, 'female criminality [can be] interpreted as the logical outcome of certain bio-psychological traits: weakness, limited self-consciousmess, incapacity of choice' (2002:24). This perception, however, does not necessarily lead to an easier path to forgiveness after their supposedly unwilling lapse. Parents were generally seen as more lenient with sons than with daughters, and all the women interviewed felt that cultural traditions made men feel as if they were always to be forgiven. This supported the idea that social control was deeply gendered:

> If the Asian males of the community commit crime, it's not looked down as bad as if it was a woman. (Mahima, shop assistant in her late twenties)

Considering the widespread belief that women are the carrier of the family *izzat*[1], the damage to reputation created by the bad behaviour of a son seemed to be retrievable, but the actions of a woman to carry bigger consequences for her parents. This view was supported by an anecdote recurrently told during fieldwork:

> I know of this family. They don't live in our neighbourhood but people used to . . . the story used to circulate from Bradford 8 to Bradford 1, so you're bound to hear somewhere along the line. This family . . . they were an Asian family, they weren't very religious and they weren't really bothered about the way they were. A lot of people said they were Westernised, but Westernised is what you think is Westernised, not . . . so, they were just themselves, they were free people, they weren't Eastern, they didn't have Eastern values or culture, what our parents believe to be Eastern. So they were just themselves, and . . . their sons started taking drugs, being smoking, they were very light, you know, 'We need to do something about him, we need to make him get off this drug'. The daughter started to take the drugs as well. She was kicked out of the house, like you said you heard. She had nowhere to go, so she ended up with her drug dealer. They said this was her ultimate decision, 'This is what she wanted from day one, that's why she made us kick her out . . .', and excuses for covering up why they kicked her out. 'This is what she wanted and that's why we've done it.' The son was continuing still taking the drugs, no matter what they'd do to stop him because it's very hard unless you get proper help, but the son was sort of . . . I don't know what it is with boys in Asian family . . . they're seen as better assets. And she was like . . . all her focus was on the son, but none on the daughter. The daughter was kicked out of the house, it doesn't matter about her, it doesn't matter. It's like she was replaced . . . they didn't need her. She ended up with her drug dealer and she ended up in a very bad state. Had she got the help she needed from the family or whoever . . . she would have maybe you know . . . did something about it. She ended up with someone who wasn't going to really get her off it, because he needs her. In fact he made her go back home, steal gold, Asian gold is like . . . very valued in family . . . made her steal all the gold, everything, so basically her life was . . . because to this day she isn't allowed to go to her family now. As far as they're concerned she's dead. (Zaara, shop assistant and special constable in her early twenties)

In this story, the lack of discipline ('they weren't really bothered'), the effect of Western culture ('people said they were Westernised'), the fact that parents were 'light' on the boys and harsh on the girl, even if she had been introduced to drugs through them, and finally the soft attitude of the mother towards her sons, exemplify once again the helplessness of a woman who becomes deviant. This anecdote, recounted more or less in the same way by different sources, seems also to convey the idea that rehabilitation of a daughter is more difficult than rehabilitation of a son. It may be for this reason that preventive social control appears stronger for girls, who are generally more limited in their freedom of movement than their brothers. The expulsion of a daughter from the family seemed to be an extreme and rare resolution, as it may be a very publicly recognisable sign of the breach of family *izzat*. On the other hand, a family who had expelled their daughter might hide it in various ways; for instance:

> They say she's studying, she's gone to stay with an auntie somewhere. If she's in Bradford they say she's gone to London, if she's in London it'll be Bradford. (Ali, artist in his late twenties)

Other families may choose to send the daughter back to Pakistan for 'rehabilitation', or ask for religious or magical help (see below). Parental strategies appeared to be varied, but dictated by the common concern of protecting *izzat*.

7.2 Social Control through the Family: Three Case Studies of Parental Strategies

Prompted by my questioning about parents' knowledge, resources and strategies beyond gender, community worker Adam introduced me to three individuals to explain his view of parenting as potentially the main source of social control.

The three men introduced belonged to well-known local families who had developed businesses and achieved an economic status described as 'middle class'. The first was Iqbal, a businessman engaged in local politics, born in the Mirpur District, who migrated to the UK as a child. According to Adam, he had managed to involve all his children in the family businesses (even the one who had graduated) and had always managed to stay close to them. None of them had ever been involved even in the minor crimes quite common amongst Pakistani teenagers in the area who wanted to have 'a bit of fun' (*sic*). Indirectly, Iqbal described his ethos as a parent by attaching it to two discourses already analysed in Chapter Five: the side-effects of the

'Asian economic niche' and of the 'generational gap':

> I think that parents have to be strict and I think strictness is something that doesn't come about at the age of 16, it has to start at a very early age, but the problem that has been with . . . how shall I say . . . with the Muslim community was the father was too busy working, because the mother wasn't allowed to work, or the mother wasn't in the position to work, and . . . but the basic education, where does that come from? How do you discipline the child . . . how does that come from? The mother wasn't able to do it, and the father was too busy working. I think the Asian community has come to thinking, 'Well, the Muslim community, we were too busy working and we neglected the children. . . . I realised that when my son was born . . . and I realised that wasn't the way forward, I think my children have to come first, so I'd better be with him. But sometimes when you have like mother and father back home, your family here, so you are torn between those two things . . . (Iqbal, entrepreneur and politician in his mid-fifties)

In order to show me a comparative example for the idea of good parenting as the simple act of spending time with one's children (especially sons, according to the quote) from early childhood, Adam presented the author with the example of 23- year-old Azad, unemployed. At the time of the interview Azad was busy gathering his friends (and personal driver) to arrange the Saturday-night drug business. Azad's father was described by Adam as a famous mullah respected by the whole local community as somebody who had 'made it big' at an international level, and was very respected. According to Adam, Azad's father spent most of his time abroad, preaching from California to Malaysia; he earned a fortune, but completely neglected his sons, who turned into drug dealers. Instead of completely rebelling against the family, Azad had decided to preserve the family *izzat* by accommodating the parents' desires, such as going to Pakistan at least once a year to visit relatives. During these absences, he would 'sell up to a friend', that is to say he would rent his phone where he received the orders and would get the phone back once he returned to Bradford.

Azad's brother had been arrested for an armed robbery before becoming a Quran *hafiz*[62]. Azad, who himself could have fitted in Wardak's 'accommodationists' category (see Table 6.1), justified his new life-style by saying that he had worked for too long for a local greengrocer's and now it was time 'to chill'. Allegedly, his father said to him that he could do whatever he wanted as long as he did not get to know about it. Adam's critical view of a parent who is too involved in religion to look after his children was mentioned also by a Londoner, a newcomer to Bradford:

> The other extreme dimension is when people have kids. I have a personal example, a very, very close friend of mine since uni, his father would go ... Tableeghi Jamaat ... He has got four kids, married man, who goes to Tableegh for nine–ten months a year. Two months he'll come back and then he'll go again to different countries, yet there isn't father figure at home ... Tableegh is where people believe you have to dedicate at the minimum 30 days a year of your life to the mosque where you go ... for example, you're in Bradford, you go to the mosque in London, in Malaysia, and you invite people from that area to come to the mosque. This is your top priority. Some people have taken it to such an extreme that they won't do 30 days, they'll do nine–ten months a year, but they'll only come back just to like . . . recuperate, and then go back again. That's the other extreme, they don't work, they become very lazy, they give nothing back positively in the community. (Imran, teacher in his early thirties)

The third example Adam presented in order to make his point about parenting concerned another local businessman who, according to local residents, had shared much of his good luck in business with the neighbourhood, providing jobs to many young people and improving the reputation of the area with a well-established business venture. Although Jamil was only 36, he seemed to embody all the essential characteristics that people tend to ascribe to the 'first generation': hard-working, not tempted by quick money and expensive commodities, and concerned about the well-being of his community (cf. the concept of 'putting things back into the community', or *khidmat*, in Chapter Four). Adam's view of the man as a businessman was very respectful:

> I think in the community at the moment everybody are driven by their own interest. They're not interested in what the community's doing. I've seen him [Jamil], he's got businesses and he's done a lot for the community, he's brought young lads from the community in here and he's helped them to gain that experience ... he educated them, gave them a chance to develop life skills! ... He's been an inspiration for the young lads in the area, but then again [Jamil] has got his life, he can't be there for them all the time. He's been a role model for the young kids, he's done really well for himself, and he's got his business

set up and everything. His brothers are all here, they're all working, like he was saying, 12–13 hours shift. He says he's here all the time, he only goes home to sleep. Then he comes back here . . . it has a knock-on effect on the community where people see that and they want to do better and go forward and open businesses. (Adam, community worker in his late twenties)

On the other hand, the view about the man as a parent was quite critical: Adam wondered whether his children would see enough of him. Again, as in the quotes discussed above, the time spent with one's children became of major concern as one of the variables that would secure good parenting:

> A lot of things today [are] about bad parenting. No matter how good the parents are as people, if they don't spend enough time with children, they can't grow up straight. (Adam, community worker in his late twenties)

The lack of time spent with children was linked by one informant to the erosion of the family system:

> We've broken the family system, there's nobody in the family who's solely responsible for the upbringing of the child; we've created the stigma of one parent, if he or she says, 'I look after children' we think he's useless, or she's useless, wasting time, so you wouldn't hear, maybe, a very happy response to say 'I'm a housewife' or maybe 'I'm a father, my wife works and I'm doing this'. (Tahir, teacher in his late thirties)

The position of Jamil himself on the matter was based on a belief that role models in the family, no matter how present they are in their lives, will automatically dictate the good path to their children:

> MB: 'So what do you think went right for you and wrong for the others who hang out on the road? Is it because you're assertive and they aren't or . . .'
> Jamil (entrepreneur in his early thirties): 'There are two things. When I was at school, I was still at school, after school, go to the shop, help out in the shop. It just came, you know, just naturally came to me that we had to work for a living. And from that day on we just worked. Because our parents always worked, from day one. It just came from

there, and then when I grew up I thought, "I have to work" and I just had to put the hours in, and not everybody wants to put them hours in.'

Overall, there seemed to be a popular understanding that the problem was the result of a very carefree upbringing and rooted in either the fathers' absence (cf. reference to the 'Asian economic niche' in Chapter Five), the lack of discipline and norms, and often the mothers' attitudes (see below), or the erosion of ethnic networks (see Chapter Five). Such a 'laid-back' trend set in early childhood was considered difficult to reverse later in the teenage years, especially for boys (see the quote from Iqbal above). Bad parenting was normally equated with giving too much freedom to children, whether examples referred to children running unsupervised in a shop, to children whose playmates were not controlled and were outside at all hours, or to young boys who were allowed out for the whole night:

> I think the kids are out of control of the parents and I think it comes from when the child is very small, as a baby and when he's growing up, how the parents discipline the child and sometimes, three–four years old, he's ruling and he's the boss and they're just doing . . . it comes from an early age when parents should discipline them and keep an eye and give them a good atmosphere at home, good education and just work towards that, but I noticed that in some families they have kids and it's just normal, they get up in the morning and they do their routine . . . they're doing their own things and parents let them. So I blame the parents, who aren't strict with them, they should discipline them so then they could avoid . . . (Shamim, community worker in her early forties)

This seemed to some as unrelated to bad will, but resulting rather from a lack of understanding of a different environment and its necessities[63]. This attitude could be labelled 'passive bad parenting':

> I think it is just lack of education for parents, they have no knowledge. . . . I'll just tell . . . you know, in Pakistan, in India . . . you know children can play out, and here the houses are all closed in and sometime people have like six kids in one room and for parents and for kids it's not good, not healthy, and therefore at an early age, parents will say, 'Go on, play out', where in Pakistan they are not allowed to play out like that, you know, because the extended family is there, and they're

safe there, but here, because they can't cope with so much, people just sitting in one room, so I think that's one of the reasons, that they don't have enough space to play with . . . a play area, and the weather as well, so parents are frustrated and they think, 'Well, let them go out and do what they can do, so at least I can get on with my house work', and therefore kids are left on their own for too long . . . they're left too long. In Pakistan, if a child stays out for more than half an hour, everybody will say, 'Oh, he hasn't come home yet', but here, because there's so much going on, so much on parents' mind as well. (Shamim, community worker in her early forties)

Some relevant observations were made by a woman in her forties who had attended a majority-white school in the years when the local 'bussing' policies were in force, aimed at increasing ethnic interaction by sending students to schools in other wards. She stated that she realised how much less discipline she was subjected to, compared to her English counterparts:

The school was very difficult because there seemed to be a sense of . . . you know for the white kids it was really different because their life used to be more structured than ours, in the sense they'd go home, have tea, have supper, da-da-da, they were set into a routine and that was represented in the way they came across. For us there was nothing like that, it was sort of like . . . you went home, you didn't have tea, you had a cup of tea and biscuits and then you had your roti at half-past seven, eight o'clock, that was our main meal. And instead of going to bed . . . you know . . . for my mum it was you go to bed when you're tired. You weren't sent to bed if you had school in the morning. So at half-past nine, ten o'clock, my younger sister and my younger brother I'd put them to sleep myself and then I'd come down and watch telly till midnight, and in them days everything switched off at half-past 11, 12 o'clock, you didn't have all-night telly. (Ayesha, community worker in her early forties)

While the above views might be ascribed to a feeling of frustration promoted by the unused potential of social control within the traditional family structure, some respondents were inclined to blame a more 'active' or 'conscious' form of bad parenting, in their opinion produced by some features of rural-Pakistani family structure:

Zameer (community worker in his early thirties): 'I think we have to take some responsibility for ourselves on that, the way we portray ourselves, and the thing is, at the end of the day, we're a law-abiding community, because if you look at the Indians, Indian Muslims, and the Indian Hindu population in West Yorkshire, you don't get to see many of them misbehaving, the way the Pakistanis do . . . they don't, do they? You don't see many of them involved in drugs.'

MB: 'Why?'

Zameer: 'That's a good question, why. That . . . because you see an Asian, physically, you're not gonna know if this guy is a Muslim or Hindu or Sikh, but why is it that the Muslim Pakistani kids may potentially misbehave much more than the Hindu or the Gujarati kid? It is a big question, because the Gujaratis, right, some of those are Muslims, so there's something which isn't right here...if a Gujarati kid from India in general do much better than Pakistani kids....is that something to do with the make-up of the families? Where your mentality, it is something to do with your clan, where you live? . . . I think it is, it's the way we may be behaving in our families, the way some of it's acceptable, some of that so-called deviant behaviour is acceptable.'

Chapters Three and Five have already highlighted some perspectives extant in Bradford concerning the lack of education in the Mirpuri heritage, the prioritising of biraderi interests at the expense of the common good, and the 'cultural' practice of Islam. There follows an analysis of what the gendered division of parental roles based on cultural tradition may mean for social control.

7.3 The Mother's Roles

The division of the living quarters is an effective image in helping to understand the gendered roles in the Mirpuri family. In Mirpur, men normally take care of the external world and the family connections to it; they lead a social life that goes beyond the walls of the home, and their reputation and honour is expected to be constructed or challenged in the public sphere, in contrast with women's domain in the private sphere (cf. Gilmore 1987; 1990).

Women are however generally in charge of certain matters within the home (Saifullah-Khan 1974; Afshar 1994; Wardak 2000; Ballard 2001). They are seen as the principal educators of the children as far as behaviour and values are concerned (Afshar 1994), and at the same time they seem to be the most responsible for the family honour (*izzat*). This is why the level of danger to the community from crime is often expressed in terms of the threat posed by it to women (cf. Chapter Six).

> A lot of issues that came up while visiting homes . . . you could tell there were problems they were reluctant to talk about, it showed whatever tension or . . . problems . . . so we got involved to find out what the problem was and found out that they [some women] weren't allowed to go out, and the family was afraid that they'd mix in with the society and that would mean that they'll misguide them (Shamim, community worker in her early forties)

In Adam's examples above, the point about good and bad parenting was made partly on the basis of reference to the fathers. In almost all interviews, however, respondents tended to talk about parents in general, and when questioned about the different roles of mothers and fathers in raising children there seemed to be unanimity in describing a division in parental roles. Mothers were the worrying, listening and forgiving side; fathers were more strict, and inclined to impose punishment in the form of physical chastisement (cf. also Irfan and Cowburn 2004:96):

> My mum [laughs], she always says, even if I'm 18, what I should do or shouldn't do. Sometimes I go out and see my friends and if I'm late she's always calling me, 'Where are you?' in case I'm in an accident somewhere, she's always worried. . . . I think it's everybody, in the majority it's always mothers who get worried, you know. (Yousef, student, 16 years old)

The widespread belief that in Pakistani culture, or even more generally in Muslim culture, the man has a more public role and the woman a private one seemed to be backed up by many interviews in a way that is consistent with relevant literature (Irfan and Cowburn 2004). The mother is supposed to represent a 'softer' traditional culture, the father authority and prescription:

> My dad is more educated than my mum, and he's been brought up in England, that plays a big factor on my dad's character. My mum tends to have a big part in our culture, whereas my dad doesn't. (Mahima, student in her late twenties)

It was felt that while fathers might be more or less present in the upbringing of children (and that their absence would lead to a lack of discipline) the more stable presence of the mother may fail to provide an adequate upbringing, because of either her softness or her being unprepared to deal with the problems facing the young. This may be related to the essentialised perceptions of gender characteristics (as outlined in Chapter Six): women may be in fact considered softer, more passive, and passively involved in deviant behaviour. So women taking drugs may be seen as victims of a polluted society, and mothers who do not adequately discipline their sons are considered victims of their soft nature.

So far preventative social control has been discussed, while the actions that families may take once the children have already been involved in illegal activities have only been hinted at. Some forms of retrieval strategies will be evaluated below.

7.4 'Home-made Rehabilitation': 'Village Rehab' and the 'Marriage Cure'

Some elders seemed to retain an idealised concept of 'back home'. In many families it is still the custom to send children back home during their holidays in order to enhance their 'real life' and show how 'lucky they are' (Kalra and Mcloughlin 1999; Bolognani, 2007d):

> At one time all the children were encouraged to go to Pakistan for a holiday, during the summer, but nowadays the tendency is getting less and less. . . . It's because the children don't wanna go, but by not going they're missing out on something, like you know . . . I'm sure it helps your education and it helps by understanding other people's problems, you know, you understand how other people live, and it's not all the same. (Iqbal, entrepreneur and politician in his late fifties)

Whether the idealised morality is supposed to simply rub off on the young *vilayatis* (foreigners), or there will be a rational realisation of their privileged condition in the UK, the results of these 'travels of knowledge' are quite controversial. According to some young men who had recently been, such visits could become counter-productive, and they believed that the idealisation of 'back home' was misplaced:

> MB: 'There's nothing like this [pointing at his vodka and Red Bull] in Pakistan, is there?'
> Khalil (quoted in Bolognani 2002): 'There is! A lot stronger than this! It's called kuppi . . . you know, if you had that much, you wouldn't wake up for about two–three days. I've got two of my friends who've

come back from Pakistan now, two weeks ago, one of them has been drinking and smoking so much . . . smoking that black . . . he's been smoking so much of that, he was taken to hospital. Because it's warm as well, innit? So you're always sweating and stuff, and it dries you out, innit? I've never drank in Pakistan because I go with my uncle and with my family, d'you know what I mean? But this time we go we aren't gonna go home, we go home for the first week or somewhat, and then just stay out and enjoy, see places and everything, and have a good life.'

Azad recounted how much 'chilling' he is used to doing in Lahore, where 'everybody' (*sic*) is on drugs. Some literature on the subject refers to anecdotes about the development of a 'holiday habit' (Pearson and Patel 1998:218), an addiction developed during a sojourn in Pakistan. Hussain, when asked about drugs in the community, answered by saying that it was quite natural for Pakistani people to use drugs: evidence of that lay in the natural, lush growth of marijuana in the Indian sub-continent. However, the practice of sending children back home to wean them off drugs was still in use at the time of the fieldwork. Of particular interest was the news reported by some tabloids after '7/7' that one of the London bombers from Leeds had been sent to Pakistan by his family to wean him off alcohol, but there he might have developed an interest in discourses that played a part in his terrorist action. During the fieldwork, however, some respondents recounted stories of successful 'village-rehabilitated' acquaintances as well as failed ones. Interestingly, different strategies of rehabilitation seem to have grown out of the original one, including the use of clinics in Pakistani cities:

> Fatima (student, 19 years old): 'I have one cousin, not cousin, but like family cousin, who lives just a few streets away. I think he's in his thirties and something and he used to take drugs and he actually went to Pakistan to get rehab from there and I was there in Pakistan at the moment so . . .'
> MB: 'Do you mean he went to a clinic?'
> Fatima: 'Yes, in Pakistan. They have rehab there. Then . . . they sent him into a rehab clinic and stuff like that and I think the wider community, the elder generation, they're aware that there's a problem with drugs, and that there are institutions to deal with it, but in the past, or even now in the present there's been this sense of hiding, put it under the carpet, "He'll be OK, we'll deal with it ourselves." So say for example if you've been affected in a family with drugs, and you

put it under the carpet and you see, you know, two doors away from you, that the same ... people from the same background, people have got the same problem with drugs, that family ... family A won't go to family B because first they'll keep their problems to themselves so they don't want to go to them people and help them, because this family's got this concept of "We dealt with it ourselves, they can deal with it themselves" ... d'you get it?'

In this way the rehabilitation may be kept secret from the rest of the community who do not have contacts in Pakistani cities.

Sometimes rehab back home may be paired with marriage:

MB: 'What if parents found out about a son taking drugs?'
Jamal (student in his early twenties): 'I'll give you an example. I've got someone I know and he found out that his son was smoking cannabis when his son was only 14, so he sent him off to Pakistan and got him married at the age of 14! This was years ago, we were kids, I was about 14, no 16, he was two years younger than me, that kid . . . he was smoking some weed and his dad saw him and he got his passport, took him to Pakistan, kept him there for one year, got him married, brought him back, set him to work in a restaurant, the guy's now about 20 now, he brought his missus over . . . and he's got a kid! He's a father by the age of 17.'
MB: 'Do you think it worked?'
Jamal: 'No, because he still does it.'
MB: 'What's the reasoning behind it?'
Jamal: 'Discipline. The eldest . . . for them, it's a real discipline. 'Oh well, if I give him some responsibility and get him married and having a family, he might just stop it because it's your responsibility'. . . It's about discipline. Sometimes it works, sometimes it doesn't. I know people for whom it worked, man. I know people who were drunkies, I know one at the bottom of our street, my friend's older brother and he's a drunkie and heroin, cocaine and all sort and drinking . . . everything. Partying . . . going out every night, not coming home for three, four days . . . his dad took him to Pakistan, got him married, came back now and you won't believe he's the same person. He stopped drinking, stopped the drugs, stopped everything. . . . Yes. Sometimes it works . . . but at the age of 14, what do you know about life? You try to enjoy yourself . . . I used to do all sorts that my mum and dad don't know about.'

Some would argue that there is a value of treatment attached to these types of marriage (cf. also Werbner 2004:903), but such understanding is quite controversial:

> The mother's crying, 'My son, why did you go to jail, come on, let's go to Pakistan and get you married', as if marriage is some miracle cure that suddenly the son becomes a doctor and goes to university when he comes back . . . I'm sorry but it doesn't work like that. (Mahima, student in her late twenties)

However, reflecting on Jamal's accounts, it is interesting to see how, apart from giving responsibility to the 'derailed' child, there are other advantages: the whole biraderi is kept happy and the 'prodigal son', through the rite of marriage, is reintegrated into his family, whose wishes he accepts:

> I think parents, they feel they owe it to their family back home, that's sense of guilt, I think that's what it boils down to. Is the sense of 'We're here, you're there, so if we intermarry and your kids come over. . .', and I think a lot has to do with that. (Ayesha, community worker in her early forties)

7.5 Means of Social Control: Gossip and Scandal

In the anthropological literature, both theoretical (see Gluckman 1963) and ethnographic (see Lyon 2004), gossip has been considered a very effective means to check behaviour and keep track of status competition. In the fieldwork reprted here, gossip and moral panic appeared as an instrument of social control. As argued by Saeed (2002:310), patriarchal societies sometimes pose psychological and physical boundaries by creating taboos, stigmas and urban myths. The exaggeration and ubiquity of the perceived drug threat against females in the fieldwork seemed to follow a similar pattern. Stories (with a similar core, but changing fringe details) recounting parables of fallen women, victims of drug dealers from their own community, recurred. The link between drug consumption, 'grooming' and prostitution was part of the wide-spread moral panic about British Pakistani women being drug-raped and subsequently blackmailed and introduced into prostitution[64] (see Chapter Six):

> The Asian girls, now . . . I've seen myself they're all taking drugs and everything it's unbelievable. What's happening at university now, four years ago it wasn't like that, but the culture at university has com-

> pletely changed, it's unbelievable. You see, with me I've got friends in Manchester, people in Birmingham, London, when I go there, ah, it's just completely different culture shock, they're smoking heroin, and spliffs and everything . . . but I'm talking about the grooming . . . they'll start with a cigarette and then the boy will say let's smoke a spliff, the spliff is like cannabis, and they put a line of heroin in it, and it's like a drink, if you have a drink and someone spikes it with a bit of vodka you don't realise they're doing it. That's what they do, they put a line of cocaine so it makes it stronger, so when you take it, you're put on it, so you'll always take it, more and more and everything. (Adam, development worker in his late twenties)

One imam was told by taxi drivers that Asian girls are to be found working in saunas as prostitutes in Bradford to pay for their drug habits. These may have been urban myths, but in the research context, the existence of such rumours seemed to be an important fact in itself. The author believes that such rumours have an actual social impact on the community, as they feed into the moral panic about the hazardous environment of Western urban settings and have consequences for young women's autonomy. Exposure to the inner-city world, indeed, seems by itself to be a hazard for women; moving to other cities to attend university can only increase the danger (see also 'Poisoning the community' in Chapter Four).

Gossip can be treated, then, as part of social-control strategies, and we have mentioned that a sense of taboo, stigma and scandal can be diffused by both men and women. However, it seems that other informal social-control strategies are gendered in a way that mirrors the dichotomy of women as private and soft, men as public and strong.

Respondents often referred to sanctions that were activated against families whose members had been, for example, arrested. Some would not be invited to functions such as weddings, and reciprocal visiting would be interrupted. When reciprocity in invitations to weddings was interrupted, the signs of a breakdown in *lena dena* ('taking, giving', see Chapter Three) would become obvious. This, according to some respondents, would only happen when there was formal public evidence of the offences committed (i.e. incarceration or information published in the local papers). Where judgements were made according to rumours circulating in the community, sanctions would be less definite. Mothers would ask the children not to go out with members of the rumoured family, for instance, but no public shaming would take place. According to Bano, her parents would be very cautious as gossip might irreparably and unfairly damage a whole family:

When my mum and dad say that they would think about it one hundred times, because in my family it is wrong to talk about people, because if they talk of so and so's daughter, they've got a daughter at home and if they talk of so and so's son they've got two sons at home, so that's why they don't tend to talk about things because anything could happen. (Bano, student, 18 years old)

Rumours were also considered a form of envy, and therefore not always accurate. As Alexander noted in the Bangladeshi community in London, the ubiquity of gossip may make it void (Alexander 2000:128). During the fieldwork, rumours about well-known entrepreneurs being involved in money-laundering were compared, and it was sometimes argued that this was malicious information spread by competitors:

Jamil (entrepreneur in his early thirties): '[Here there is] too much gossip! If you can get to the *izzat* of any family, you'll just go for it, innit?'
Adam (community worker in his late twenties): 'Yeah, you'll go all the way to Pakistan to find out! [laughs]'

It may perhaps be interesting to note that the crime committed may be of relevance to the intensity of community sanctions. For example, as already mentioned in Chapter Four, riots were not generally considered a major law infringement (see also Bolognani 2007c):

Obviously there's the sense of this person being in the riot and it was quite bad at the beginning. But people keep quiet about it; they might talk about it behind our backs [but will not shame us in public]. (Fatima, student, 19 years old)

In the process of public shaming therefore, a form of collaboration between institutional sanctions (i.e. arrest and prison) and informal sanctions seemed to be vital, as the former triggered the latter (cf. Braithwaithe 1989:97).
Word of mouth could take the form of negative gossip, but also that of an informal source of knowledge and support (see also media and the word of mouth in Chapter Eight). This seemed particularly developed amongst women, who seemed to have less access to imams and may be less likely to consult practitioners and privileged informal support networks (cf. Orford et al. 2004:25):

MB: 'Do you think the ones who've got a doubt will feel comfortable and close enough to the imam to ask about these questions?'
Aqdus (student, 16 years old): 'I'm not really sure.'
MB: 'Do you think they'll ask somebody else?'
Aqdus: 'I don't think they'll go to the imam because they don't wanna tell them that they're doing it, but I think they'll ask people, so somebody else, yeah.'
MB: 'Are there any religious people you can speak to about these issues?'
Aqdus: 'Yeah.'
MB: 'So if you had a doubt, would you go to the imam and discuss these things?'
Maria (student, 16 years old): 'I wouldn't personally go to the imam and discuss these things. I'd ask my parents . . . my mum, and then she'd look into it for me. She can ask other women as well, you know . . . who know more about Islam.'

7.6 Importing a Communal System of Social Control

In Chapter Three the particularity of biraderi as an institution half-way between family and community was discussed. While the preceding section focused on the more familial aspect of social control, here we will concentrate on its community aspects.

Chapter Four highlighted how respondents tended to agree on the fact that the Pakistani community had the same problems as any other, but we have also seen that some aspects of Pakistani culture (such as *izzat*) may play a role in social control. Cultural features of this kind appear in some of the literature as advantages for crime prevention (see for example Mawby and Batta 1980:18, discussed in Chapter Two).

How biraderi can be seen as providing a 'cushion against difficulties experienced' has been discussed in Chapter Three. Here we will focus on how the 'social structure of the country of origin . . . may protect' the community.

A different form of collaboration between informal and institutional sanctions was also cited in the case of 'mediation'. With mediation it is possible to define an informal system of restorative justice bearing similarities to an institutional practice in the Indian sub-continent, the *panchayyat* (Chaudhary 1999:85). Whilst restoring rights or order in general may be considered a form of social control, as it prevents the development of further feuds, this is more about resolution than 'group harmony' (Lyon 2004:185). And while in the Indian sub-continent the village *panchayyat* is made up of a group of elders, and both victim and perpetrator appear in front of them to give evidence and discuss what will make amends for the contentious deed in contention, mediation in the diaspora is less formally organised:

> Mediation is somebody just sitting between parties and trying to resolve it. (Ayesha, community worker in her early forties)

> If something big comes up normally my mum gets called as a mediator because she's neutral, so people get her to sit down and kind of keep the diplomacy . . . but in general it's elder figures like grandma, grandpa . . . because they'll have more authority over everyone. (Bashir, student, 19 years old)

> It's the pain of our life . . . because our granddad says, 'So-and-so came, they respect me, they've come to see me, they respect my opinion, my own children and my own grandchildren won't take me . . . they'll take me for granted and you don't respect me.' But itsn't that, sometimes it's just wrong. It happens quite a lot. I can't say . . . but I would say, it's 99 per cent, I bet every Asian family's got someone who's a mediator. Someone to look to if something goes wrong. (Zaara, shop assistant and special constable in her early twenties)

> I think it's less now, but mediation used to take place when there was a break down in marriage relationships. It did work, but now with the third generation, kids don't want that mediation, they don't wanna know. I don't think that goes on a lot now. But mediation does take place, but obviously on smaller issues, where there's misunderstandings between two or three parties . . . it's only for minor cases. Cases where . . . murder and attempted murder, I think it'd be unwise to get involved with that sort of things . . . it's better to let the police to deal with it. (Iqbal, entrepreneur and politician in his late fifties)

Anecdotes reported during the research referred to episodes of mediation only in conjunction with the formal criminal-justice system. For example, the potentially violent confrontation between two families who both wanted to sell ice cream in the same area (an episode widely known as the 'ice-cream war') was dealt with through the mediation of an elder who was considered wise and neutral, but during the mediation a legal discussion of what the law implied also took place.

Sometimes mediation was the name given to the help given by a third party in dealing with the police:

> In the summer, a particular family approached me because I'm an educated person so maybe I could help, I think it was a mother who was feeling very vulnerable, teenagers were playing football, throwing the ball on the walls . . . white teenagers, I think . . . there was one Asian as well. . . . again she's very unhappy with the police, they haven't helped her and haven't responded to her calls. She's highly educated but her English is not as fluent as maybe required to persuade the police [laughs]. (Tahir, teacher in his late thirties)

At other times, mediation is a corollary to a case dealt with by the police:

> The person who threatened to shoot my brother in the head, my grandfather knew his father from Pakistan as well (my granddad is from Pakistan), he's a Raja[65], [Rajas] are perceived high in Pakistan. So as a Raja, in Pakistan he had a lot of say . . . like here, well, here it's not as much, but in Pakistan is unbelievable, so . . . he called that boy's father to his house, after the police had gone, and he made that boy, drug dealer, apologise because he was rude to my mother as well, so he called my mother, my brother, apologised to them and he actually apologised, saying, 'I didn't know whose daughter you were', he said to my mum, and his dad was there, and he said to his son, 'You don't know but this man in his time, he has knocked a few heads together as well' and everyone . . . it came to an end. He said, 'In the future don't be rude to this family. (Zaara, shop assistant and special constable in her early twenties)

Mediation, however, seemed to be used more in marriage matters than in anything else. Some mediation would take place while a divorce was already being discussed in court, with sudden reconciliations when one of the parties accepted the other's conditions (for instance the newly wed couple would buy a house by themselves and stop living with the in-laws). In cases of domestic violence, mediation seemed to be considered more a patriarchal feature rather than a useful instrument, unless accompanied by the law in the form of action by the social services or the presence of a police officer:

> MB: 'Is mediation successful to any extent?'

Alina (community worker in her late thirties): 'Unfortunately not. It's not mediation, I wouldn't call it mediation, it's sheer blackmail, emotional blackmail by the elders. Obviously they're not worried about the woman, how this violence is emotionally or psychologically impacting on the woman or the children, all they're worried about is honour, what people would think. Obviously emotional blackmail can't work together and there's a time when the woman says, "Enough is enough, I have to do something about it now." Because my experience is that the elders aren't addressing the issues, they're only waffling basically to protect the honour of the family. Also the majority of women who come over from Pakistan, India and Bangladesh, they want to take some steps, but they have this immigration threat over their heads, the family uses it as a threat and the majority of them don't know what their rights are, they only know what they're told by the partners' families. They don't even have their passport, they're kept in custody. ... Sometimes women who know these are their options, they're too scared to do that on their own so they need somebody to guide them through the whole process. ... It's very hard, and unfortunately in the Asian community ... we've had some success stories, but when a woman lives in an extended family, for her to go down this route is highly difficult and her options are that she either moves into a refuge or goes to a separate property. But women who live in a nuclear family, for them is much easier. That is where we have some success, where women live in a nuclear family.'

Ayesha (community worker in her early forties): 'It's really difficult, because for some women ... one woman for instance, she said, "I don't wanna leave my home, I just want the beating to stop. I've got two kids, I live with my husband and my father-in-law and both beat me, I just don't want to leave my home, go and talk to them" ... and in this case I said, "What do you want me to do?" and she said: "Go and talk to him."'
MB: 'Was it a kind of mediation?'
Ayesha: 'Mediation is just something I don't believe in, I'm not really interested in it. Mediation is somebody just sitting between parties and trying to resolve it. But I remember what the Southall Black Sisters said, they said mediation doesn't work, because when she comes to you, she's already passed all them stages, she's tried to resolve it and because it isn't resolved is the reason why she has come to you, and the family might force mediation to get her to come back home. So

anyway I went, I said, "Go on then, pick up your stuff and we'll see." I went. The police officer who used to work with, very close, I told him . . . he said "I'll come with you." So they came with me. But the main thing was, I knew the woman, I knew the family and they knew me. . . . so I went to their house, and the father-in-law was there and the husband and me and the police officer went in and she goes to me in our language, "Talk to them first see what they've got to say." I says, "You know what? If she wants to, she can have you outside of this bloody house and she can live here on her own until her kids are 16, 17 and you'll have to pay the mortgage and the maintenance. We can do that. I can do that within days. Give me a week and I'll have you out of here." Because she was bruised, because he'd pushed her downstairs. So I said, "You know what? You really have to re-decide what you want, because I'm not here to sweet talk anybody." I was really furious and my temper was . . . mmmhhh . . . and he looked and goes, "No, no, *putter* [child], I'm really sorry."...I said, "Don't apologise to me, you haven't done anything wrong to me, I'm doing my job, but when I'm doing my job I see what you're doing and what effect do you think that has on the kids?" 15 years down the line, this woman still lives in the house, she's still got the kids.'

Involving an authority may be the only guarantee of fairness:

MB: 'So let's say something happens in your family . . .'
Maria (student, 16 years old): 'It depends what kind of problem it is. If it's a problem that can be solved without the police getting involved . . . otherwise you don't have a choice.'
Aqdus (student, 16 years old): 'If there's a rape you don't wanna call the police because you're gonna be put in papers and stuff.'
Maria: 'But then if you want to have justice, you've got to call the police.'

7.7 Between Culture and Religion: *Taweez*

Religion may be an effective means of social control. Aware of the debate that has been labelled 'religion vs. Culture', before analysing the real impact of faith we will describe a feature of social control that rests between the two: *taweez* or, as some would call it, 'black magic' (Mcloughlin 1998a:99). *Taweez* literally means 'amulet', but by extension a number of practices that have to do with the alleged healing power of Quranic verses are grouped under that term. The following quotation seems to embody the blurring boundaries between magic and religion implied by *taweez*.

> I can't really explain because it's weird and wonderful, it's one of those magical things that happen and make you believe in religion. (Amir, unemployed in his mid-thirties)

Some respondents were aware of the practice of having a *taweez* made for children who were on drugs, but also for depression, relationship problems, illnesses, exams and in one case even to try to break a love marriage that had taken place against the will of the family.

In Islam there is a tradition of spiritual healing (*rukhia*) through the reading of the Quran, as Shamim says:

> God has said that if you . . . for every bad thing or illness if you read it properly and follow those things, there's a cure, there's a cure for everything in Quran, is a complete book. (Shamim, community worker in her early forties)

The difference between *rukhia* and *taweez* lies in the different use of the Quranic verses; while in *rukhia* the Quran is read by or to the person to be healed, *taweez* may consist of the action of wearing, displaying on a wall or even swallowing some verses. Scholars are divided about what is to be considered consistent with religious teachings, and many consider *taweez* as it is practised by many in Bradford as *jaddu* (magic).

Many anecdotes gathered during fieldwork told of parents who as soon as they found out about their children's drug habit consulted mullahs in order to have prayers read or *taweez* made. Often the request for amulets implies the belief that a *jinn* (spirit) has been the cause of the problem:

> For good health they use *taweez*, for anything that's going wrong they'll try to sort out through *taweez*, and somebody who's on drugs they'll say, "It's not his fault, it's somebody who's done something to him" [laughs]. (Shamim, community worker in her early forties)

> They may look to that thing, "Somebody's put them up to it, or some bad thing's happened and they're taking drugs." They'll look at an excuse, put it in that way, and *taweez* is one thing, the jinn, and this and the other, something has got hold of this individual and that's why he's taking drugs. (Zameer, community worker in his early thirties)

[The reason why people take drugs is] mostly because they're weak and the parents haven't been teaching how to do correctly. What you normally find is people possessed by *jinns* are normally the good, law-abiding, religiously [interrupted]. (Amir, unemployed in his mid thirties)

Two imams said that they would not make amulets, but would agree to offer special prayers for the young men in trouble; this would be used as a strategy to get to speak with the family and the person in question, and to start suggesting other means of dealing with the problems.

7.8 Religion as a Protective Factor

If the deep, albeit controversial faith in *taweez* was certainly popular, faith itself was another element of potential control. Religion and religious institutions were often mentioned as one of the variables of social control. Elders would recall the role that mosques played in 'keeping the community disciplined' in the first years of migration, when 'young men at the time were wild, with all the *gores*[66] and needed the 'discipline Islam provides' (Umar). Younger respondents would instead be familiar with narratives of 'redemption' (see below) through the re-discovery of faith. For example, in 2003 a youth centre in Girlington staged a play written by local members about a drug dealer who discovered religion after his father's death, repented and became a very observant Muslim. A similar paradigm of sin and potential redemption was narrated in the Keighley-based film *Yasmin*[67], where the protagonist's brother is a dealer but gives it up once he is involved in an extremist Muslim organisation (although he ends up going to Afghanistan to join the *jihad*).

Although it was clear that religion was widely considered as a 'protective factor' (Orford et al. 2004:23), how this worked was rather obscure. Views about what religion is and what it prescribed were very varied. Interviewees disagreed on many aspects of religion; from the possibility of enforcing religious practice to matters like 'is marijuana allowed in Islam?' The way madrassas were organised was blamed by some for the failure of mosques to exercise social control on youth, something which will be discussed in the next chapter. However, here it is important to point out that the idea that a better understanding of the Quran or a higher attendance at the mosque would make youth more law-abiding was controversial:

I think it's true in some of the cases. I think the issue you're presenting is brought up by the '*Edge of the City*' programme because a lot of madrassas and community leaders then came out and said, 'These kids need to learn these things from the mosque', some sort of values have to be instilled in these people. And then other said, 'Well, these kids were involved in paedophilia, they'll never gonna go near a mosque anyway so . . . one of the biggest misconception amongst the Pakistani community is that Islam is a very forgiving religion. A lot of people are out drinking, they'd commit adultery, they'll commit illegal acts on the basis, 'I am fallible, I make mistakes, and God will forgive me.' So religion is very conveniently put aside, especially among people who are gonna go out and break law so they'll use religion when it suits them, they'll put it aside when it doesn't suit them. Religion, I believe, plays very little part. I think is the lure of big things, money, cars, nice clothes, status, recognition. I think it's the lure of those things why people do illegal things, because then they become recognised . . . of the community, become highly respected; if you've got money, you've got clout. (Abdul, community worker in his early forties)

While faith might help individuals who had taken a wrong path, it was generally considered a variable independent of human will, and therefore could not directly be used in crime prevention; humans cannot control faith. However, many believed that an upbringing that emphasised Muslim identity might lead to some positive results.

7.9 Purification, Reintegration and 'Reconversions'

Although they may wish for more investments in their areas and 'pumping more money into the community', interviewees generally related crime to the lack of moral values and the prominence of individualism and avidity. Iqbal theorised this by mentioning the cross-cultural effect of Thatcherism, which affected youth in terms of aspirational frame, as they shared the same aspirations of higher classes but had not been given the means to achieve them (see strain theory in Chapter Five). Respondents engaged in revivalist Islamic groups also referred to 'moral values', and identified the need for them to be 'pumped into the community':

I'm a Muslim, I'm aware of whom I am, my identity is either Muslim or Pakistani, or as an Arab, and Muslim is my identity and I haven't adopted my identity from my fathers as my father is Pakistani. My identity is Muslim. So it gives me the confidence of a Muslim. I don't want to succeed in life, my success is my progression . . . how well do I do in pleasing my creator? And part of that pleasing is that you have to be successful in this life and the one after. So you do whatever you can in the best way; for example my belief encourages me, whatever I do, to do it best, so if I'm cleaning the roads I should do it as best as I can, there's no shame in cleaning roads or cleaning toilets, that's my job and I should do it the best as I can, so it really gives you comfort in that way. So really it's a combination of both, and at the same time I should actively interact with the community I live in, because I believe there are common problems which in a community . . . I do believe that that's the right direction to go towards, rather than isolation in both ways. (Imran, teacher in his early thirties)

Moral values often had a religious connotation, and ideas of good and bad seemed directly derived from one's knowledge of what Islam said. Most of the time this would overlap with Christian or even secular values, but the language in which it was expressed was of clear Islamic derivation (see discussion of the *haram/halal* dichotomy in Chapter Four).

Reintegration into the family and community life, as we have already seen in examples of 'home-made rehabilitation', appeared to be possible even after major *haram* deeds. Purification could be exercised through religious pilgrimages (i.e. the *Umra* or *Hajj*), or even by 'visible' conversions. For example, girls might start wearing the hijab and boys would perform daily prayers, attend the mosque and even grow a beard. These processes were commonly called 'reconversions', a term that alludes to the common belief that every human being is born as a Muslim but may abandon the Muslim ethos or beliefs. In some cases prison sentences triggered reconversion (see next chapter), but in others, individuals narrated an epiphany, a sudden enlightenment:

My cousin, when he got caught doing something he started getting into religion and stuff . . . they made him go to mosque and things . . . and then stopped it because he got into religion . . . [There is another case of a] guy . . . but that was murder. What happened was that this . . . I can't remember actually if it was a Pakistani guy or a white guy, he came to his house and threatened his mother, and he came out and he stabbed him. and then he was in prison for a while. When he came out, he embraced Islam. (Ali, artist in his late twenties)

I've got a very close friend who's actually, I think he's about 25 now, but he's only come to Islam recently; I tend to go to mosque myself and I've started talking to him etcetera, and he was involved in this kind of stuff, if you know what I mean, but at a young age he actually got involved in a wrong group of people, and he got involved in drugs and crime, and he's only recently started to get away from it all, and he's started coming to the mosque etcetera, and he says the majority, they do actually come to the mosque, it's only for the Friday prayers etcetera, they do tend to come to the mosque but I mean, it's no use, if you know what I mean, if you're gonna go, if you're gonna come to the mosque and ask for forgiveness for your sins, but if you're gonna get out there and do the same thing again, there's no point for it . . . He actually went to an Islamic talk and he heard the speaker in English. I mean, I think the thing with our mosques is that . . . especially for the young people, for the young generation, they'll go for Friday prayers and you have the imam and you'll have them talking in Urdu if you know what I mean, and it's a very strong Urdu that they're using, they use . . . they tend to use the slang amongst themselves . . . I think what we need is we need some English speakers . . . and like this friend of mine, he actually went to this talk and he heard a very good English talk and afterwards he got together with that English talker, the speaker, and he actually got a one-to-one with him, and he got him thinking and he got . . . and after that he started coming to the mosque slowly-slowly . . . it was actually that talk that changed him . . . and it is actually pretty amazing, some of the stories that he tells, but what he's told me is that it's very tempting, you know . . . there are always temptations out there, to go and do the wrong thing, but you know . . . if you've got what it takes . . . he used to say, when he goes out there, the world . . . his mates are gonna come back to him and say, 'Let's go for a night out and this, that and the other' and it's gonna be really hard for him to see, and stay away from it all . . . but if you come to Islam then what we believe in, is God's gonna help you, you know, and he's actually making an effort, and he's actually OK, he makes time to come to the mosque every so often and he's actually away from the wrong path and it's actually helping him. (Yousef, student, 16 years old)

I don't know . . . a lot is . . . when I turned 17, I started looking at things in a different view and . . . because I've got like two other brothers and they respect me so much for what I do and it's . . . when you're an Asian girl and you have family traditions and family values, people look at you in a lot of ways, and I realised . . . obviously what I wear [a hijab]. (Bano, student, 18 years old)

Between the ideas of passivity that both British Pakistani commentaries and British white mainstream views seem to construct, Islamist discourses seem to have created a different space for Pakistani women. Afshar in 1994 and McLoughlin in 1998 talk of a cathartic use of Islam for Bradford Muslim women. For instance:

> For at least some women, 'reinvented', 'authentic' accounts of their religious experiences are the most organic feminist tools that they have to 'think' alternatives with. (McLoughlin 1998:103)

> My respondents . . . experienced Islam as a set of discourses and practices which could be deployed both hegemonically, in an attempt to control and discipline young women, and counter-hegemonically, so as to legitimate their concerns about issues such as higher education and marriage. (Ibid:105)

Many female interviewees said they found inspiration for assertiveness and independence in the Quran. Regardless of the contested status of women's roles in Islam, clearly some of them have found grounds for autonomy in familiarising themselves with a translation of the Quran. Many women used the same example to describe how this reading made them grow in autonomy:

> The Prophet's wife was a merchant banker, she proposed to him (Mahima, shop assistant in her late twenties)

Amongst young Muslims the idea that Islam in South Asia has been profoundly influenced and 'contaminated' by local cultures, and that there should be a process of purging from it what is not consistent with the Prophet's teachings, is very common[68]. 'Spurious' Islam would affect the lives of Muslims in a very different way from the original, as one informant put it:

> . . . they should give girls some autonomy because Islamic law allows girls some autonomy . . . Bradford's conservative, the community's conservative. The biggest problem I think is the culture, and culture has nothing to do with religion. For example, weddings. The tradi-

tions [of weddings] are Hindu traditions . . . [it is something] that's been inherited and it sticks, like culture. (Sadiq, student in his midtwenties, quoted in Bolognani 2002)

An attempt to go back to 'the original Islam' has been adopted by movements and associations of young people in Bradford—for example Young Muslims UK, the Muslim Women Forum and the Islamic Society of Britain (cf. McLoughlin 2006)—and is the cause of most of the changes in women's practice of Islam, but also of wider practices and beliefs. For example, in 2002 the Muslim Women Forum was promoting the creation of areas for women in the local mosques, as only a minority of buildings provide this facility. One of the changes in perceptions of Islam by the younger generations is that. while for a large part of the older generation Islam becomes important during life-cycle rituals (McLoughlin 1998:99), for an increasing part of the younger generation who read the Quran in translation, religion is apparently an integral part of their daily life and has a constant bearing on it. For these individuals religion becomes a public and political matter. For some women, it is the gateway to much more freedom of choice and movement. Furthermore, 'fallen' Pakistani women may go through rituals and adopt visible signs of their 'redemption'; this, according to the above analysis, is much harder to come by through the 'cultural' community of their heritage. Fatima, a university student in her early twenties and an active member of an Islamist organisation, described her 'reversion' to Islam in this way:

> I can give you a personal example. Before when I was 16, I was really confused. . . . So I didn't know how to deal with my problems because I couldn't turn to my parents because I know what they'd say, I couldn't turn to my grandparents, because I know what they'd say and I wouldn't have liked to hear what they wanted to say. But I still knew, even if I turned to my friends they wouldn't tell me something that's correct as well, so I could only trust the one thing, which is my religion, my Islam, which could guide me out of my confusion that I was living in. So now when I did start talking with these girls, you know, my friends I knew who used to take lower-class drugs, like smoking spliffs and . . . just, you know, a bit of fun here and there . . . . when I did start talking about religion to them, to them it was only a laugh and a joke, but to me it was becoming serious so I started to change in a different way and they started to advance in their drugs and stuff like that . . . I think . . . my experience, especially with . . . be-

cause I went though, even after *Umra*, after basically becoming more religious and practising . . . I realised when I went back into sixth form or college and I saw a difference . . . not a difference . . . but the way I started to think now was more Islamically . . . (Fatima, university student in her early twenties)

Fatima who, by her own definition, used to live 'a life at odds with Islam', after *Umra* started wearing the *hijab* and moved freely around Bradford, organising meetings for her association and planning to go and study abroad, hopefully in Syria. Islam offered her a tool for negotiating her independence with her parents and the means of redemption so hard to find in her traditional community. Pilgrimage and the act of covering her head with the *hijab* rehabilitated her into her family and community. Whether this kind of Muslim discourse—allowing a specific form of autonomy and independence for women—is only typical of one class is a controversial matter. While a large part of activities by Islamist movements happen on campuses, there is evidence that at a global level these discourses are likely to be embraced first by the educated upper-middle class, but are also conveyed to different classes through the inherent 'outreach programmes' (Ahmad, forthcoming). One of the most successful such groups, Al-Huda, offers a moving example by promoting quranic classes in disadvantaged areas and jails (ibid.)

Some respondents argued that some religious groups deliberately target young drug addicts because they are perceived as easier to involve in their doctrines. This appeared to informants to be the case of Hizb-ut-Tahrir. On the other hand, some imams who believed more in prevention than rehabilitation seemed to have acquired great popularity. Hussain, himself redeemed from a cannabis habit while developing a deep reconversion that took him on the *Hajj*, introduced the presdent author to the work of a very popular Bradford based-imam, Sheikh Ahmed Ali.

7.10 Popular Preaching: Sheikh Ahmed Ali – a Case Study

Sheikh Ahmed Ali is a British Muslim who was religiously educated in Bury *dar-ul-oom*[69] and in Cairo. He founded the Islamic Academy in Bradford, and is not associated with the conservative approach of elder local Muslim leaders (Lewis 2006). The aims of the Academy are to convey much of the religious education in English, and engage youth with their faith through a number of activities such as summer camps, day trips and sports tournaments (ibid.). Ahmed's tapes sell worldwide and are particularly concerned with youth (two popular titles are: *Muslim Youth* and *Drugs, the Mother of All*

Evils). Ahmed's approach is not institutional: his tapes are heard in cars or at home and his sermons are made at informal gatherings, not necessarily in mosques. However, his messages tend to reproduce the criticism of bad parenting and family-exclusive bonding (see Chapter Five), and his praise of strict adherence to the Quran and the *hadith* is supported by detailed description of punishments in hell. His sermons nevertheless represent an attempt to talk with youth more or less as an equal—albeit sometimes in a controversial way, adopting a view of Muslims as in opposition to the West—and refer to real-life situations. His knowledge of urban British life and young people's aspirations is conveyed through vivid language, a diffusion facilitated by means such as CDs and Internet marketing. Local contemporary knowledge (such as the latest fashion items sought by petty drug dealers) is reinterpreted through Islamic tradition and is articulated through the *hadith*.

Sheikh Ahmed Ali repeats themes addressed in Chapter Five, such as the generation gap and the alleged helplessness of parents. In addition he shows a deep knowledge of a variety of activities in which young Muslim men are said to be engaging. As we have previously seen (in Chapters Four and Six), women are thought to be of increasing concern for the community; daughters gone astray and irresponsible mothers are often referred to in his sermons (see for example the opening quote in Chapter Six). However, the main culprits of a 'gangster' culture (see Chapter Six) seem to be both parents, either passive or complacent:

> Who is to blame? Who is responsible? Who has made these children drug pushers, thieves and gangsters, who is the one who taught them to break the laws of Allah? Who is the one who turned a blind eye when his son had a £40,000 car outside his house and he knew that his son did not work? Who is the one who did not question his son when he put £1,000 on the table when he knows that he doesn't work? . . . And the truth is that nobody is to blame for this outcome except for you and I, the mother and father. (Sheikh Ahmed Ali, *Muslim Youth*)

The contrast between a 'Pakistani culture' and Islam (cf. 'religion vs Culture', Chapter Five) is one of the main points of Sheikh Ahmed Ali's preaching:

> Why? Because we are the ones who neglected these children, the ones who taught them how to break the laws of Allah and his message, the lesson of disobedience . . . Many of us are from Pakistani background. In this background the child is only six months and you will

see a golden ring on his finger, a golden chain around his neck. This child did not purchase it! . . . It was mother, father or one of the relatives. (Sheikh Ahmed Ali, Muslim Youth)

Religious expressions such as *haram* become the pivot for labelling:

> You know, I know that gold is *haram* with a male. It will become a means to him to go to hell. . . . We say: 'He is only a child, when he grows up he will realize'. This is the first time we tell this child that we break the laws of Allah. . . . Now it is time for the child hair cut. We know this modern day style hair cuts are *haram* . . . Who pays for these haircuts? Who goes with his child to the barber's? It is the father . . . And what do we say? 'It is only a child, when he grows up he will stop doing this' . . . The kid wants his ears pierced. . . . We teach him this lesson so well that he breaks the rules of Allah by taking intoxicants, by selling drugs . . . he begins to break the law of Allah with fornication, he begins to commit adultery, he begins to break the law of Allah with regard to interest, he begins to wheel and deal. (Sheikh Ahmed Ali, *Muslim Youth*)

However, the final and greatest condemnation is for the phenomenon that we have seen described as *biraderism* (see Chapter Five):

> When do we realize that our child is out of control? When do we start teaching him the lesson of obedience? When there is the million dollar question. And what is the million dollar question? 'Son, now you are 20, the time has come for you to marry. Your uncle's daughter is good looking, she will make you a good wife.' The child turns around and says, 'Abba, no thanks, not for me.' Now we begin to teach him the lesson of obedience. Not because he does something which displease Allah and his messenger, but because he has done something that displeases me. Because he won't agree to marry the uncle's daughter now, we will begin to teach him the lesson of obedience and we will say 'Do you know what the Quran says about respecting the mother and father?' (Sheikh Ahmed Ali, *Muslim Youth*)

7.11 Conclusion: Informal Control as a Partial Solution

This chapter has looked at how informal social control is exercised through family, community and certain interpretations of religion. These three elements seemed to be perceived as having the potential to help, in terms both of preventing crime and of reintegrating criminals. However, all three ele-

8.1 Mosques: Caught between the Local and the Global

At the time of the research, faith communities were increasingly being considered at a social-policy level as one of the agents that can help *community* cohesion and the development of communities (Furbey and Macey 2005). The idea behind it would seem to be that:

> Our major faith traditions – all of them more historic and rooted than any political party or ideology – play a fundamental role in supporting and propagating values which bind us together as a nation (Blair 2001, quoted in Furbey and Macey 2005:97)

Some informants believed that Islam in particular had a structural organisation that may be ideal for the policy needs of the state:

> I think Islam has got very strong influence or infrastructure in place to tackle these kinds of [criminal] things. And again Friday is an institution; I wouldn't say that in other religions it doesn't happen, but it's heavily attended, maybe 4,500 people attending, so if mosques want to do something they can play a very positive role in educating, tackling these things. I'd say it's very complex, actually. You have people who are really doing their reciting and here, yes, kids aren't on the streets, they aren't involved in any other activities, police is very pleased with that, I've discussed this with some people, because for two hours they aren't on the streets, so they're doing a great job in terms of keeping kids off the streets, and not only that, the whole ethos, it's a religious place, and there is very strong discipline. (Tahir, teacher in his late thirties)

Mosques' activities that may be linked to social control are principally organised in two parts: through preaching (especially on Fridays during the sermon) and through religious education in the madrassas.

Friday prayers and the Friday sermon have lately been in the limelight as a possible means for the glorification of terrorism, such as the sermons of Abou Hamza, put on trial in February 2006. According to interviewees, mosques in Bradford differ a great deal in how the Friday sermons are organised, and over the last 20 years the themes tackled by prayer leaders have significantly changed. Some informants pointed to the detachment of the preaching in the mosque from local issues, while more and more attention is paid to the *Umma* (the virtual Muslim global nation):

> I know some mosques when for example in the eighties there was the AIDS campaign, they were telling about the disease that was discovered. This was in the eighties. If you go to mosques, especially nowadays, I think they have much more discussions than they had in the past, I can't remember in the eighties that many discussions . . . there was the occasion of the eighties, but . . . everything that was going on outside the world . . . there will always be, 'Oh, the West is gonna corrupt you.' 'Don't drink, don't take drugs, don't do this, don't look at white women' and then . . . but nowadays, especially in the nineties I realised there was much more talks, much more . . . and more people were going there to watch videos and things, or having people who talk about Americans and stuff . . . they scare people, just like Fox News scares the Americans in a very extreme way, you get some mosques will scare the local members of the community on the opposite really. And then I think, when these things like that . . . especially very right-wing news channels, they'll say 'we're right, look what they're doing, look what they're preaching.' (Ali, artist in his late twenties)

> You'll find it surprising, they don't mention about drugs and what's going on in the community and everything . . . they'll give a speech on what's happening in Israel, Palestine and places like that, but they don't address the community, the problems facing the community. So they don't mention in duah, in the prayer, people who're poor, people who're going the wrong way. But like I said, in mosques they don't know how to address that. (Zaara, shop assistant and special constable in her early twenties)

Some respondents believed that in many cases mosques failed to address local issues, not out of ignorance but out of fear:

> Akbar (retired, in his early seventies): 'Maulvis try to [make] people to come to mosque and pray, try to [make people to] remember God, bring the children for pray, reading Quran, the maulvis cannot do more than that. If they do anything strict maybe they [will be] kick[ed] off from the mosque.'
> Amir (unemployed, in his mid-thirties): 'That's true, they'll get kicked out and also the parents . . . because there are so many mosques around . . . they'll go to another mosque. "This maulvis is harassing us, we don't want to go there, everybody's children are dealing

with drugs, we don't want him to preach to us, we will go to another mosque."'

Some mosques are concerned with the well-being of their community: our treasurer [reference to a grass-roots organisation] is the secretary of the local mosque. But also the imams are scared to say things in the mosque because they don't want bricks through the window. (Kamran, community worker in his early thirties)

MB: 'But who decides who's going to be the maulvi of the mosque?'
Amir (unemployed in his mid-thirties): 'There's a committee . . . for example there's one here . . . I've seen them fighting in the street over it . . . control of the mosque. People's legs have been broken, stuff like that. So this is control of the mosque? So you think at that level . . . how the hell are they gonna be able to control . . . ?'
MB: 'But what do they gain . . . ?'
Amir: 'It's prestige, the name, it's "our mosque". We do what we want to do in our mosque. If we say you can't have a chat afterwards, read the *hadith* afterwards, you've got to get out. So they have full control of the mosque. Ridiculous. If the mosques are in that state, if we can't sort the mosques out, what chance have we got to sort out the community? It's very difficult.'

Sometimes imams would mention local problems in very general terms so as not to upset any members who might be involved:

When I go to mosque on Friday the *mufti*, the imam at the mosque, tends to mention it: 'Young lads now are turning to self-employment' and self-employment meaning drugs, working for themselves, selling drugs . . . (Jamal, student in his early twenties)

I am quoting Spider Man here [laughs] but with great power comes great responsibility and it [is] the case that they've got to be very, very careful because they're in a position where they're talking through the whole of the community. (Amir, in conversation with Mahima, student in her late twenties)

In these cases, mosques may be a comfortable space for drug dealers too, as one recounted:

I go mosque when I wanna go mosque (to be honest with you I haven't been for a long time . . . once a year, do you get what I mean? On Eid only. I know I should, but what can you do, innit? Everyone's different, innit? Well, it's all right [when you go to mosque] it's a good atmosphere, innit? Everyone who's gonna be there is who you know or from your area, do you get what I mean? so you don't have no problems, everyone you know go there, you look, 'All right?', 'All right?', 'All right?'—safe, you know what I mean? Ten minutes and you're out of there. Think about it, it's ten minutes, so it doesn't really matter. (Khalil, 19 years old, quoted in Bolognani 2002)

Allegedly, local drug dealers were involved in the administration of some mosques, and this had a definite consequence for what themes would be discussed:

When I go there [to the mosque down the road] . . . I haven't gone to the mosque again. Shall I tell you why? Because I don't like seeing what I see when I go there. I go in there, I have a wash, I look around, and there are the thugs . . . giving you dirty looks, talking during the *hazan*, while you have to keep your mouth shut. And they're talking and talking. No one tells them to shut up, not even . . . these groups are getting bigger and bigger, they've found the place where the police can't come in and they don't come in because if they do it'll be all over papers. But they are dealing drugs in mosque. No one is gonna question them. . . . I know for example some mullahs whose sons are all criminals. Do you know why? Because they're known, they think they can't be touched. They think the people respect the mullahs and their sons can get away with anything, so they remember them days when there was a set of patterns going on even them . . . again we're generalising again, but the ones I know, their sons are all criminals. So who are they to talk and tell other people how to run their lives if they can't control their own lives? Just because they're mullahs it doesn't make a good parent. . . . People know the sons are drug dealers. He loses his face. They won't say it in front of his face, they'll say, 'It's God's will, it's not your fault', but really, I'm sorry, it is his fault. It really is. (Amir, unemployed, in his mid-thirties in conversation with Mahima, student in her late twenties)

So this inward-looking nature of certain communities, centred around their mosques, seemed to present a problem even for those maulvis who may be willing to tackle local problems but fear for the future of their mosque, or live under pressure from the mosque committees. This problem, which may again be ascribed to excessive bonding (cf. Chapter Five), was, according to many interviewees, emphasised by the importing of imams who had privileged connections to some biraderi (cf. also McLoughlin 1998c:222). In these cases, mosque policies were influenced by these clerics:

> The Pakistani community is very close-knit; you need to go back and look at how . . . in Pakistan and that's based on the biraderi system, tribal . . . That's very much continued, I think that's breaking down radically but there's still a sense of 'blood's thicker than water' try to exploit . . . There's no such thing as priesthood in Islam. You don't have to go through schools and qualify and sit exams as you do in Catholicism and other religions. Yes, a lot of times you have the Carlisle Mosque, the Manchester Road Mosque, these are village communities all made by biraderi groups, so they're self-managed, self-financed so they'll want to bring a maulvi from the village back home. . . . [In the same way] a lot of brothers, I'm thinking of an example of three, four brothers who've got two sisters, they all married their children to each other so that would[n't] need anybody else. It's respectable for the drug dealer in his close group and everything is OK. (Abdul, social worker in his early forties)

Importing imams from 'back home', then, may create mosques which cater only for small communities, and which may not be able to relate to current local issues, advise youth or even make their sermons understandable:

> I've been to quite a lot of Friday speeches and what I used to . . . basically I used to go to a local mosque, on Barkerend Road, and he used to speak in Urdu and I could understand but I'm sure that a lot of the youth who used to go there, they probably didn't understand. That's why there was a very low attendance from the youth themselves and with . . . I think there's a majority of mosques who're like that and resemble that . . . you know, like, Urdu-speaking and . . . you know, the secular Islam that they give, so it's always wishy-washy, it's always stories of the past . . . but how these stories affect you today! That's not given. (Fatima, student, 19 years old)
> MB: 'Do you think the imams, you know, would accept [discussing drugs and sex]?'
> Maria (student, 16 years old): 'No, because it's mainly because . . . the

imam in my area is the language barrier, they don't understand. Most of them come from back home, innit? And it's like . . .'

Rhya (student, 16 years old): 'You know . . . it's mostly guys, if at all, speak to the imams, innit? Like the women . . . I don't know, I think you've got a bit mixed up, like the actual mosque where the prayer's read, obviously only men are allowed to go there.'

It's a channel of communication, you know, and it's partly . . . have you got the right imam there? In the sense that . . . things are changing, but some of the imams, obviously, come from Pakistan and their command of the English language is non-existent . . .'[70] (Zameer, community worker in his early thirties)

8.2 Madrassas and the Understanding of Islam

The problem of the teaching in madrassas was a very hot issue in Bradford (cf. Lewis 2006), and the mosques where the teaching is done in English currently have a long waiting-list (for example Abu Bakr in Leeds Road). Preaching in English did not necessarily mean a more liberal approach to life, but was widely considered an important variable in maximising the effect of Quranic teachings on everyday life (ibid.).

None of the members of the sample who grew up in Bradford had had their religious teaching in English or had to learn the contents of the Quran on top of learning how to read Arabic. The ones who had studied Islam in depth had all done so after leaving the madrassa. As one interviewee put it:

Have you ever seen a parrot? They can talk . . . you can teach a parrot to talk and it'll regurgitate whatever you taught it, but it doesn't understand a word of it. It's exactly how the youth are today . . . exactly the same way. They'd know more of the Arabic language than I would. A nine-year-old, in many cases that I know, knows more than what I do about the Arabic language and yet he doesn't understand nothing. I know people with big beards, you ask them why have you got a beard? 'That's because my religion wants me to', and yet that same individual deals in drugs, simply because he hasn't built a criteria that this is *halal* and this is *haram*, not allowed. *Halal* or not *halal* is restricted to what I can do in the mosque, or . . . 'I can't eat this chocolate because it has E45 number on it', or 'I'm not allowed to eat pork', that's it. This is the limitation of what I can or can't do. Outside of that they've never been taught, they've never been cultured that you have dos and don'ts outside that environment. (Imran, teacher in his early thirties)

Respondents who engaged with mosques for work affirmed that they were starting to see changes in some madrassas:

> In my work I had the opportunity to go out to a number of mosques and simply talked to maulvis about professional criteria for what's acceptable, for example it's against the law to give corporal punishment to children. We were getting referrals by children who'd been smacked on their hands with sticks, and that's clearly against the law, it's a crime. Now, in a lot of instances the maulvi will want to learn about the law. Because they have actually no idea about child development, how children grow, how children learn . . . different perspectives. (Abdul, community worker in his early forties)

At the same time, the theme of the delegation of moral teachings to mosques (Bolognani 2007a) was reinforced by the lack of parental involvement in the madrassa. The more conscientious parents, for instance, would organise private tuition rather than engage with changes in the local madrassa. Others emphasised how the average parent would keep sending children to the madrassa but would not follow its tuition:

> Such is the concern we show to our children that the child will go to the madrassa when he is five, he will remain there for ten years, and such is the love that we have for our child. In these ten years not once we will visit the madrassa to visit the teacher of our child and ask about the progress of our child. . . . Never mind monitoring the child education on a daily basis, never mind on a weekly basis, we won't even walk in there in a period of ten years, so busy we are. And this is the love we've got for our child, such is the love we've got for Allah. (Sheikh Ahmed Ali, *Muslim Youth*)

> But I think if in certain areas they're not discussing then it's up to parents, the parents go and raise . . . say, 'We'd really like you to mention this because there's a problem in this area' and it's about people getting together and bringing it to the maulvi's attention. (Shamim, community worker in her early forties)

For this reason, some argued, the responsibility was unfairly placed on maulvis, while parents and the whole community were also responsible, as they did not encourage reform within mosques through the mosque committees.

8.3 Mosques as Community Centres

Mosques seem to be run by the mosque committees rather than the imams, the authority of whom, in many cases, is strictly subordinate (cf. McLoughlin 1998c:215, 2005:1061):

> Some of the speakers from the mosques might not give interviews without permission of the committee, it happens all the time, and you can understand why as well. If I'm interviewing any practitioners without permission of the line manager, it's exactly the same. (Tahir, teacher in his late thirties)

The Mosque committees also seem to have control over the duties that mosques attend to, from the organisation of life-cycle rituals (McLoughlin 1998a:99) to charity (Kalra and Rehman 2006). Many, however, complained that local mosques were not taking full advantage of their potential and were not developing their role as a point of reference for those seeking advice:

> It's more [about] giving Islam in a secular way, it's just personalised in your own home, it's praying your *salat* (your obligatory prayers) and respecting your elders, it's just picking certain things that are taught, and that doesn't equip you with problems that you'll face in the wider society. As Muslims we should accept Islam in its totality so we shouldn't be nit-picking so you're going to find at home somebody who's totally different, but when you're outside in the wider society, if you've got drugs problems, girlfriend-boyfriend problems, society problems, free-mixing problems, you know, all this type of different problems, we're not gonna see them, we're not gonna see Islam dealing with these problems because our institutions like madrassas or these mosques are little study circles that . . . they haven't taught, they haven't equipped us with the true Islamic ideas to deal with those problems because it's been given in a very secular way. (Fatima, student, 19 years old)

> MB: 'What do you think about the role of mosques?'
> Maria (student, 16 years old): 'In the Muslim community the mosque is meant to be the central and direct . . . nobody should feel like they

can't go to the imam and ask him a question like you said before, and the mosque should be more open and open to everybody.'

This was especially cogent as some who had been in mosques outside Bradford had heard of or experienced a much more active approach that involved campaigns against drugs, domestic violence, etc.:

> MB: 'You think mosques can really be the agents of change?'
> Ayesha (community worker in her early forties): 'Of course they can, but you know what it is, the mosques . . . some of them they're doing absolutely an amazing job, some of the mosques down London, in Tower Hamlets. They say there one member in every four households is a heroin user. So the mosques had to become the vehicle of change. In Bradford they'll only become the vehicle of change when the same epidemics will hit here because nobody really wants to know at the moment.'

Given the lack of forums for discussion, consultations with imams who had a reputation for being able to address the needs of young people may be organised through email or by phone:

> I would speak with . . . the imam's wife as well. We often go to her because I go to mosque a lot and we have classes on Wednesday for little girls . . . just starting . . . about ten years old . . . Quranic classes. We teach the girls, but we're learning ourselves as well . . . we need volunteers to help for little girls. So we go to the imam's wife because she's got a lot of knowledge because of her husband and you can ask her and she tends to know a lot more than we do. (Rhya, student, 16 years old)

> You know, normally women get to ring the imam at the mosque. Abu Bakr Mosque on Leeds Road, that's what happens, like after he's done his prayer, he just stays in that room for a few hours and he gets called. (Sundas, student, 16 years old)

The ideal of a mosque, as a community centre providing for almost all community needs (McLoughlin 1998c:211), was described in this way:

> Your *masjid* [mosque] isn't only a place to worship, a community centre, it's where your affairs should be dealt with, and if there are is-

> sues, that's where it should be dealt . . . it's like your social club; it's a place for worship first, secondly it's a place where the imam on Friday should be giving the *khuthba*, the speech which tackles the problems in the streets, where issues should be resolved in the community, but I don't think this is happening personally, it's very easy to give a good speech by the imam, very easy for us to go on Friday, do our prayers and then come out again. (Zameer, community worker in his early thirties)

> You know one of my ideologies, my ideas, my protocols was . . . these mosques they're building, they're spending thousands and thousands of pounds, if they had the education facilities, the computers there, where young kids could go in there and access . . . you know, like the mosque is like the way to the future now, mosques with facilities like sport centres, getting kids in there to do certain things, then they could pray, mosque's not just a place where you just go to pray, what counts . . . it's the place where you get knowledge and experience. This is how it was going back in history, so much people used to come from different countries to go to the mosques and there were books in different languages where you can learn certain subjects and everything, written in different languages, and this is how people got the knowledge from. (Adam, community worker in his late twenties)

The fact that most mosques in Bradford do not have female spaces, however, reduced the feasibility of mosque community-centres that benefit women as much as men (cf. 'word of mouth' and 'network reliability' for women, Chapter Seven):

> It's a problem, a lot of *masjids* don't have access for women, which is not ideal, I have to say, but the issue predominantly is with male, isn't it? I think the indigenous white population, you have white women using drugs, but I think it's a lot less, far less in the Asian community . . . (Zameer, community worker in his early thirties)

Women cannot take advantage of the mosque centres, and must therefore rely either on a supporting network of acquaintances to improve their knowledge and seek advice, or look for help in the information industry.

8.4 Media

Some media have given explicit and public recognition to some problems and have upheld something of a mandate to provide instruments for both parents and the youth themselves to deal with their problems.

In the previous chapter it was pointed out how many women may find it difficult to break the ice and speak with professionals when they face a problem; they seem to be more likely to rely on strong personal ties rather than dealing with practitioners (Orford et al. 2004:25). We have also seen above how access to religious institutions and authorities may be problematic, and sometimes is even bypassed by asking the imam's wife for advice. Other means of accessing information to exercise better-informed social control were radio and television:

> I think now the word is going around because they're discussing it on radio, you know like in Ramadan, in our fasting month, and the people listen more to the radio and this programme on Islam and religion and fasting and what God wants you to do, not just 'you have to be a good Muslim' . . . some people listen to it, and every day they do bring something like those issues and people would ring in . . . people who're doing the radio programmes are from Bradford and sometimes they invite certain persons, and sometimes it's somebody who knows more about certain issues . . . I don't know about the youngsters, but during Ramzan ['Ramadan'? ??] there is that sort of atmosphere where everybody is enjoying that more than television, so maybe I've noticed in that month people bring a lot of things up because the radio's on most of the time, so that's the best time, and now I'm very happy that things have changed because now people are talking openly about it. Before they weren't. Because it's affecting everybody, so everybody's concerned, so every day now . . . on television there's an Islamic channel on, where people can ring in and talk about any issue, and people ring for different things, 'Oh, my son . . .', there are different channels . . . and there're regular programmes every day, for women as well, there's a lady who does all issues to do with . . . and it's in Urdu. And in different languages, you see it in Bengali as well . . . (Shamim, community worker in her early forties)

The popular access to satellite programming included not only Islamic and Bollywood channels: an increasing number of families seemed to follow news channels. During interviews, documentaries and TV programmes were often quoted as sources of knowledge, and enhanced by word of mouth—summaries of what was being broadcast, watched by some members of the community and then recounted after mosque, in cars, in restaurants or after football matches (see for example recurrent references in Chapter Four to the documentary *Edge of the City*).

Some TV programmes appeared to make up for deficiencies in madrassas:

> Now on television they do this programme where they teach children to learn Arabic and they go through one sentence and then they'll explain in Urdu, they'll explain in English, and it's like half an hour, teaching kids, so they're working towards it. I think people in the Pakistani community have realised there's a problem. (Shamim, community worker in her early forties)

While some respondents shared sociological criticism of television, like Putnam's (Boggs 2001:288; Field 2003:31; Kivisto 2004:16) and blamed TV for the erosion of social networks (cf. Chapter Five), others saw it as an up-to-date device able to maximise the delivery of their cultural and religious messages. 'Virtual' consultation through phone, email or messages from other continents seemed at first glance to be valued more than local institutions run by individuals who might be too young to bear much authority.

8.5 Local Institutions

Some mosques in Bradford have now got facilities such as computers and libraries. In other areas, however, very similar 'learning centres' are run by the council, but their popularity varies from ward to ward:

> Theres an advice centre [in the BD8 district], the youth club, hardly anyone goes there now, and the guys hang around on street corners. 11, 12 [at night], one in the morning, you see them there hanging around smoking, drinking, dealing in drugs, or just hanging there doing nothing, because there's nowt there for them. (Jamal, student in his early twenties)

Others suddenly become popular when day-trips or journeys to Europe are organised, according to Salman and Munir, both 16 years old, who would attend one of the youth centres in Bradford 3 and who said that they spent most of their time either there or at mosque.

According to some, one of the main benefits of youth centres was to 'keep the kids off the streets', but nobody would rely on them for active and strategic social control. Young men (for whom the majority of centres seemed to be catering) could be 'kept off the streets' by other agents:

> There's a very nice snooker place they opened now ... in West Bowling ... I think it's opened by a private person, I've never been myself, my brother's going to it, but they've opened that and it's really good because guys who used to hanging around on street corners they're actually going in there and just have a laugh. (Bano, student, 18 years old)

> People my age group, 19–20, especially the ones who're starting to practise Islam, we believe that ... I don't think even a greater police influence or setting up a youth centre down the road, they can actually truly solve the problem. Yeah, you can have these institutions to get people off the street, but what's gonna stop them from taking drugs inside the centre itself? ... I don't think the centres work at all. I think it's a good tool that can be used, a good style that can be used, but if the youth are still having the ideas of having ... if the youth don't need free time ... I mean, we don't need time to play pool or basketball or tennis ... yes, that's fun time, but what gonna stop that person from now after basketball just taking the spliff or marijuana in the cloakroom? Unless that person's equipped with the correct ideas to solve these problems correctly, then he's not gonna basically see a problem. He's just gonna keep carrying on. He doesn't care. He will be good at basketball but he'll be good at taking spliffs or whatever. (Fatima, student, 19 years old)

The activities of one youth centre were described in this way:

> [The centre in the BD8 district] did help a lot in keeping people off the street ... first it used to be guys hanging around street corners and even if they weren't doing anything wrong, just the walking past them, walking down the street and seeing ten, 15 young lads with hoodie tops on and trainers and stuff, smoking, you'd feel intimidated by them, regardless whether they were being doing something or not, and the youth club was open six till nine, so the lads would say, rather than hanging around, why don't we just go there and play football, basketball, pool, table tennis, just chill out, playing the computer, just doing some uni, college work, get some work upstairs because we had IT facilities and internet upstairs so people could come in on a night and do college work or school work. We had three workers at the youth club, employed by the council, and then we had me and my friends who were volunteers. Some helped the lads out with their

lay nights were for girls only, then on weekend we'd have
a club for girls and boys, ten to 11 you do your homework,
12 you do whatever you want: pool, football, whatever.
(......, student in his early twenties)

If council-run centres where mostly young youth workers were employed did not provide the assurance of formal social control, then views about the roles of schools and teachers were just as controversial.

8.6 Schools

There was a widespread scepticism about the possibility of schools being able to exercise social control. Many parents seemed to believe that when schools did not teach discipline (and given the bad publicity for Bradford schools in the national media it seemed evident they did not) then they could not rely on schools to promote moral values:

> I'm not talking . . . I don't know generally, but my family . . . my parents . . . my parents wanted my brother to come out with a good education because they can get a better job and they can live the life they want. They don't rely on school and that, they rely on the person: they rely on me, they rely on my brothers to have that, because education's a gift, and if you want to take that gift you can take it . . . (Bano, student, 18 years old)

> Kids'll be brought up by schools, society, by media and that parents have no control on that, and I'm not talking about Pakistani parents, I'm talking about parents in general. And I think [it is] schools which are failing all kids in Britain, and that's why if you do a careful study of the statements we hear, we expect prisons to bring up our children, we have a solution: schools, and if not, they go to prison and we expect the prisons, they're now doing their job: education, opportunities, employment, training, everything's taking place in prisons . . . and our government proposal to extend school to six p.m., we'll realise very soon it's wonderful experiment, it'll bring its own problems, and children need love, care, people to show that they're caring for them, they care for them, they cook meals for them, and this is how children love the person who cares for them, and if they see that everybody's busy with their own . . . and 'we aren't priority', they'll find their recreational activities somewhere else. (Tahir, teacher in his late thirties)

Much of the impact of school on young people seemed to be seen as dependent on how parents valued school:

> I think that because the parents don't have much interaction with the teachers . . . so the children don't take that notice as well. But I don't think that school has a big influence on them. (Aqdus, student, 16 years old)

> I wanted to become parents' governor several months ago. That's the kind of thing, it's very easy for parents and stuff like that to say 'schools don't do anything', but hang on, you've got responsibility as well to make contact with the school and do things at home with kids . . . if you're not approaching, you know, maybe the school should be also approaching the community and the parents and stuff like that, and providing information, but the question is, why don't you go and ask? Why don't you get involved? You don't have to become necessarily a parents' governor, but there is no reason . . . why not going and ask 'How's my child doing?', 'What's his behaviour like?', 'Who does he hang around with?', because, you know, we come to work, we spend a lot of time with our colleagues at work, seven, eight hours a day, same thing kids spend a lot of time with teachers at school, don't they? That's a good place to know whether . . . hang on, is my kid at school first of all, is he there regular . . . is he . . . how's his conduct at school, is he studying, is he not studying, who does he hang around with, what influences are out there? Does it make sense? It's very easy to blame other people, but I think you have to take some of the responsibility for yourself as well . . . (Zameer, community worker in his early thirties)

When Kamran was asked to comment on the paucity of Muslim governors, the reply was: 'Now you show you're a *gore*', as if to imply that, traditionally, family focus would be on other matters, but not on interacting with their children's school.

An interesting example was presented by Tahir who described, how one mosque engaging with the school attended by its young students had triggered positive effects for both institutions:

> There are excellent examples of mosques which are doing very good jobs in Bradford and you can't get admission there, 300, 400 people on the waiting-list, you can't because these people are full-time teach-

ers and *maulana* as well, for example on Leeds Road there're two, one's the head teacher of maths in a school, and in this they have a partnership with the school, so for example when children perform very well in the mosque, the school knows the result, so the teacher is praising them, 'Well done at the mosque', and at the same time, when they perform well at school, the imam knows as well. So they're working in partnership, this is what we want, whereas other than that, this is my very informed view, that a lot of head teachers, they [slag off] mosques in schools, they think that kids are wasting time, they have extra burden; you'll come across all sorts of issues. And when you say, OK, extend the school hours for another hour, [unclear] then Mr Head Teacher is lost again. (Tahir, teacher in his late thirties)

When social control failed to be an effective means of crime prevention, then the penal system would have to intervene. On this matter, views were quite surprising, as they seemed to contradict previous research on minority ethnic groups and the criminal-justice system.

8.7 Prisons

In the quote opening this chapter, Tahir indicated how he thought that society was requiring prisons to do the job of schools, implying that rehabilitation could have been avoided by a thorough process of prevention.

Prison sentences, however, often appeared as an effective, albeit not always durable way of changing matters. According to the Armley prison Muslim chaplain, many British Pakistanis 'as prisoners find their identity as Muslims'. Sometimes a return to the religion of their birth produced long-lasting effects through the phenomenon previously called 'reconversion' (see Chapter Seven), but at other times did not survive their release. When the shame of incarceration triggered community shame (Braithwaithe 1989:97), families might not accept their children back and consequently they were pushed towards illegality as soon as they came out of jail.

Some families had been known to hide the prison sentences of their members by mentioning trips to Pakistan or work in London, but the growing interest of the local press in crime amongst Asians seemed to have made this strategy less feasible, as photos and details of offenders were now often published:

If I say, 'Where have you been all this time?', 'Oh, I've been to Pakistan', 'I've been on holiday', 'I was working outside the country', stuff like that, this is what they'll tell you. They won't tell you the truth. And you hear stuff like your next door's neighbour's been drinking and driving their car, they've been caught, before you didn't know they'd been drinking and driving, but now they have this crime column in the T&A, and the name's printed, how much fine they get, and they're like 'Wow!', d'you know what I mean? People, they don't expect their neighbour to do that. (Adam, community worker in his late twenties)

Unless, while in prison, a reconversion took place, perception of the penal system was not very positive:

[Going to prison] is more bad! Because they want holiday! They have good food there, play football, watch television, they don't bother. In Pakistan, if you go to jail you'll never do it again because they start from morning work, and finish evening and they give *dhal* and just water for food, they never go there again ... other people [first-time offenders] yes, but them no. If anybody wants food they go to jail because it is more better. (Akbar, retired, in his early seventies)

Bano (student, 18 years old): 'My uncle went to jail for beating someone up and he said you can get heroin, anything in jail.'
Safina (student, 17 years old): 'Yes, there was that programme that came on BBC 4 with hidden video cameras and the person going undercover ... and actually the police asked the prisoners to open the window while they were smoking the weed. The coppers can smell everything and they [only] told [the inmates to put it out] ...'

Prison sentences therefore seem to be effective only given certain collaboration from the outside world—support, shame, etc.:

For people I know who went to prison, they do come out to a much more stronger family support, they will have ... the Asian community's very strong in terms of family values anyway, they're a lot more closer ... you know, there's no way I would put my mother in a nursing home, you know, that kind of mentality, we don't do things like that, so we ... like, your mum looks after you, brings you up, your father ... you do the same when you grow up, you look after them and the network, the family, what you call biraderis or your clan ... they're quite close, they'll support each other ... maybe if you commit an offence, some kind of a sexual offence, something very extreme, you can understand that, you'll be stigmatised, shut on the side, but generally we'll come out to much more support, to much more structure in terms of what's available for us. (Zameer, community worker in his early thirties)

8.8 Policing

The policing of minority ethnic communities in Bradford has generated a long history of grievances, from the rumours of mistreatment of females that led to the 1995 riots (Macey 1999a; 1999b) to complaints about stop-and-search policies still in operation. For this reason, some commentaries by interviewees are surprising. For some, the police force seemed to be considered as the only way forward for these communities, despite the acknowledgement of past conflicts with it. However, there was certainly a negative inheritance too:

> My dad's like second generation, while I'm third, and people like my dad in their forties or thirties and everything, they have this sense that they can't rely on the police, or we can't rely on these other institutions. (Fatima, student, 19 years old)

> I strongly, personally, I can't say it's a fact, but from experience from living there 22 years of my life, is very close knit and any outsiders . . . and I don't mean as outsiders people who come to live in the neighbourhood, but I mean as outsiders the police . . . anything to do with the law is very unwelcome because maybe in the past the older generation've had problems with the police and they've been passed on these views and thoughts, have been passed on to the younger generation. (Zaara, shop assistant and special constable in her early twenties)

Yet many respondents seemed to recognise the potential role that the police could play, although the majority complained that, at the present time, there was not enough patrolling in some areas and that police intervention was not always satisfactory. Although many complaints about stop-and-search policies were registered, there were as many complaints to do with the supposed lenience of the police:

> I personally think, I know it's heavy-handedness, but the police need to make a stand. They promised they would after the riots and they haven't. . . . I think they need to enforce, for example pulling cars over, punishing people, you're speeding, you've no insurance? Right, go to

prison for months, put points on your licence. (Amir, unemployed in his mid-thirties)

[Police] is not racist, they are doing their jobs! Why are you doing bad sins? If you don't, they stop. In 40 years nobody stopped me on this road or they never asked me, 'Why do you do that?'. If the police come, I am happy you know, but the people who don't want the police involved, they are drug dealer and all. Now they have let people, mostly in Bradford, the most people, now it is our people, you know, they do a lot of bad things. And if the police care, they just say, 'Oh, they are racist . . . not true! because they do bad things. If they never do anything . . . the police force in Bradford is not only English, they are Pakistani, Indian, Sikh, my son is a policeman. (Akbar, retired, in his early seventies)

Some were persuaded that sometimes police turned a blind eye:

The police aren't doing much, I think they're just ignoring some of the things. (Shamim, community worker in her early forties)

The fact is a few years ago, if West Yorkshire police had reached their quota of arresting Asian people . . . if they'd arrested any more people after reaching their quota, they would've been considered as a racist police force, and that's why they don't arrest anybody else. (Amir, unemployed in his mid-thirties)

If the police actually try harder, and not just, like . . . suspect certain people and they suspect everyone, maybe they can get something out of it. . . . They could [do more], because they're doing a lot, like night watches, cameras and CCTV everywhere, and that really helps but they could do more, they could do a lot more, 'cos that's what the police are there for, this is what they're getting paid for. They're getting paid for looking after the community, not for sitting on their backs, not having a cup of coffee, they get paid so they can get look after the community and the community feel secure to live in their own houses. (Bano, student, 18 years old)

You know sometimes I've heard many times many people saying that the police encourage it, but obviously I don't know how to believe that. But . . . sometimes it makes you wonder . . . There was a case . . .

very serious case . . . it needed involvement of local councillors, local MP before the police came out, and when they came out they didn't do nothing . . . it was a very serious case, the police was called and they never came around, very serious case where there was attempted murder and they never came round. And they came round after the local councillor and the local MP were involved and when they came out after four days they didn't do nothing and that was . . . I was very surprised. (Iqbal, entrepreneur and politician in his late fifties)

The idea that police would not deal properly with problems seemed to have more to do with a sort of perceived incapability rather than institutional racism or an unfair approach, but also some might fear repercussions as police intervention was perceived as a last resort, resorting to an extraneous force:

In my own family, three months ago, my auntie was assaulted in her own home by someone in her neighbourhood, and it started off really silly. It started off over their . . . these two people . . . my auntie's son and this other lady's son arguing . . . they are only five, six years old, they had an argument, they hit one another . . . the lady came over to complain to my auntie. My auntie said to come inside and said, 'They shouldn't do that, let's speak to them, listen to their parents' . . . she was trying to put some sense in their heads. When they came they had a bit of a dispute and started smacking my auntie so my auntie called my family. I was at work, I couldn't leave and so my auntie called my family, she didn't call the police. . . . To be honest, as a family we have no problems calling the police. If we need the police, we'll be there to call them. A lot of people have problems, they're very afraid to call the police because they're scared of repercussions, not only in the sense of what'll happen with the community, because the police have been called the community's gonna sort of stop talking to us 'cos we've got outside that boundary. The police are seen as the last resort, but the last resort that should never be taken . . . that step should never be taken. Then, there's also that sense that the police come and the Asian community feel that the police haven't done their job to the satisfaction of what the people should think the police should do. Then, they think it's a waste of time to call the police. There are many reasons why people won't call the police, but if they do and then don't get the right results they're hoping for, then that's it, from that experience the police won't be called again. (Zaara, shop assistant and special constable in her early twenties)

Wherever the community felt that the police were engaging with them there seemed to be positive results. Officers on the beat who were willing to get to know their culture seemed to be much appreciated:

> I think at the end of the day, what it boils down to is that there has to be more visible policing. (Iqbal, entrepreneur and politician in his late fifteies)

> The particular policeman I dealt with I found him extremely helpful, not only that, he was learning Urdu, taking Urdu lessons, so I was really impressed. The thing is, he was from a business background, he had a very good customer focus, I asked him what was his reason. And he said that his learning Urdu was not really viewed as something of a normal good thing, because he was on a customer-relationship background, he thought he would be more able to talk with people and people would be more 'acceptive' if he spoke their language, which is sensible, very clever, so . . . (Tahir, teacher in his late thirties)

In particular, the existence of the Minorities' Liaison Committee (Bradford and District Minority Ethnic Communities/Police Liaison Committee Constitution: 1998) was generally positively acclaimed as an example of the police force engaging with and consulting the local communities, and acknowledging their needs. The committee was founded in 1998 after recurrent episodes of violence had focused the attention of the police on the frustration of minorities in Bradford, especially in 1995, first with vigilantism on Lumb Lane and then with the summer riots (see Chapter Three):

> Lumb Lane campaign was the result of frustration of non-intervention of the police, people took action in their hands, so now the prostitutes are in an industrial area where they don't disturb families. Now the police is talking more to the community, but it's not sure if the relation between the two has improved. (Umar, civil servant in his late forties)

8.9 Conclusion: Complementarity of Formal and Informal Social Control

This chapter has looked at the relation between different structures of social control in the areas touched by the research. The analysis started from data regarding mosques, where according to many participants, messages are often delivered by ignoring local 'hot' issues such as drugs. The potential enjoyed by such spaces was therefore often considered wasted in relation to prevention and discussion of the most preoccupying problems of the community. The lack of knowledge and skills in dealing with young people ascribed to many imams was also mentioned as a factor that kept many mosques alien to a process of change that instead seemed to be carried out by pilot projects like the one in Batley, where one madrassa is running a drug-awareness course. The majority of madrassas in Bradford, instead, were thought to concentrate on a learning process based on memorising Quranic verses rather than discussing them.

While the preoccupation with Muslim youth was measured by the increasing attention to drugs given by some Muslim media and by the increasing funding given to youth centres, opinions about the effectiveness of many 'top-down' social-control strategies were controversial. In particular, a widespread mistrust of schools and teachers was recorded across the sample. Perhaps surprisingly, many research participants looked to the police as one of the most potentially effective means of social control, in spite of the history of mistrust between the Pakistani community and police officers. Prison sentences, on the other hand, often appeared as an effective, if not always durable way of changing deviant individuals, for example through the phenomenon called 'reconversion'. Overall, research informants seemed to see potential for change in both public and cultural institutions, but especially in the collaboration of the two. The complementarity of the structures appeared to articulate a meaning of 'community' that went beyond an ethnic projection, but included all the resources (public and cultural) available in one's area, as will be discussed in the conclusions to this study.

9

THE POLITICS OF CRIMINOLOGY: FROM BIRADERI TO COMMUNITY

> The title of this series of lectures signals the existence of what is very widely felt to be a growing challenge in our society – that is, the presence of communities which, while no less 'law-abiding' than the rest of the population, relate to something other than the British legal system alone. But, as I hope to suggest, the issues that arise around what level of public or legal recognition, if any, might be allowed to the legal provisions of a religious group, are not peculiar to Islam: we might recall that, while the law of the Church of England is the law of the land, its daily operation is in the hands of authorities to whom considerable independence is granted. And beyond the specific issues that arise in relation to the practicalities of recognition or delegation, there are large questions in the background about what we understand by and expect from the law, questions that are more sharply focused than ever in a largely secular social environment. (Williams 2008)

This book has shown how the concerns spread by the media and by policy-makers are not necessarily always congruent with the ones described by the Pakistani community of Bradford. One of the aims of the study was to record local knowledge, beliefs and informal practices related to crime and social control. This has contributed to one of the first systematic collections of ethnic-minority people's perceptions about crime. By doing that, not only were their ideas of crime deconstructed and contextualised, but these ideas informed a series of discourses on the aetiologies of crime and its possible solutions. These discourses mainly referred to their family system and to a vague sense of 'community' that we have yet to pin down.

Theoretically, we have worked with two main concerns: the criminological and the diasporic. Methodologically, the book has applied an emic and ethnographic strategy to the Bradford Pakistani context, and considered the effectiveness of that strategy in terms of analysing knowledge of crime held by minority ethnic groups (see Chapter One). Empirically, such knowledge held by Bradford Pakistanis has been explored through the analysis of their views about crime construction (Chapter Four), crime production (Chapter Five), and informal and formal social control (Chapters Seven and Eight). This concluding chapter will illustrate the intertwining of cultural and social variables of the above-mentioned discourses as the main factors contributing to the politics of criminology amongst Bradford Pakistanis.

9.1 Breaking the Taboo, through Empirical Considerations beyond Anti-Essentialism

In Chapter One we argued that in criminology there is a gap in the study of race and crime. While there is a substantial body of literature on discrimination against minority ethnic groups in the criminal-justice system, there is still a need to incorporate the (cultural) knowledge held by such groups. Some have argued that this deficiency may be traced back to the fear of pathologising minority ethnic groups in relation to crime (see Phillips and Bowling 2003). While this debate can be compared to the one about essentialising and pathologising minority ethnic groups that occurred in the 1990s (see Chapter One), we have throughout this book argued that academics should move beyond anti-essentialism. For example, neglecting the fact that minority ethnic groups have at their disposal internalised, shared and similar experiences, throughout the stages of settlement, may be detrimental to the understanding of the dynamics of their engaging with crime. Although we have discussed evidence of the heterogeneity and fragmentation of Bradford Pakistanis (see Chapter Three), we still argue that the term 'community' may be of use in this field.

The discourse about community (Hoggett 1997:3) has been very important in recent times in the Bradford context (see for example Ouseley:2001). This northern city has been considered an important place for implementation of community cohesion strategies, in the aftermath of the 2001 riots (Pankhurst 2002). Nonetheless, community crime prevention has not received as much attention in the public agenda. This has perhaps been due to the fact that identifying a 'community' is a difficult task when the group informally described as 'Bradford Pakistanis' embodies a high level of fragmentation across regional, religious and generational lines. Other reasons may lie in the fear of racialising boundaries that are at the same time ethnic and geographical (with most Pakistanis clustered in inner-city areas), or perhaps in the distrust apparently developed towards representatives of

the community or community leaders (Ouseley 2001, Kundnani 2002). On the other hand, during the research on which this book is based, the Pakistani community was confirmed as an important element in the study of deviance for three reasons:
- the perceived effect on the community appeared to be the measure for classifying the seriousness of crimes (the greater the threat to the community, the greater the crime);
- the diffused panic about the 'erosion of community' (see Chapter Five); and
- the community's distinctiveness in dealing with crime (see Chapter Seven).

Despite an interest in community discourse, community crime-prevention strategies have not been institutionally or openly discussed in relation to the potential of the local Muslim population. Studying the specificities of a minority ethnic group does not necessarily arise from the will to 'collude' with social-control agencies (cf. Sharma et al. 1996, cited in Chapter One); instead, it follows from reviewing the general literature and understanding the need to include more minority ethnic perspectives in this field. Analysing local history, and knowledge produced and re-invented in the community (practical concerns, cultural and religious beliefs, and moral dilemmas), plays a crucial part in the study of the relations between Bradford groups and crime. It would be useful for policy-makers to see how these factors work in local grassroots organisations.

The second part of the book was based on an analysis of the data collected during the fieldwork. The analysis developed through the concerns that emerged (Chapter Four), the views on the aetiologies expressed by the respondents (Chapter Five), an overview of how formal (Chapter Eight) and informal (Chapter Seven) control is currently working, including the supposed solutions to the crime problem.

Labelling seemed to be based on a classification of potential dangers to the community: the higher threat seemed to be perceived as the one that was potentially more destabilising for the group. At the same time, community resources and networks were described as essential to articulate discourses around crime, principles similar to the ones on which national community crime-prevention strategies are based (Burnside and Baker 1994:19).

The social production of crime seemed to be discussed in either ecological or cultural terms. Some participants tended to see a combination of structural and cultural factors as the most accurate aetiology of crime in the community, reproducing discourses that were more similar to recent New Labour policies such as the 'respect agenda' (Knight 2006) than to deprivationist views. Others, like Imran, seemed to refer to discourses of Islamic revivalism. Similar attitudes of resistance through one's cultural background, in other studies (Tatum 2002:16), have been described as a 'post-colonial theory of crime violence and minority youth' since, like other post-colonial theories, they account not only for structural constraints but also for responses to oppression coming from the oppressed and their support systems[71] (for example, in the case of Imran, from religion). Ethnic resources and networks seemed the most common factors mentioned in the process of attribution of blame for crime. This may be a significant switch from 1980s deprivationist discourses (see Aldrich et al. 1981) to more 'cultural' ones. Further research might complement these findings by investigating how far public-policy discourses post-2001 may have influenced in a hegemonic way the preference given to culture and identity rather than objective structural disadvantage.

Public discourses about 'male youth as a problem' seemed another concern shared by 'mainstream' British society or media and many Bradford Pakistanis. In certain descriptions it emerged that male youth sub-cultures among Bradford Pakistanis may be seen as a product of environmental and cultural interaction. Here competing resources and networks seem to co-exist in the choices of young men as to how to engage actively with the local social environment.

In the last two chapters formal and informal social control were discussed in relation to potential solutions to crime. The solutions were grouped around four agents: the family, the mosque, the public institutions (services and educational systems) and the police. These elements had been mentioned in the previous chapters both as perceived causes of problems and as being faulty in exercising social control, but the research highlighted that by complementing each other they are believed to retain still some positive potential as agents of solutions to crime problems. This also confirmed that openly taking up a study that relates certain minority ethnic groups and crime does not have necessarily to lead to pathologisation, but rather it may on the contrary unveil appropriate and informed solutions to the problems considered a priority by the group itself.

Families were seen as closely tied to the main concerns around drugs; they were mentioned as the main target of drugs, whose ramifications in society would eventually undermine progress and family stability. At the same time, families were part of the aetiologies of the perceived rise in crime: they were seen as having been passive in their omissions in upbringing, and in some cases as complacent of criminal activities in order to protect their *izzat* or improve their financial status. On the other hand, they were

from concentrating on one single community organisation, with the risk of reproducing a hegemonic point of view that claims to be widely representative (see for example Bagguley and Hussain's prolific writing on the 2001 riots in Bradford). Doctoral students might be more fortunate, as their status allows them to interact with the community over at least a two-year period, but these issues need to be taken seriously by funding bodies, as already indicated by Gilliat-Ray (2005:29). The time and the level of closeness with respondents helps informants to give reliable accounts as the rapport with the researcher ideally does not end in the formal interview, but lingers and repeats itself on a number of occasions. The high degree of personal involvement of ethno-anthropological strategies helped to facilitate the development of participant observation, and of an understanding of the material offered by interviews, that surveys and quantitative methodology might struggle with, given their degree of detachment (Lee 1993:119). The reliability of the data also lies in the personal rapport between researcher and respondents, while participant observation offers a means of triangulation of what is expressed in formal interviews when respondents are likely to portray certain views influenced by the surrounding political context and (in this case) its understanding of Islam.

Ethno-anthropological methods were especially significant for this research in deconstructing the essentialised 'Muslim community'. 'Accessing all areas' (in terms of environments and groups of individuals), and stock-taking to avoid a self-appointed (and not necessarily representative) and highly politicised sample, seemed the keys to challenging the monolithic public discourse about 'the Muslim community'. This could be considered an ethical issue of representation as, especially after 7 July 2005, the idea of a 'Muslim community' has provided grounds for inaccurate generalisations, and consequent grievance among Muslims. The issue of adequate representation, especially as a sampling concern, is a political problem that puts the burden of political responsibility on the researcher.

9.3 A 'Community Criminology'

Perhaps there is a general tendency for sociologists of complex societies to study formal control and anthropologists to study informal control (Krase and Sagarin 1980:211). For example, research in the British Pakistani setting of Edinburgh narrowed its focus down to 'the community's social institutions (or agencies of social control) [that] promote order and regulate behaviour through the social bonding of members/participants to its moral and social order' (Wardak 2000:16), instead of the community's evaluation of formal institutions. In the present research we have explored a general pluralistic discourse that considered a combination of formal and informal structures as the most effective social-control repertoire. While some respondents looked at formal social-control systems as more efficient and fairer—'if you want to have justice, you've got to call the police', Bano, student, 18 years old—the government may look at informal cultural means such as faith communities to enhance crime prevention. This, however, may create controversies, as Tahir described when criticising those who see mosques as infrastructure but do not help them financially as they would other institutions with the same function:

> In terms of the comments this person made, 'These people don't have any moral teachings in the mosque', I'd say it . . . you have an emotional response and say, 'No moral teaching's going on', but this is not the case, because the nature of these imams . . . if you maybe hold a conference and present this statement to maybe 30 maulanas, they'll jump up and down and say, 'Look, we're doing the best we're doing', yes? Now, with regards to the question whether they go to learn the Quran, the mosque is providing that service and this is what parents expect. So parents haven't said, 'Do something else as well' . . . so there's a contract and the contract's being fulfilled and again if you only pay one pound to the mosque to do this service you shouldn't expect the high-quality education, because they can't provide it. The reason I'm saying it's a very, very complex issue, is . . . for example if we want to do shopping we're going to Tesco or Asda, or maybe other stores, you tell me there's a good store there, I'll try that, but why don't we do it for our own kids? Who are our future, and city's future, and country's future, we don't pay them serious [money] . . . and when we ask the mosques to do that, they can't do this because they don't have resources. We're very keen to jump and criticise mosques, and churches, *gurdwaras, mandirs*, but we don't give them funding to provide that work. Why do these educational institutions exist? Because the mainstream education is not catering for the children need, then government's not supporting them financially, council isn't providing any resources, so what do you expect? . . . [They live on] donations, so every Friday, I think mosques are very concerned about getting 400, 500 pounds a week, and that'll go for bills, maintenance, everything. And if you go to a mosque and you smell a disgusting smell, you know that the money isn't being spent, but we're very quick to make legislation, saying these maulana are coming from that country . . . (Tahir, teacher in his late thirties)

Other respondents saw a solution in a partnership between mosques and the police, where part of the deal would be some drug-awareness training delivered in or through mosques, by officers (as for instance the Armley prison's Muslim chaplain is doing in Batley):

> Like going in and explain it. When these attacks [shootings] happened I said to a police officer, a sergeant, 'Go into the community, go into the mosque and deliver a speech or give a presentation, "This is what happened and we want people to come forward"'. I haven't seen that.
> (Adam, community worker in his late twenties)

In this book we argue that the emic analysis of criminological discourses has highlighted the presence of a variety of approaches within the same community. However, in comparison to previous research it appears that the sense of bridging between different resources within one's locality is generally considered to be the most effective approach, and that this may have led to a different construction of the idea of community at this stage of the post-settlement era in Bradford: community is no longer only biraderi, but rather an ensemble which includes even those local institutional bodies which are inclusive.

The emic analysis of criminological discourses has highlighted the presence of a variety of approaches within the same community. The initial question of whether in Bradford there is cohesive community criminology with reference to the Pakistani community has been problematic, in the sense that the views across generations and occupational groups were very varied. The terms in which the function of family was described, for instance, fluctuated from positions where the traditional structure was blamed (as inconsistent, inapt, and therefore counter-productive, in the ccontext of necessarily British life, see Chapter Five), to views according to which the erosion of that very system had led to the drift towards crime (see Chapter Five). On the other hand, more coherence was to be found in the process of delineating which agents could potentially make a difference in this respect: families, mosques, public institutions and the police. Some of the more critical views about the 'original' culture of the majority of the community were paralleled by a belief that where such culture failed, there should have been a different and more assertive intervention from what used to be the host society. If many families failed for some time, for instance, to see British formal education as a way to improve oneself, the educational system, social services and even the government should have paid more attention to the problem, and prevented it from persisting.

In comparison to previous researches it appears that the sense of bridging between different resources within one's locality was quite generally considered to be the most effective approach, and this may have led to a different construction of the idea of community at this stage of the post-settlement period in Bradford: community is not only biraderi (see Chapters Three and Five) any more, but an ensemble which includes even institutional bodies operating in one's locality. While there is a tendency to see Muslims as the ultimate others (Alexander 2000:6), the dimension of the combination of traditions in the diaspora has somehow become lost or undervalued in the analysis. This study has shown how formal and informal, or British and 'traditional' Pakistani, can be combined, and are no longer separable in the dynamics of social control.

The emic of cultural agency can be said to legitimise the term 'community criminology', but not in the sense that Bradford Pakistanis demonstrate exclusive criminological discourses, labelling, preventive strategies and rehabilitation practices. Rather, they engage with mainstream criminological and policy discourses in a way that might well be considered a kind of reflection representative of the position of their diaspora: 'community' for them does not only include their traditional structures but all the intra-communal and inter-communal relations that are meaningful to them, both as resources and constraints.

The term 'community' in Bradford, in relation to the stage of settlement, may be better understood by comparison with another Pakistani transnational setting. In December 2005 the present author attended a public meeting with the small Pakistani community of Desenzano del Garda, in northern Italy. The members of that community present at the public event were all male, apart from two teenage girls; there was an interpreter, who described the ten years' history of the migration to the Brescia county. He had to translate everything said that evening for his countrymen, who did not speak Italian. The choice of words was particularly interesting as he decided to translate the word 'community' (*comunità* in Italian) as *biraderi*. He also introduced a *rappresentante della comunità* ('community representative') who declared himself to be the only link between the local 'Pakistani *biraderi*' (*sic*) and Italian society. At a very early stage of migration, where families have yet not been reunited, mosques have not been built and community relations are organised on the basis of self-appointed representation, the term used to describe community is biraderi, or 'brotherhood', 'extended family', 'closed blood-cum-caste unit'. This definition is now far from the Bradford Pakistani one. In the latter context, the term 'community' covers family, and specific cultural and religious institutions (mosques), but also public services and police. This definition helps us to understand the difference between a positive connotation of 'community' and the negative connotation of biraderi illustrated above.

NOTES

Chapter One
1. By 'racial' we refer to an identity based on 'supposed physical or biological groupings linked to skin and bodily features' (Harrison 2005:2).
2. The same concern will emerge in some of the data collected by the present researcher:
   MB: 'Is it true that there's a Pakistani gang?'
   Jamil (entrepreneur, in his mid-thirties): 'No. I would say *gang*, but there isn't a *Pakistani* gang, no . . . They're all races . . . but around here there are all Pakistanis . . when you see a group of lads together they're all Pakistanis . . . so you really can't call them a gang. They grew up together and they stick around together, so it isn't really a gang . . . it's friends, you know . . . like a bunch. And anybody who drives around they think they're a gang. But it's not a gang.'
3. Here we may disagree with Alexander, as in Chapter Three it will be argued that the local context of Bradford and its being so compact is important insofar as the notion of 'community' bears a significance that goes beyond race, while including locality and intracommunal relations. In Bradford the idea of community is only relatively an abstract construction; apart from being a term that is used by Bradford Pakistanis themselves, the pockets of high concentration of the same ethnic group with their semi-autonomous associations, structures and economic networks can justify the use of 'community' without worrying too much about the accusation of 'imagining a community'.
4. It may be interesting to note how a study that theorises West Indians' lives as 'disordered' and in many ways pathological is actually an insider sociologist's study of a Bristol community; see Pryce (1979/1986) above.

Chapter Two
5. In 2002 Macey published another study, including an analysis of the 2001 riots, but the considerations expressed with regard to the use and abuse of religion are substantially the same as the ones discussed in 1999a and 1999b, and on which this section is based.
6. The film *My Son the Fanatic* by Udayan Prasad, based on the eponymous short story by Hanif Qureishi, although not mentioning Bradford, represents very clearly the religious discourses manifested amongst the protesters in the Manningham area at the time.

7 Syleth is an area in Bangladesh; Chachchis are members of an ethnic group located in the Attock district of the Pakistani Punjab.
8 'Mohajjirs' is the name (whose use is sometimes controversial) given to the people who moved to the new Pakistan from India in 1947, and their descendants. It literally means 'migrants'.
9 This is a technical term in Islamic law that describes the process of making a legal decision by independent interpretation of the legal sources, the Qur'an and the Sunnah. The opposite of *ijtihad* is *taqlid,* Arabic for 'imitation'.
10 *Izzat* can be broadly translated as 'family honour', 'status', 'respect' or 'face-saving'.
11 The etic approach assumes that there is always a possible degree of abstraction in the analysis of a behavioural structure, and that through abstraction the social scientist can impose models aligned to a specific structure; a theoretical framework constructed in totally different situations may be applied to a community that has a very distinct history, for instance. Consequently, an etic approach is concerned with generalised statements about the data in order to compare them with other communities' (Pike 1954:8).
12 Amongst the studies about young Muslim men that give complex accounts of their lives, moving from gender, generation, identity and masculinity to racism, it is important to remember Archer's contribution (2003) in the field of education. She in fact follows Alexander in her theorisation of ethnic studies that should account for 'shifting discourses of the family, politics, age and territory' (ibid:161).
13 Such distinction can be made clear by paraphrasing these labels as 'Muslims by birth and Muslims by choice'.
14 In an introductory example, Pike says that an analysis of a language that does not include an analysis of behaviour is bound to have theoretical and methodological discontinuities, and vice-versa: 'the activity of man [sic] constitutes a structural whole, in such a way that it cannot be subdivided into neat "parts" or "levels" or "components" with language in a behavioral compartment insulated in character, content, and organisation from other behavior. Verbal and non-verbal activity is a unified whole, and theory and methodology should be organized or created to treat it as such.' (1954:2)
15 The terms 'etic' and 'emic' were at the centre of anthropological debate for a while after Pike's publication of his 1954 work. Critics of Pike's theory have often been accused of having misunderstood his writings and misrepresenting his concepts of emic and etic. The most famous controversy was the one stirred by Marvin Harris, who wrote about his own understanding of the two concepts in *The Rise of Anthropological Theory. A History of Theories of Culture* (New York, Thomas and Y. Crowell, 1969). Harris's version of emic and etic is still considered by Pike's followers as a gross misunderstanding of the original concepts.
16 Given the political implications of the debate on inter-continental marriages, the author feels it is important to note the heterogeneity of the stories of 'imported partners'; amongst the people interviewed, one woman who arrived in her late teens is, 25 years later, completely fluent and literate in English, working each week as a volunteer in more than one local community group; one woman who comes from a city in Pakistan, after eight years in the country, works in social care and leads a life that could be labelled 'middle class'; a woman from a village

in Mirpur has slowly learnt English, got a job, bought a house in a middle-class area with her savings and divorced her husband. Although these are not representative of the majority of cases, it seems important to remind the reader that 'imported partners' are not necessarily contributing to deprivation and lack of integration, as has been claimed recently (see Alibhai-Brown, Y. (2001) 'Mr Blunkett has insulted all of us', *The Independent*, 10 December).

17 In this book, the only term used to refer to generation is 'first-generation', by which people born in Pakistan and naturalised British are described. It is important to establish this convention, as a few interviewees understood 'first-generation' to mean the first individuals of Pakistani origin to be born in the UK.

Chapter Three

18 Although the term 'riots' has been disputed by academia (Burlet and Reid 1996:155), public opinion categorises such events under this label and, more importantly, 'rioting' has been the charge levelled against young men convicted in 2001.

19 Although in the Bradford district 'Asian' is commonly used to refer to Pakistanis, in this study the term will be used for people who were born in South Asia or who trace their descent from there. The term 'Indian' will include Sikhs and Hindus. When not specified, the term 'Pakistani' will refer to Pakistani Muslims independently of their sub-group (i.e. Pathan, Kashmiri, etc). The term 'Kashmiri' will refer in particular to people from the Mirpur district, who are the majority group within the Pakistani population of Bradford.

20 The extended family of agnatic descent (see below).

21 Until 1977, the year of Bangladesh independence, the term 'Pakistanis' included Bengalis.

22 By 'multiple deprivation' we refer to a situation of disadvantage in more than one field: poor housing, overcrowded households, malnutrition, illiteracy, educational underachievement, unemployment, etc. Note that the background of the observer might alter perceptions of the criteria used to measure these factors; for instance, a household might perhaps be defined as 'overcrowded' more easily by a white British person than by a British Asian; but statistics use established UK official standards.

23 More recent data are not available, but during fieldwork the impression was that a great number of marriages are still transcontinental.

24 For a non-romanticised account of bachelors' houses in Yorkshire, see *Brothers in Trouble*, directed by Udayan Prasad and based on a short story by Abdullah Hussain.

25 'kameti' (or 'committee') is an informal mode of credit rotation.

26 Literally: 'out of one's group'. The term can refer to inter-ethnic marriages, but in this case refers to cross-caste ones.

27 Exchange of gifts or services and extensive exchange of visits.

28 According to the 1962 Commonwealth Immigration Act, category-A visas were given to people who had been offered a job in the UK, category-B to people with qualifications and category-C to unskilled workers (Siddique 1993:22).

29 'Mela' is the Indian term for 'fair', from the Indo-european root 'ml' (to meet).

30 The author is aware of the controversial use of the term 'caste' in Pakistani studies. However, its use here reflects that by research participants.

31 Manningham was the centre of the 1995 and 2001 riots, and its history and demography has made it a popular setting for research and media accounts of Bradford problems. Locals strongly believe that there is serious 'postcode discrimination' against people from Manningham (Harrison and Phillips 2003:200). The area is one of the most deprived in Bradford, with 32 per cent unemployed compared to the West Yorkshire average of ten per cent (Phillips 2001). Amongst young Manningham Pakistanis the situation is even worse: unemployment is calculated at around 45 per cent (ibid).

32 This seemed to be the general perception. However, the police publicly declared that four NF members arrived at Bradford Interchange station and were sent back from the same platform (Bagguley and Hussain 2003c).

33 This refers to a racist attack carried out by a white man on a Pakistani man in the early afternoon of the first day of the riots. The perpetrator's membership to the BNP has not been confirmed.

Chapter Four

34 The documentary was the account of the working lives of Keighley social workers fighting against a spiral of 'grooming' of young girls by Pakistani men (see Hall 2004).

35 Similar views seem to be expressed in Bradford amongst the white community (cf. Harrison and Phillips 2005:183).

36 Pollution as a threat to society order is common coinage in anthropology. Douglas has argued that the fear of 'dirt' is fear of 'disorder' (1966/2002:2): 'Eliminating it is not a negative moment but a positive effort to organise the environment' (ibid). And again: 'The ideas about separating, purifying, demarcating and punishing transgressions have as their main function to impose system on an inherently untidy experience. It is only by exaggerating the difference between within and without, about and below, male and female, with and against, that a semblance of order is created' (ibid:4); 'Disorder spoils pattern' (ibid:95). These are in fact dynamic features: 'There is every reason to believe that they are sensitive to change. The same impulse to impose order which brings them into existence can be supposed to be continually modifying or enriching them' (ibid:5). 'The idea of dirt is not only to do with hygiene, but also with respect of conventions' (ibid:7). 'Propriety' (appropriateness, conformity with conventions, etc.) may be a form of purity, as it seems relevant to this context.

37 Thanks to Philip Lewis for alerting me to the concept of *ghanimat* and to Mazhar Malik and Tajul Islam for their help in coming to terms with it.

38 The annual amount of charity compulsory for all Muslims, and one of the five pillars of Islam.

39 *Hafiz* refers to those who have learnt the Quran by heart.

Chapter Five

40 It is clear that the Pakistani community has a very young population:

Table 5.1 Population of Bradford district in 1998, by age and ethnic group

Ethnic group	Age 0–15	Age 16–17	Age 18–24	Age 25+	TOTALS
Afro-Caribbean	1,685	203	573	3,751	6,212
Bangladeshi	2,163	269	858	1,901	5,191
Indian	3,387	504	1,430	8,106	13,427
Pakistani	26,166	3,043	9.426	26,999	65,634
White	78,375	9,784	32,734	268,353	389,246
Other	2,374	310	845	3,162	6,691
TOTALS	114,150	14,113	45,866	312,272	486,401

Source: Bashford et al. 2004:7

41 This perception is consistent with Bourdieu's definition of cultural capital and has been widely used in ethnic studies; cf. Modood 2004:88.
42 Most informants complained that in the community there was a widespread ignorance of drugs and their effects (see Chapters Eight and Nine).
43 It has proved impossible to construct a consistent use of a time or a culturally uniform unit called 'generation'. For this reason, the term is used by different respondents in different ways, and the author prefers to use 'younger' and 'older'. In this instance the term is used to describe the general divide between parents and their children.
44 Alexander (2000:240) has argued that the essentialisation of 'first generation' and discourses based on the dichotomy traditional/non-traditional are paramount in contemporary ethnic studies.
45 For similar, more theoretical findings cf. Bankston and Zhou 2002:290.
46 The expressions 'mafia culture' or 'gangster culture' were widely utilised during the research, maybe also because of my Italian identity; see Chapter Six.
47 I must thank Keir Martin from Manchester University for sharing with me his research notes on kastom and social change in Papua New Guinea. Although a systematic comparison of our data has not been attempted, many of his reflections have helped me in finalising the analysis of the label 'Culture' in the Bradford setting.
48 The example of people belonging to Tableegh Jamaat was brought to my attention many times; see for example Chapter Seven.
49 At the same time Tatum argues that lack of expectations may lead young people to form minority ethnic groups at a stage where they struggle to recognise oppression (Tatum 2000:23).
50 While in American sociology the relation between social capital and ethnicity is nowadays an established field (Bankston and Zhou 2002:289), it has been argued that in the UK this is still virtually unexplored (Modood 2004:98), making the deprivationist analysis the most subscribed approach, in spite of the 1990s recommendations about what has been called 'ethnicity as a resource' (Werbner

1990; Ballard 1996). Combining environmental constraints with social and cultural capitals, therefore, has been perceived by some as the only answer to empirical questions that still have counter-intuitive answers for many—for instance, why, in the same originally economically disadvantaged group, there are both a high concentration of high achievers and a high concentration of underachievers (Modood 2004:88).

Chapter Six

51 Recently, a growing number of pieces of research about Muslim male sub-cultures seem to have developed in the UK. Among these are Archer's research on Muslim boys and education (2003) and Shah and Dwyer's Leverhulme-funded research in Slough (2006).
52 The label 'coconut' describes an individual who is 'brown outside and white inside' (Asian in appearance but English in life-style), cf. Imtiaz 2002:125.
53 Some girls may utilise their growing knowledge of Islam to convince their parents to change some traditional norms and expectations that they feel are unfair or even inconsistent with their religion (McLoughlin 1998a:103).
54 A preliminary version of the following paragraphs on Bradford Pakistani women and deviance was published in Bolognani 2008.
55 Some research participants were keen on telling stories of drug dealers who used women in order to transport and sell drugs, in the strong belief that the police never stop Pakistani women; if that belief is well-grounded, it would help to account for the infrequent mention of cases of women convicted for drug offences. On the other hand, some sources have revealed a sharp increase in convictions of Muslim women in West Yorkshire, even leading to the appointment of a female Muslim chaplain in Wakefield female prison.
56 Chaudhary (1999:64) considers three types of 'shame': *izzat* ('prudery or consciousness of what constitutes shame'), *haya* ('inner modesty') and *ghairat* ('successful defence of honour and women'). In my research, the term *izzat* seemed to cover all three concepts, although occasionally *ghairat* was used, sometimes in the slang expression 'g factor'.
57 Declan Walsh, in an article in *The Guardian* of 9 December 2005, reports that every year about 100 British Pakistani women are saved from forced marriages by the Foreign Office Forced Marriage Unit. Walsh also claims that some 60 per cent of all the cases handled by the Unit involve British Pakistanis.
58 Chaudhary (1999:64) considers three types of 'shame': *izzat* ('prudery or consciousness of what constitutes shame'), *haya* ('inner modesty') and *ghairat* ('successful defence of honour and women'). In the fieldwork and in the diasporic literature-review I have only encountered the term *izzat*, which seemed to cover both *haya* and *ghairat*.
59 For the difference between *Gemeinschaft* (community) and *Gesellschaft* (society) see Tonnies, F. (1887) *Gemeinschaft und Gesellschaft*, Leipzig, Fue's Verlag.
60 Cf. Hanif Kureishi's interview with the boxer Amir Khan, The Observer, 12 February 2006.

Chapter Seven

61 Saeed describes the concept of honour as carried by females in a very effective manner: 'Men created this concept and housed it in women's bodies. . . . Have

you heard the story of the *jin* [genie] and the *tota* [parrot]? The genie's soul was in a parrot. No one could kill the genie unless they reached the parrot. So the genie built a secret den in a big mountain and hid the parrot. Once the parrot was hidden, the genie was indestructible, free to move around and do whatever he liked. It's the same idea here. A man places his honour inside a woman's body and hides her away in his house, freeing himself to go around and do anything he wants' (2003:306, 307).

62 A Quran *hafiz* is one who knows the Quran by heart.

63 Observations on very relaxed attitudes towards disciplining very young children in rural Punjab have been discussed by some anthropologists (Lyon 2004). Lyon recounted episodes when serious mischief by his hosts' youngest son was laughed at, and the guest was reprimanded for trying to stop the child touching his computer: the child was not believed to be capable of understanding (ibid:75–8).

64 For a Pakistani parallel of moral panic diffused as gossip or even as urban myth, see the discussion of the parables of prostitutes' recruitment in Lahore, diffused by women as much as men, in Saeed (2002).

65 Rajas or Rajputs are one of the *zamindaar* (landowner) castes.

66 *Gore* is the singular ('white woman'). The plural should be *gorian*; *gores* is the anglicised form.

67 *Yasmin* is based on a screenplay written during a workshop organised by the film director with local members of the Pakistani community (Bolognani et al., under submission).

68 For an account of how Islamist discourses spread in Bradford after the Rushdie affair, see Herbert 2003.

69 'Seminar' of the Deobandi tradition, see Gilliat-Ray 2005 and Lewis 2006.

Chapter Eight

70 Similar problems of language affected some parent-children relations. The language used by the parents appeared sometimes less than completely intelligible to young people. Many younger respondents in fact said that they could speak Punjabi, but were not confident enough to have conversations that went beyond food, plans and inquiring about family well-being. Some older people, instead, confessed that whenever they felt like having a heart-to-heart with a younger person, they would switch to English, no matter how unproficient they were in it. The sudden switch to the language commonly perceived as informal would give out a sign to the younger person that the conversation did not have to be affected by rigid rules of respect for elders, and was supposed to encourage them to open up and liberally express their opinions. The existence of only one form to address a second person ('you') instead of the three in Urdu (*tu* for younger or subordinated individuals, *tum* for people one may be intimate with and *ap* for the elders or authorities), as well as the use of first names rather than titles, are all characteristics that contribute to the feeling that some conveyed to me by saying 'English is a very disrespectful language'. Communication in English based on parents' good will, however, was not always successful: some young men said that their parents would not be able to empathise with their problems, not even when they encouraged communication in English, and therefore there was no point in opening up.

Chapter Nine

71 At the same time Tatum argues that lack of expectations may lead young people from minority ethnic groups to a stage where they struggle to recognise oppression (Tatum 2000:23).

BIBLIOGRAPHY

Adler, P.A. and Adler, P. (1991) 'Stability and flexibility: maintaining relations within organised and disorganised groups'. In Shaffir, W. and Stebbins, R. (eds.) *Experiencing Fieldwork*. London: Sage.

Afshar, A. (1989) 'Gender roles and 'The Moral Economy of Kin' among Pakistani women in West Yorkshire'. *New Community*, 15(2), 211–25.

Afshar, A. (1994) 'Muslim women in West Yorkshire: growing up with real and imaginary values amidst conflicting views of Self and Society'. In Afshar, A. and Maynard, M. (eds.) *The Dynamics of Race and Gender: Some Feminist Interventions*. London: Taylor and Francis.

Ahmad, S. (forthcoming) 'Of Al-Huda and the Powerpoint'. In Ahmad, S. (ed.) Oxford in *Pakistan: Readings in Sociology and Social Anthropology, volume on Gender*. Karachi: Oxford University Press

Akhtar, N. (writer) (2003) 'The biraderi'. *BBC Radio 4*, 26th August.

Alam, M.Y. (1998) *Annie Pott is Dead*. Glossoughton: Route.

Alam, M.Y. (2002) *Kilo*. Glossoughton: Route.

Alexander, C.E. (2000) *The Asian Gang: Ethnicity, Identity, Masculinity*. Oxford: Berg.

Alexander, C.E. (2004). 'Imagining the Asian gang: ethnicity, masculinity and youth after the riots'. *Critical Social Policy*, 24 (4), 526–49.

Alexander, C.E. (2006). 'Introduction: mapping the issues. ethnic and racial studies'. *Writing Race: Ethnography and Difference*, 29(3) (special issue), 397–410.

Aldrich, H.E., Cater, J.C., Jones, T.P. and McEvoy, D. (1981) 'Business development and self-segregation: Asian enterprise in three British cities'. In Peach, C., Robinson, V. and Smith, S. (eds.) *Ethnic Segregation in Cities*. London: Croom Helm.

Ali, Y. (2000) 'Muslim women and the politics of ethnicity and culture in Northern England'. In Sahgal, G. and Yuval-Davis, N. (eds.) *Refusing Holy Orders: Women and Fundamentalism in Britain*. London: Virago.

Alibhai-Brown, Y. (2001) 'Mr Blunkett has insulted all of us'. *The Independent*, 10 December.

Allen, S. (1996) *The Bradford Commission Report*. London: HMSO.

Amin, A. (2003) Unruly strangers? The 2001 urban riots in Britain. *International Journal of Urban and Regional Research*, 27(2), 460–63.

Anderson, L.S., Chiricos, T.G. and Waldo, G.P. (1977) 'Formal and informal sanctions: A comparison of deterrent effects'. *Social Problems*, 25, 103–14.

Anthias, F. and Yuval-Davis, N. (1996) *Racialised Boundaries: Race, Nation, Gender, Colour and Class and the Anti-racist Struggle*. London: Routledge.

Anwar, M. (1979) *The Myth of Return*, London: Heineman.

Apaxton (2002) 'Drugs in Bradford'. At *www.student.brad.ac.uk/apaxton/DrugsInBradford.htm*.

Archer, L. (2001) "Muslim brothers, black lads, traditional Asians': British Muslim young men's construction of race, religion and masculinity'. *Feminism and Psychology*, 11(1), 79–105.

Archer, L. (2003) *Race, Masculinity and Schooling: Muslim Boys and Education*. Maidenhead: Open University Press.

Back, L. (1996). *New Ethnicities and Urban Culture: Racism and Multiculture in*

Young lives. London: University College London Press.

Bagguley, P. and Hussain, Y. (2003a) 'Citizenship, ethnicity and identity: British Pakistanis after the 2001 'riots''. *Working paper, School of Sociology and Social Policy*, Leeds University.

Bagguley, P. and Hussain, Y. (2003b) 'Conflict and cohesion: constructions of community around the 2001 'riots''. At *http://www.leeds.ac.uk/sociology/people/pbdocs/Conflict%20and%20Cohesion%204%20conference.doc*

Bagguley, P. and Hussain, Y. (2003c) 'The Bradford 'riot' of 2001: A preliminary analysis'. *Paper presented at the Ninth Alternative Futures and Popular Protest Conference*, Manchester Metropolitan University, 22–3 April.

Ballard, R. (1990) 'Migration and kinship: The differential effect of marriage rules on the processes of Punjabi migration to Britain'. In Clarke, C. and Vertovec, S. (eds.) *South Asian Overseas Migration and Ethnicity*. Cambridge: Cambridge University Press.

Ballard, R. (1992) 'New clothes for the emperor? The conceptual nakedness of Britain's race relations industry'. *New Community*, 18, 481–92.

Ballard, R. (1994) 'Introduction'. In Ballard, R. (ed.) *Desh Pardesh: The South Asian Presence in Britain*. London: Hurst.

Ballard, R. (1996) 'The Pakistanis: Stability and introspection'. In Peach, C. (ed.) *Ethnicity in the 1991 Census*, vol. 2. London: HMSO.

Ballard, R. (2001) 'The impact of kinship on the economic dynamics of transnational networks: differential trajectories of adaptation amongst Mirpuris, Jullunduris and Sylethis', at *http://www.bradford2020.com/pride/docs/3.doc*.

Bankston, C.L. and Zhou, M. (2002) 'Social Capital as process: The meanings and problems of a theoretical metaphor'. *Sociological Enquiry*, 72(2), 285–317.

Barth, F. (1969) 'Introduction'. In Barth, F. (ed.) *Ethnic Groups and Boundaries*. London: Little, Brown.

Bashford, J., Kaur, J., Winters, M., Williams, R. and Patel, K. (2004) *Healthy Minds. What Are the Mental Health Needs of Bradford's Pakistani Muslim Children and Young People and How Can They Be Addressed?'*. University of Central Lancashire.

Basu, A. (1998) 'An exploration of entrepreneurial activity among Asian small businesses in Britain'. *Small Business Economics*, 10, 313–26.

Becker, H.S. (1963) *Outsiders: Studies in the Sociology of Deviance*. New York: Free Press.

Bell, C. (1976) 'Community, communion, class and community action: The social sources of the new urban politics'. In Herbert, D.T. and Johnston, R.J. (eds.) *Social Areas in Cities: Processes, Patterns and Problems*. London: Wiley.

Benson, S. (1996) 'Asians have culture, West Indians have problems: Discourses of race and ethnicity in and out of Anthropology'. In Terence, R., Samad, Y. and Ossie, S. (eds.) *Culture, Identity and Politics*. Aldershot: Avebury.

Beteille, A. (2006) *An Anthropologist in His Own Country*. Keynote address, ASA Conference, Keele University, 12 April.

Blaikie, N.V.H (1993) *Approaches to Social Enquiry*. Cambridge: Polity.

Bisi S. (March 2002) 'Female criminality and gender difference', *International Review of Sociology / Revue Internationale de Sociologie*,12 (1), 23-43 (21)

Boggs, C. (2001) 'Social Capital and political fantasy: Robert Putnam's bowling alone'. *Theory and Society*, 30, 281–97.

Bolognani, M. (2002) 'Bradistani: casi di etnicità pakistana' in Gran Bretagna. *Unpublished tesi di laurea, Dipartimento di Filosofia e Scienze Etno-antropologiche*, Università di Siena, Italy.

Bolognani, M. (2005) 'Attitudes towards crime and crime Prevention in the Bradford Pakistani community'. *Research Findings, Centre for the Study of Racism and Ethnicity*, University of Leeds.

Bolognani, M. (2006) 'Social construction and social production of crime amongst Bradford Pakistanis: Extended view. *Sage Race Relations Abstracts*, 31 (3), 19–27.

Bolognani, M. (2007a) 'Community perceptions of moral education as a response to crime amongst Bradford Pakistanis'. *Journal of Moral Education*, 36 (3), 357–369.

Bolognani, M. (2007b) 'Islam, ethnography and politics'. *International Journal of Social Research Methodology*, 10 (4), 279–93.

Bolognani, M. (2007c) Les 'désordres ethniques' en Grande-Bretagne: le cas de Bradford. *Espaces et Sociétés*, 128, 103–18.

Bolognani, M. (2007d) 'The myth of return: dismissal, survival or revival? A Bradford example of transnationalism as a political instrument. *Journal of Ethnic and Migration Studies*, 33(1), 59–76.

Bolognani, M. (2008) "These Girls Want to Get Married As Well': Normality, double deviance and reintegration amongst British Pakistani women'. In Kalra, V. (ed.) *Pakistani Diasporas: Culture, Conflict and Change*. Karachi: Oxford University Press.

Bolognani, M, Haider, E., Iqbal, H. and Sabri, Z. (under submission) *101 Damnations: Being a Pakistani in British Cinema*.

Bourdieu, P. (1986) 'Cultural capital and education'. In Richardson, J.G. (ed.) *Handbook of Theory and Research for the Sociology of Education*. New York: Greenwood Press, 241–58.

Bradford Chamber of Commerce and Industry (2003) *Business Crime Survey Results*. Bradford: BCCI.

Braithwaite, J. (1989) *Crime, Shame and Reintegration*. Cambridge: Cambridge University Press.

Burdsey, D. (2004). "One of the Lads?' Dual ethnicity and assimilated ethnicities in the careers of British Asian professional footballers'. *Ethnic and Racial Studies*, 27(5), 757–79.

Burlet, S. and Reid, H. (1996) 'Riots, representation and responsibilities: The role of young men in Pakistani-heritage Muslim communities'. In Shadid, W.A.R, and van Koningsveld, P.S. (eds.) *Political Participation and Identities of Muslims in Non-Muslim States.* Kampen, Netherlands: Kok Pharos.

Burnside, J. and Baker, N. (eds.) (1994) *Relational Justice.* Winchester: Waterside.

Cain, M. (2000) 'Orientalism, occidentalism and the sociology of crime'. *British Journal of Criminology*, 40, 239–60.

Careers Bradford (2002) 'Busibytes'. At *www.careersb.co.uk/Imi/busibytes/pdf/2002/Jan%2002.pdf.*

Carlen, P. (1985) *Criminal Women.* London: Polity.

Cesari, J. (2004) *When Islam and Democracy Meet.* New York: Palgrave.

Chakraborti, N., Garland, J. and Spalek, B. (2004) 'Out of sight, out of mind? Towards developing an understanding of the needs of 'hidden' minority ethnic communities'. *Criminal Justice Matters*, 57, 34–5.

Chaudhary, M. (1999) *Justice in Practice.* Karachi: Oxford University Press.

Collison, M. (1999) 'In search of the high life: Drugs, crime, masculinities and consumption'. In South, N. (ed.) *Youth Crime and Delinquency*, vol. 1. Aldershot: Ashgate.

Curtis, L.A. (1975) *Violence, Race and Culture.* London: Lexington.

Darr, A. and Modell, B. (1988) 'The frequency of consanguineous marriage amongst British Pakistanis'. *Journal of Medical Genetics*, 25, 191–4.

Denzin, N.K. (2001). *Interpretive Interactionism.* London: Sage.

Dhaya, B. (1970). 'Pakistanis in Britain: transients or settlers?' *Race*, 14, 241–77.

Dhaya, B. (1974) 'The nature of Pakistanis ethnicity in industrial cities in Britain'. In Cohen, A.P. (ed.) *Urban Ethnicity.* London: Tavistock.

D'Orban, P.T. (1991) 'Women, violent crime and the menstrual cycle', in *Medicine, Science and Law*, 31 (2), 353-359.

Douglas, M. (1966/2002) *Purity and Danger*. London: Routledge.

Eadie, T.M.R. (1999) 'Crime, justice and punishment'. In Baldock, J., Manning, N., Miller, S. and Vickerstaff, S. (eds.) *Social Policy*. Oxford: Oxford University Press.

Edmunds, J. and Turner, B.S. (2002) *Generations, Culture and Society*. Buckingham: Open University Press.

el-Zein, A.H. (1977) 'Beyond ideology and theology: The search for the anthropology of Islam'. *Annual Review of Anthropology*, 6, 227–54.

Erickson, R. (1977). 'Social distance and reaction criminality'. *British Journal of Criminology*, 17, 16–19.

Eriksen, T.H. (1993) *Ethnicity and Nationalism*. London: Pluto.

Fabietti, U. (1991) *Storia dell'Antropologia*. Bologna, Italy: Zanichelli.

Fallaci, O. (2005) *La Rabbia e l'Orgoglio*. Milan, Italy: Rizzoli.

Field, J. (2003) *Social Capital*. London: Routledge.

Furbey, R. and Macey, M. (2005) 'Religion and urban regeneration: A place for faith?' *Policy and Politics*, 33(1), 95–116.

Gabbidon, S.L. and Taylor Greene, H. (2005) *Race and Crime*. London: Sage.

Garland, J., Spalek, B. and Chakraborti, N. (2006). 'Hearing lost voices: Issues in researching 'hidden' minority ethnic communities'. *British Journal of Criminology*, 46, 423–37.

Geertz, C. (1973) 'Thick description: Towards an interpretive theory of culture'. In Geertz, C. (ed.) *The Interpretation of Cultures*. New York: Basic Books.

Gibson, M. (2002) *Born to Crime: Cesare Lombroso and the Origins of Biological Criminology.* London: Praeger.

Gilliat-Ray, S. (2005) '(Not) 'Accessing Deobandi dar ul-uloom in Britain'. *Fieldwork in Religion,* 1, 7–33.

Gilmore, D. (1987) 'Introduction'. In Gilmore, D. (ed.) *Honour and Shame and the Unity of the Mediterranean.* New York: Academic.

Gilmore, D. (1990) *Manhood in the Making: Cultural Concepts of Masculinity.* London: Yale University Press.

Gilroy, P. (1993) *The Black Atlantic: Modernity and Double Consciousness.* London: Verso.

Goffman, E. (1968) *Stigma. Notes on the Management of Social Identity.* London: Penguin.

Goodey, J. (2001) 'The criminalization of British Asian youth: Research from Bradford and Sheffield'. *Journal of Youth Studies,* 4(4), 429–50.

Goulding, C. (2002) *Grounded Theory.* London: Sage.

Granovetter, M.S. (1973) 'The strength of weak ties.' *American Journal of Sociology,* 78(6), 1360–80.

Grillo, R. (2004) 'Islam and transnationalism'. *Journal of Ethnic and Migration Studies,* 30(5), 861–78.

Hall, A. (writer) (2004) *Edge of the City.* Channel 4, 26th August.

Harrington, B. (2003) 'The social psychology of access in ethnographic research' *Journal of Contemporary Ethnography,* 32, 592-625.

Harrison, M. (2005) 'Introduction'. In Harrison, M., Phillips, D., Chahal, K., Hunt, L. and Perry, J. (eds.) *Housing, 'Race' and Community Cohesion.* Coventry: Chartered Institute of Housing.

Harrison, M. and Phillips, D. (2005) 'Perspectives from the 'grass roots': A Bradford case study and its implications'. In Harrison, M., Phillips, D., Chahal, K., Hunt, L. and Perry, J. (eds.) *Housing, 'Race' and Community Cohesion*. Coventry: Chartered Institute of Housing.

Herbert, D.E.J. (2003) 'Bradford after Rushdie: Islam, civil society and the public sphere in Britain'. In Herbert, D.E.J (ed.) *Religion and Civil Society*. Aldershot: Ashgate.

Herzfeld, M. (1982) *Ours Once More: Folklore, Ideology and the Making of Modern Greece*. Austin, TX: University of Texas Press.

Hirschi, T. (1971) *Causes of Delinquency*. Berkeley, CA: University of California Press.

Hoggett, P. (ed.) (1997) *Contested Communities*. Bristol: Policy.

Hooper, S. (writer) (2005) *Safe and Sound in Bradford 3*. Bradford: Age Concern.

Hope, T. (2001) 'Community crime prevention in Britain: A strategic overview'. *International Journal of Policy and Practice*. 1(4), 421-39

Ilahi, N. and Jafarey, S. (1999) 'Guestworker migration, remittances and the extended family: Evidence from Pakistan'. *Journal of Development and Economics*, 58, 485–512.

Imtiaz, A. (2002) *Identity and the Politics of Representation*. Unpublished PhD thesis, London School of Economics.

Irfan, S. and Cowburn, M. (2004) 'Disciplining, chastisement and physical child abuse: Perceptions and attitudes'. *Journal of Muslim Minority Affairs*, 24(1), 89–98.

Jacobson, J. (1997) 'Religion and ethnicity: Dual and alternative sources of identity among young British Pakistanis'. *Ethnic and Racial Studies*, 20(2), 238–56.

Jan-Khan, M. (2003) 'The right to riot?' *Community Development Journal*, 38(1), 32–42.

Kalra, V. and McLoughlin, S. (1999) 'Wish you were(n't) here'. In R. Kaur,

Hutnyk, J. (eds.) *Travel Worlds: Journeys in Contemporary Cultural Politics*. London: Zed Books.

Kalra, V. (2000) *From Textile Mills to Taxi Ranks: Experiences of Labour, Migration and Social Change*. Aldershot: Ashgate.

Kalra, V. (2003) 'Police lore and community disorder: diversity in the criminal justice system'. In Mason, D. (ed.) *Explaining Ethnic Differences: Changing Patterns of Disadvantage in Britain*. Bristol: Policy.

Kalra, V. S. (2006). 'Ethnography as politics: A critical review of British studies of racialised minorities'. *Ethnic and Racial Studies*, 29(3), 452–70.

Kalra, V.S. and Rehman, S. (2006) 'Earthquake: Transnationalism from below'. In Bolognani, M. and Lyon, S. (eds.) *Contemporary South Asia*, 15(3) (special issue on Pakistan), 173–288.

Khanum, S. (2000) 'Education and the Muslim girl'. In Sahgal, G. and Yuval-Davis, N. (eds.) *Refusing Holy Orders: Women and Fundamentalism in Britain*. London: Virago.

Kivisto, P. (2004) 'Immigrants, Citizenship and the Declining of Social Capital' Thesis. Paper presented at the *Leverhulme Programme on Migration and Citizenship Seminar*, University of Bristol, 1st April.

Knight, S. (2006) "Problem' families face eviction as Tony Blair demands respect'. *The Times*, 10 January.

Krase, J. and Sagarin, E. (1980) 'Formal and informal social control in cross-cultural perspective'. In Newman, G.R. (ed.) *Crime and Deviance: A Comparative Analysis*. London: Sage.

Kundnani, A. (2002) 'The death of multiculturalism'. At *www.irr.co.uk*.

Kureishi, H. (1996) *Bradford. In My Beautiful Laundrette and Other Stories*. London: Faber and Faber.

Lee, R.M. (1993) *Doing Research on Sensitive Topics*. London: Sage.

Lederman, D.L.N., Menéndez, A.M. (2002) 'Violent crime: Does social capital matter?' *Economic Development and Cultural Change*, 50, 509–39.

Lewis, P. (1994). *Islamic Britain*. London: I.B. Tauris.

Lewis, P. (2001). 'Between Lord Ahmed and Ali G: Which future for British Muslims?' At *http://bradford2020.com/pride/suplimentary.html*.

Lewis, P. (2006) 'Imams, Ulema and Sufis: Providers of bridging social capital for British Pakistanis?' In Bolognani, M. and Lyon, S. (eds.) *Contemporary South Asia*, 15(3) (special issue on Pakistan), 173–288.

Lien, I.L. (2005a) 'Criminal gangs and their connections: Metaphors, definitions and structures'. In Derek, A. and Weerman, T. (eds.) European Street Gangs and Troublesome Youth Groups. San Francisco, CA: Alta Mira.

Lien, I.L. (2005b) 'The role of crime acts in constituting the gang's mentality'. In Derek, A. and Weerman, T. (eds.) *European Street Gangs and Troublesome Youth Groups*. San Francisco, CA: Alta Mira.

Lyon, S. M. (2004) *An Anthropological Analysis of Local Politics and Patronage in a Pakistani Village*. Lewiston: Edwin Mellen.

Lutz, H. (1991) 'The myth of the 'other': Western representation and images of migrant women of so-called Islamic background'. *International Review of Sociology*, 2, 121–32.

Macdonald, J. and Macdonald, P. (1962) 'Chain migration, ethnic neighbourhood formation and social networks'. *Social Research*, 29 (4), 433–48.

Macey, M. (1999a) 'Class, gender and religious influences on changing patterns of Pakistani Muslim male violence in Bradford'. *Ethnic and Racial Studies*, 22(5), 845–66.

Macey, M. (1999b) 'Religion, male violence and the control of women: Pakistani Muslim men in Bradford'. *Gender and Development*, 7(1), 48–55.

Macey, M., Beckett, C. (2001) 'Race, gender and sexuality: the oppression of multi-culturalism', in *Women's Studies International Forum*, 24 (3), 309-319.

Macey, M. (2002) 'Interpreting Islam: Young Muslim men's involvement in criminal activity in Bradford'. In Spalek, B. (ed.) *Islam, Crime and the Criminal Justice System.* Cullompton: Willan.

MacPherson, W. (1999) *The Stephen Lawrence Inquiry.* Report of an inquiry conducted by Sir William MacPherson, advised by T. Cook, J. Sentamu and R. Stone. Cm 4262-I. London: Stationery Office.

Malik, Z. (2004) 'My £1.40 ride through Muslim Britain'. G2, *The Guardian*, 1st July.

Malinowski, B. (1926) *Crime and Custom in Savage Society.* London: Routledge.

Mamadouh, V. (1999) 'Grid-group cultural theory: An introduction'. *GeoJournal*, 47, 395–409.

Mason, J. (2002) *Qualitative Researching.* London: Sage.

Mawby, B. and Batta, I.D. (1980) *Asians and Crime: The Bradford Experience.* Middlesex: Scope Communication.

McGhee, D. (2005) *Intolerant Britain? Hate, Citizenship and Difference.* Maidenhead: Open University Press.

McLoughlin, S. (1996) 'In the name of the Umma: Globalisation, 'race' relations and Muslim identity politics in Bradford'. In Shadid W.A.R, Van Koningsveld, P.S. (eds.) *Political Participation and Identities of Muslims in non-Muslim States.* Kampen, Netherlands: Kok Pharos.

McLoughlin, S. (1998a) "An underclass in Purdah?' Discrepant representations of identity and the experiences of young-British-Asian-Muslim-women'. *Bulletin of the John Rylands University Library of Manchester*, 80(3), 89–106.

McLoughlin, S. (1998b) "A part of the community?' The politics of representation and a Muslim school's application for state funding'. *Innovation*, 11(4), 89-106.

McLoughlin, S. (1998c) 'The mosque-centre, community-mosque: Multifunctions, funding and the reconstruction of Islam in Bradford'. *Scottish Journal of Religious Studies*, 19(2), 211–27.

McLoughlin, S. (2000) 'Researching Muslim minorities: Some reflections on fieldwork' in Britain. *Journal of Semitic Studies*, Suppl. 12, 175–191.

McLoughlin, S. (2005) 'Mosques and the public space: conflict and cooperation' in Bradford. *Journal of Ethnic and Migration Studies*, 31, 1045–66.

McLoughlin (2006a) 'Towards a cosmo-political Islamism? 'New' middle-class activists and cross-cultural engagement in Britain'. Paper presented at the *ASA Conference*, University of Keele, 12 April.

McLoughlin (2006b) 'Writing a 'Brasian' city: Ethnicity, 'race', culture and religion in accounts of postcolonial Bradford'. In Ali, N., Sayyd, S. and Kalra, V.S. (eds.) *A Postcolonial People*. London: Hurst.

Mehmood, T. (1983) *Hand on the Sun*. London: Penguin.

Melossi, D. (2000) 'Changing representations of the criminal'. *British Journal of Criminology*, 40, 296–320.

Merton, R. (1938/1995) 'Opportunity structure'. In Adler, F. and Laufer, W. (eds.) *The Legacy of Anomie Theory*. Toronto, Canada: Transaction.

Metcalf, H., Modood, T. and Virdee, S. (1996) *Asian Self-employment: The Interaction of Culture and Economics in England*. London: Policy Studies Institute.

Miller, L.L. (2001) *The Politics of Community Crime Prevention*. Aldershot: Ashgate.

Modood, T. (1988) "Black', racial equality and Asian identity'. *New Community*, 14 (3), 397–404.

Modood, T. (1990) 'Catching up with Jesse Jackson: Being oppressed and being somebody'. *New Community*, 17 (1), 87–98.

Modood, T. (1992) *Not Easy Being British: Colour, Culture and Citizenship*. Stoke on Trent: Runnymede Trust.

Modood, T. (2004) 'Capitals, ethnic identity and educational qualifications'. *Cultural Trends*, 13(2), 87–105.

Muncie, J.M. (1996) 'The construction and deconstruction of crime'. In Muncie, J.M. (ed.) *The Problem of Crime*. London: Sage.

Murphy, D. (1987) *Tales from Two Cities*. London: Murray.

Murtuja, S.B. (2004). *Pakistani Muslim Communities in Britain and Germany: Informal Familial Care of Elders and Processes of Social Exclusion*. Unpublished PhD thesis, University of Leeds.

Orford, J., Johnson, M. and Purser, B. (2004) 'Drinking in second-generation Black and Asian communities in the English Midlands'. *Addiction Research and Theory*, 12(1), 11–30.

Ouseley, H. (2001) *Community Pride, Not Prejudice*. Bradford: Bradford Vision.

Pankhurst, D. (2002) 'Introductory lecture', *Now and After: Bradford Now and in the Future*, Bradford School of Lifelong Learning, Education and Development, Ouseley, 25 April.

Pearson, G. and Patel, K. (1998) 'Drugs, deprivation and ethnicity: outreach among Asian drug users in a northern English city'. *Journal of Drug Issues*, 28(1) (special edition on 'Contemporary Issues Concerning Illicit Drug Use in the British Isles'), Florida State University, 199–225.

Pearson, G. (1999) 'Lawlessness, modernity and social change: A historical appraisal'. In South, N. (ed.) *Youth Crime and Delinquency*, vol. 1. Aldershot: Ashgate.

Phillips, C. and Bowling, B. (2002) 'Racism, ethnicity, crime and criminal justice'. In Maguire, M., Morgan, R. and Reiner, R, (eds.) *The Oxford Handbook of Criminology*. Oxford: Oxford University Press.

Phillips, C. and Bowling, B. (2003) 'Racism, ethnicity and criminology: developing minority perspectives'. *British Journal of Criminology*, 43(2), 269–90.

Phillips, D. (2001) 'The changing geography of South Asians in Bradford'. At *http://www.bradford2020.com/pride/docs/Section5.doc*.

Pike, K.L. (1954) *Language in Relation to a Unified Theory of the Structure of Hu-*

man Behaviour, vol. 1. Gendale, CA: Summer Institute of Linguistics.

Pryce, K. (1979/1986) *Endless Pressure: A Study of West Indian Lifestyles in Bristol*. Bristol: Bristol Classical.

Putnam, R. (1993) *Making Democracy Work: Civic Traditions in Modern Italy*. Princeton, NJ: Princeton University Press.

Putnam, R.D. (2001) *Bowling Alone: The Collapse and Revival of American Community*. London: Simon and Schuster.

Quraishi, M. (2005) *Muslims and Crime*. Aldershot: Ashgate.

Ramadan, T. (2004) *Western Muslims and the Future of Islam*, Oxford: Oxford University Press.

Rosenhan, D.L. (1973) 'On being sane in insane places'. *Science*, 179, 250-8.

Russell, K.K. (1992) 'Development of a Black criminology and the role of the Black criminologist'. *Justice Quarterly*, 9(4), 667–83.

Rowe, M. (1998) *The Racialisation of Disorder in 20th Century Britain*. Aldershot: Ashgate.

Saeed, F. (2001) *Taboo! The Hidden Culture of a Red Light Area*. New York: Oxford University Press.

Said, E.W. (1985) *Orientalism*. Harmondsworth: Penguin.

Saifullah Khan, V. (1976a) *Mirpuri Villagers in an Industrial City*. Unpublished PhD thesis, University of Bradford.

Saifullah Khan, V. (1976b) 'Pakistanis in Britain: Perceptions of a population'. *New Community*, 5(1), 99–108

Saifullah Khan, V. (1979) 'Migration and social stress: Mirpuris in Bradford'. In Saifullah Khan, V. (ed.) *Minority Families in Britain: Support and Stress*. London: Macmillan.

Samad, Y. (1992) 'Book-burning and race relations: Political mobilisation of

Bradford Muslims'. *New Community*, 18 (4), 507–19.

Samad, Y. (1996) 'The politics of Islamic identity among Bangladeshis and Pakistanis in Britain'. In Terence, S., Ranger, Y. and Stuart, O. (eds.) *Culture, Identity and Politics*. Aldershot: Ashgate.

Samad, Y. (1998) 'Media and Muslim identity: Intersection of generation and gender'. *Innovation*, 11(4), 89-106.

Sanders, T.L.M. (2004) *Sex Work: A Risky Business*. Cullompton: Willan.

Sarup, M. (1996) *Identity, Culture and the Postmodern World*, Edinburgh: Edinburgh University Press.

Secret, P.E. and Johnson, J.B. (1989) 'Racial differences in attitudes toward crime control'. *Journal of Criminal Justice*, 17, 361–75.

Sengupta, K. (2005) 'The police nightmare: Home-grown terrorists'. *The Independent*, 13 July.

Shah, B. and Dwyer, C. (2006) 'Moving on: Exploring the educational aspirations of young Pakistanis in Britain'. Paper presented at *the Leverhulme Conference on 'Mobility, Ethnicity and Society'*, Bristol University, 17 March.

Shaikh, S. and Kelly, A. (1989) 'To mix or not to mix: Pakistani girls in British schools'. *Educational Research*, 31(1), 10–19.

Shallice, A. and Gordon, P. (1990) *Black People, White Justice? Race and the Criminal Justice System*. London: Runnymede Trust.

Sharma, S., Hutnyk, J. and Sharma, A. (1996) *Dis-orienting Rhythms*. London: Zed Books.

Shaw, A. (1988) *A Pakistani Community in Britain*. Oxford: Basil Blackwell.

Shaw, A. (1994) 'The Pakistani community in Oxford'. In Ballard, R. (ed.), *Desh Pardesh: The South Asian Presence in Britain*. London: Hurst.

Shaw, A. (2000b) *Kinship and Continuity*. Amsterdam, Netherlands: Harwood Academic.

Shaw, A. (2001) 'Kinship, cultural preference and immigration: Consanguinous marriage among British Pakistanis.' *Journal of the Royal Anthropological Institute*, 7, 315–34.

Siddique, M. (1993). *Moral Spotlight on Bradford.* Bradford: MS Press.

Siddiqui, M. (2005) 'Thought for the day'. *BBC Radio 4*, 19 July. At http://www.bbc.co.uk/religion/programmes/thought/documents/t20050719.shtml.

Simmons, J.L. (1969) *Deviants.* Berkeley, CA: Glendessary.

Singh, R. (2001) 'Future race relations in Bradford: factors that matter'. At *http://www.bradford2020.com/pride/docs/Section%208.doc.*

Singh, R. (2002) *The Struggle for Racial Equality.* Leeds: n.a.

Smith, A.D. (1986/1992) *The Ethnic Origins of Nations.* London: Basil Blackwell.

Spalek, B. (2002) 'Introduction'. In Spalek, B. (ed.) *Islam, Crime and Criminal Justice.* Cullompton: Willan.

Spalek, B. (2005) 'A critical reflection on researching Black Muslim women's lives post-September 11th'. *International Journal of Social Research and Methodology*, 8(2), 57-87.

Strauss, A. and Corbin, J. (eds.) (1997) *Grounded Theory in Practice.* London: Sage.

Taj, M. (1996) 'A 'can do' city': *Supplementary Observations, Comments and Recommendations to the Bradford Commission Report.* Bradford: Taj.

Tatum, B.L. (2000) *Crime, Violence and Minority Youths.* Aldershot: Ashgate.

Terence, S., Ranger, Y. and Stuart, O. (eds.) *Culture, Identity and Politics.* Aldershot: Ashgate.

Vine, I. (1997). 'Bradford's 1995 riots in retrospect: Muslim youth and civic alienation'. Paper presented at the *MOSAIC 97 Conference*, University of

Bath, 14–17 July.

Wallman, S. (1979) 'Introduction: The Scope for Ethnicity'. In Wallman, S. (ed.) *Ethnicity at Work*. London: Macmillan.

Wallman, S. (1986) 'Ethnicity and the boundary process in context'. In Rex, J. and Mason, D. (eds.) *Theories of Race and Ethnic Relations*. Cambridge: Cambridge University Press.

Wardak, A. (2000) *Social Control and Deviance: A South Asian Community in Scotland*. Aldershot: Ashgate.

Webster, C. (1995) *Youth Crime, Victimisation and Racial Harassment: The Keighley Crime Survey*. Bradford: Centre for Research in Applied Community Studies.

Webster, C. (1996) 'Asian young people and drug use'. *Criminal Justice Matters*, 24.

Webster, C. (1997) 'The construction of British 'Asian criminality'". *International Journal of the Sociology of Law*, 25, 65–86.

Werbner, P. (1980) 'Rich man, poor man or a community of suffering: Heroic motifs in Manchester Pakistanis' life histories'. *Oral History*, 8, 35–42.

Werbner, P. (1987) 'Barefoot in Britain: anthropological research on Asian immigrants'. *New Community*, 14, 176–81.

Werbner, P. (1989) 'The ranking of brotherhoods: The dialectics of Muslim caste among overseas Pakistanis'. *Contributions to Indian Sociology*, 23(2), 285–315.

Werbner, P. (1990) *The Migration Process: Capital, Gifts and Offerings among British Pakistanis*. New York: Berg.

Werbner, P. (2004) 'Theorising complex diasporas: Purity and hybridity in the South Asian public sphere' in *Britain*. *Journal of Ethnic and Migration Studies*, 30(5), 895–911.

Werbner, P. (1996) 'Essentialising the other: A critical response'. In Terence, R., Samad, Y. and Ossie, S. (eds.) *Culture, Identity and Politics*. Aldershot: Avebury.

West Yorkshire Police (2003) 'Annual report.' At *www.westyorkshire.police.uk/ annual_report/annualreport2003.pdf.*

West Yorkshire Police (2004) 'Crackdown-Bradford'. At *www.westyorkshire. police.uk/crackdown/.*

Williams, F. (2001) 'In and beyond New Labour: Towards a new political ethics of care'. *Critical Social Policy,* 21(4). 467–93.

Williams, R. (2008) 'Civil and religious law in Britain: A religious perspective'. *Foundation lecture, Royal Courts of Justice,* 7 February. At http://www.bishopthorpepalace.co.uk/1575.

Wilson, J.Q. and Herrnstein, R.J. (1985) *Crime and Human Nature.* New York: Touchstone.

Wilson, D. (1999) 'Muslims in prison.' In El-Hassan, S. (ed.) *Practising Islam in Prison.* London: IQRA Trust.

Woolcock, M. (2001) 'The place of social capital in understanding social and economic outcomes'. *Canadian Journal of Policy Research,* 2(1), 11–17.

Wootton, B. (1959) *Social Science and Social Pathology.* London: George Allen and Unwin.

Beaufoy, S. (writer) and Gleenan, K. (director) (2005) 'Yasmin'. *Channel 4 television,* 13 January.

GLOSSARY

Al-Huda: an Islamic school for women created by Dr. Farhat Hashmi in Islamabad in the early 1990s. It propagates a form of Islam heavily influenced by Wahabism, and has turned into a global social movement through the efforts of its graduates

Bains: Punjabi caste

Barelwi: name of the religious movement in South Asia originated from the city of Breilly in Uttar Pradesh, India, whose members venerate Sufi saints and shrines

Biraderi: local agnatic lineage, blood-cum-caste unit

Dar-ul-oom: institution of religious learning

Deobandi: a revivalist Sunni movement born in India around 1867 that emphasizes the Hanafi school of jurisprudence against the in-roads of non-Islamic influences

Desi: literally 'home-made', commonly used to refer to 'our own' or 'South Asian'

Fatwa: formal legal opinion pronounced by a mufti

Ghanimat: refers to the idea of war booty

Ghar: nuclear family or household

Goot: caste subdivision

Gora: white man (f. gore)

Gurdwara: Sikh temple

Hadis, Hadith: tradition from the Prophet containing his remarks on a given situation and based on a chain of transmitters

Hafiz (pl. *huffaz*): one who has memorized the Quran

Hajj: pilgrimage to Makkah, one of the five pillars of Islam

Halal: lawful

Haram: actions forbidden by Islamic law

Hijjab: Muslim woman's outing clothing hiding her hair and body contours

Hizb-ut-Tahrir: anti-nationalist Sunni international party whose aim is to recreate a caliphate

Ijtehad: 'striving', individual inquiry seeking to go back to the roots of Islamic jurisprudence, and thus by-passing taqlid, the solutions codified and accepted by one of the legal schools.

Imam: (1) leader of the ritual prayer; (2) the leader of the Muslim community; (3) an honorific for a great scholar; (4) in the Shi'ah tradition the leader of their community in the line of 'Ali and Fatima, the Prophet's daughter

Izzat: honor, respect

Jaddu: magic, sorcery

Jat: Punjabi caste

Jinn: creatures mentioned in the Quran, made from fire, and thought to be able to help or hinder human beings, who thus seek to control them.

Kafir: a non-Muslim practicing infidelity, it is often used with a pejorative meaning

Kameti: committee, rotating credit informal association

Karim: blessed

Khandan: family or family tree

Khidmat: service for the common good

Khuthba: sermon given during Friday prayers at mosques

Ladla: favourite and often youngest son

Lafanga: lazy, undisciplined

Lena-dena: taking-giving

Log: people

Madrasa: as understood in Bradford, a quranic school

Makkru: the area in between Halal (allowed) and Haram (forbidden) where what is accepted but not encouraged lies

Mandir: Hindu temple

Masjid: mosque

Maulvi: officiating priest of a mosque

Namaz: prayer

Nazar: a gaze, the evil eye

Nikkah: religious marriage rite

Panchayat: gathering of the elders or respectables of the village or biraderi

Pir: 'elder', a sufi able to lead devotees on the mystical path, also known as shaikh and murshid

Purdah: 'veil', refers to the practice of separation of women from men

Rajput: northern Indian caste

Rukhia: spiritual healing through the reading of the Quran

Shalwar-kameez: loose trousers and long shirt/blouse

Shari'a(h): the totality of rules guiding the individual and corporate lives of Muslims, covering law, ethics and etiquette.

Sharif: noble, respectable

Sharika: village provenance

Sufi: an adherent of Sufism which is widely understood to be the mystical dimension of Islam

Tablighi Jamaat: strictly non-political Muslim missionary and revivalist movement

Ulema: learned scholars and religious scholars

Taveez: an amulet, often prepared at a mazar, containing Quranic verses (etc.) for protection

Umma(h): community, especially the Prophet's community, the transnational world of all Muslims

Umra: the performance of part of the Hajj rituals at times other than the prescribed Hajj ritual dates, it is also known as 'little pilgrimage'

Vilayat: abroad

Zamindar: farmer, landowner/holder

Zat: caste

Zikkat: annual tithe or tax to charity prescribed by the Quran

INDEX

A

Access 23, 40, 41, 42, 65, 99, 135, 167, 194, 195, 212, 234
Accommodationists 37, 155
Adler, P.A. 227, 239
Aetiologies of Crime 5, 95, 207, 211
African/Caribbean 49, 51, 80
Afro-Caribbeans 12, 22, 76, 126, 128
Afshar, A. 56, 132, 137, 160, 178, 227
Age 5, 11, 14, 15, 16, 18, 25, 33, 37, 43, 44, 45, 51, 56, 85, 105, 116, 119, 130, 134, 136, 140, 151, 155, 158, 164, 177, 197, 220, 223, 235
Agency 10, 11, 15, 23, 38, 39, 41, 45, 47, 53, 74, 95, 96, 120, 134, 148, 149, 211, 216
Ahmad, S. 180, 227
Akhtar, N. 59, 227
Al-Huda 180, 227, 246
Alam, M.Y. 59, 66, 71, 113, 146, 150, 227
Aldrich, H.E. 62, 63, 121, 210, 228
Alexander, C.E. 8, 13, 14, 15, 16, 18, 21, 24, 25, 37, 38, 40, 70, 71, 75, 125, 134, 167, 216, 219, 220, 223, 227, 228
Ali, Y. 149, 228
Alibhai-Brown, Y. 221, 228
Alienation 16, 20, 28, 36, 243
  Self-Alienation 17, 20, 28, 36, 243
Allen, S. 67, 228, 245
Amin, A. 51, 62, 64, 228
Anderson, L.S. 150, 228
Anthias, F. 137, 228

Anthropology 10, 19, 21, 22, 25, 34, 39, 41, 45, 222, 227, 230, 233
Anti-Nazi League 68
Anti-Social Behaviour 85
Anwar, M. 55, 58, 59, 228
Apaxton 70, 80, 228
Archer, L. 13, 30, 109, 137, 220, 224, 228
Ashrafisation 140
Asian 13, 14, 15, 16, 21, 24, 27, 29, 30, 33, 47, 49, 50, 51, 52, 54, 56, 62, 63, 64, 65, 66, 70, 71, 75, 78, 83, 84, 85, 95, 96, 97, 99, 103, 104, 106, 114, 116, 120, 126, 128, 134, 136, 138, 141, 145, 152, 153, 155, 158, 160, 165, 166, 169, 170, 171, 177, 194, 201, 203, 204, 221, 224, 227, 228, 229, 230, 231, 234, 238, 239, 240, 242, 244
Aspirational Frame 131, 175
Attachment 9, 28, 37, 38, 53, 59
Attock 55, 58, 115, 220
Attribution of Blame 96, 107, 120, 122, 124, 210

B

Bachelors Houses 54, 57, 221
Back, L. 11, 72, 228
Bagguley, P. 68, 95, 213, 222, 229
Bains 66, 246
Ballard, R. 23, 25, 52, 54, 55, 57, 58, 95, 96, 160, 224, 229, 242
Bangladeshi 44, 52, 167, 223
Bankston, C.L. 61, 223, 229
Barth, F. 62, 108, 229
Bashford, J. 223, 230
Basu, A. 96, 230
Batley 78, 206, 215
Becker, H.S. 74, 77, 230
Bell, C. 73, 230
Benson, S. 8, 19, 20, 21, 22, 23, 25, 230
Beteille, A. 3, 230
Bhangra 36
Biological Approach to Crime 8, 9, 10, 11, 12, 13, 132, 219
Biraderi 5, 33, 48, 57, 58, 59, 60, 61, 71, 112, 114, 121, 122, 130, 146, 148, 160, 165, 168, 189, 207, 215, 216, 227, 246
 Biraderism 5, 61, 71, 96, 112, 115, 121, 122, 182, 183
Bisi, S. 132, 152, 230
Blaikie, N.V.H. 230

INDEX

Boggs, C. 61, 196, 230
Bollywood 36, 42, 118, 195
Bolognani, M. 4, 42, 47, 48, 49, 52, 53, 56, 57, 59, 62, 63, 66, 68, 70, 72, 132, 134, 135, 147, 152, 162, 167, 179, 188, 191, 224, 225, 230, 231, 236, 237
Bourdieu, P. 58, 60, 61, 223, 231
Bradford
  Bradford Pakistani 3, 28, 30, 31, 36, 39, 41, 42, 43, 45, 48, 49, 52, 58, 71, 72, 75, 76, 91, 93, 96, 138, 208, 216, 224, 230
  Bradford riots 68
  Bradford Twelve 32, 64, 70
  Council 64, 65, 67, 68
Bradistan 47, 49
Braithwaite, J. 25, 74, 77, 103, 115, 231
Bristol 12, 17, 18, 20, 219, 235, 236, 241, 242
British National Party 64, 68
  BNP 68, 69, 85, 222
Brothers in Trouble 221
Burdsey, D. 125, 231
Burglaries 85, 91
Burlet, S. 31, 221, 231
Burnside, J. 37, 71, 94, 115, 151, 209, 232

C

Cain, M. 3, 11, 34, 212, 232
Capital
  Bonding capital 5, 60, 61, 112, 115, 122, 146, 151, 181, 183, 189, 213
  Bridging capital 34, 60, 61, 73, 215, 216, 237
  Capital-rich underdevelopment 19
  Cultural capital 3, 16, 20, 28, 36, 37, 39, 58, 61, 62, 116, 122, 130, 223
  Social capital 34, 60, 61, 223, 236, 237, 245
Carlen, P. 132, 232
Car Theft 85, 104
Caste 22, 34, 54, 55, 59, 60, 140, 216, 221, 244, 246, 247
Census 44, 48, 49, 50, 51, 229
Cesari, J. 115, 116, 232
Chachchis 32, 49, 55, 123, 220
Chakraborti, N. 12, 232, 233
Chaudhary, M. 59, 60, 138, 168, 224, 232
Chilling 130, 143, 163

Class 13, 16, 17, 18, 19, 20, 30, 36, 39, 44, 47, 51, 82, 106, 126, 133, 140, 154, 179, 180, 220, 221, 228, 230, 237, 239
Coconuts 36, 127, 224
Collison, M. 91, 104, 141, 232
Commitment 37, 63
Community
  Bradford Pakistani Community 3, 28, 30, 31, 36, 39, 41, 42, 43, 45, 48, 52, 58, 71, 75, 93, 230
  Community Breakdown 87, 91
  Community Criminology 3, 151, 211, 215, 216
  Community Leaders 45, 175, 209
  Community of Suffering 53, 244
  Community Stability 91
  Erosion of Community 91, 209
  Pakistani Community 3, 28, 30, 31, 36, 39, 41, 42, 43, 44, 45, 47, 48, 52, 54, 58, 60, 63, 65, 68, 70, 71, 75, 76, 81, 83, 85, 88, 91, 93, 94, 97, 98, 104, 118, 125, 136, 144, 147, 150, 168, 175, 189, 196, 206, 207, 209, 211, 215, 216, 222, 225, 230, 242
  Poisoning the Community 86, 98, 139
  Putting Things Back into the Community 112, 138, 156
Competition 62, 63, 112, 141, 145, 165
Conflict 5, 13, 38, 51, 122, 144, 229, 231, 239
Conformists 35, 37, 129
  Part-Time Conformists 37, 129
Consumption 22, 51, 70, 72, 81, 82, 84, 110, 133, 141, 165, 232
  Unnecessary Consumption 141
Control Theory 37, 38
Criminology
  Black Criminology 11, 241
  Colonial Model of Criminology 16, 17, 18, 20, 23, 28
  Neo-Colonial Model of Criminology 17, 18, 23
  Postcolonial Model of Criminology 16, 120, 210
Culture
  Culture vs Religion 181
  Out of Place Culture 106, 183
  Pakistani Culture 135, 148, 161, 168, 181
  Western Culture 117, 118, 119, 154
Curtis, L.A. 75, 232

D

D'Orban, P.T 233
Dahya, B. 49, 50
Dar-ul-oom 180
Darr, A. 51, 232
Demographic Explaination of Crime 62, 104, 125
Denzin, N.K. 39, 232
Deobandi 225, 234, 246
Depression 82, 83, 135, 173
Deprivation 9, 23, 25, 30, 39, 48, 70, 95, 96, 98, 99, 103, 221, 240
  Deprivationism 23, 95
Desenzano del Garda 216
Deviance 3, 4, 5, 8, 9, 10, 11, 13, 14, 15, 18, 28, 29, 30, 33, 34, 35, 37, 38, 40, 71, 74, 77, 91, 95, 112, 121, 124, 125, 126, 132, 134, 136, 137, 138, 149, 152, 209, 224, 230, 231, 236, 244
Dhaya, B. 49, 54, 55, 62, 232
Diaspora 4, 6, 8, 27, 29, 33, 35, 45, 125, 169, 212, 216, 231
Divorce 170
  Divorced 45, 221
Domestic Violence 31, 83, 84, 91, 99, 170, 193. *See also* Violence, Private
Double Consciousness 130, 234
Double Deviance 132, 134, 231
Douglas, M. 88, 137, 222, 233
Drugs
  Drug Addiction 31, 82, 91, 148, 163
  Drug Dealers 85, 87, 89, 90, 93, 94, 100, 113, 126, 138, 140, 141, 142, 146, 148, 153, 155, 165, 170, 174, 181, 187, 188, 189, 203, 211, 224
  Drug Use 240, 244
  Light Drugs 102, 134
  Prescription Drugs 82, 133, 135

E

Eadie, T.M.R. 29, 74, 77, 103, 233
Edge of the City 175, 196, 234
Edinburgh 37, 38, 127, 213, 242
Edmunds, J. 43, 233
Education, Lack of 99, 103, 158, 160
el-Zein, A.H. 233
Elders 2, 5, 34, 43, 53, 59, 68, 79, 108, 110, 114, 115, 117, 121, 146, 162,

163, 169, 171, 174, 180, 192, 225, 240
Emic 27, 39, 40, 44, 45, 95, 128, 151, 207, 212, 215, 216, 220
Entrepreneur 79, 87, 92, 95, 100, 104, 109, 111, 113, 126, 138, 145, 155, 157, 162, 167, 169, 204, 205, 219
  Entrepreneurship 58, 62, 63, 96
Erickson, R. 115, 233
Eriksen, T.H. 233
Essentialism, Anti- 21, 208
Ethnic Resources and Networks 25, 40, 41, 47, 48, 52, 62, 73, 77, 96, 106, 124, 137
Ethnography 28, 33, 228, 231, 234, 236
Etic 34, 35, 38, 39, 40, 43, 128, 220
Excessive Bonding 112, 115, 189
Experimenters 35, 129, 130
Extremists 36, 37, 128, 174

F

Fabietti, U. 41, 233
Faith 38, 65, 150, 172, 174, 175, 180, 183, 184, 185, 214, 233
Fallaci, O. 233
Family 5, 6, 14, 15, 16, 18, 19, 20, 29, 34, 35, 37, 38, 40, 48, 51, 52, 54, 55, 56, 57, 58, 59, 60, 61, 62, 63, 69, 73, 78, 79, 82, 83, 86, 88, 89, 91, 92, 94, 96, 102, 103, 104, 106, 107, 108, 110, 111, 112, 113, 114, 115, 118, 122, 127, 129, 131, 132, 133, 134, 135, 136, 137, 138, 139, 147, 149, 150, 151, 152, 153, 154, 155, 157, 158, 159, 160, 161, 163, 164, 165, 166, 167, 168, 169, 170, 171, 172, 173, 174, 176, 177, 180, 181, 182, 183, 184, 198, 199, 201, 204, 207, 210, 215, 216, 220, 221, 225, 235
Fatalism 96, 120, 122
Fathers 52, 92, 96, 102, 110, 113, 124, 127, 136, 144, 158, 161, 175
Field, J. 61, 196, 233
Frustration 17, 31, 79, 88, 99, 102, 115, 159, 205
Furbey, R. 31, 185, 233

G

Gabbidon, S.L. 7, 8, 9, 233
Gang 13, 14, 15, 24, 33, 34, 81, 146, 219, 227, 237
Gangster 119, 147, 181, 223
Garland, J. 11, 23, 232, 233

Geertz, C. 41, 233
Gemeinschaft 73, 224
Gender 2, 5, 11, 13, 15, 18, 25, 30, 37, 40, 45, 51, 98, 124, 125, 132, 136, 151, 154, 162, 220, 227, 228, 230, 237, 242
Generation
 First Generation 29, 43, 44, 100, 107, 109, 110, 156, 223
 Generational Gap 53, 155
 Second Generation 29, 88, 92, 109, 112, 202
 Third Generation 43, 88, 112, 169
Gesellschaft 73, 224
Ghanimat 222
Gibson, M. 8, 9, 234
Gilliat-Ray, S. 213, 225, 234
Gilmore, D. 160, 234
Gilroy, P. 131, 234
Go-betweens 35, 36, 82, 129, 147
Goffman, E. 115, 234
Gold shops 97
Goodey, J. 14, 125, 234
Gossip 2, 57, 134, 148, 152, 165, 166, 167, 225
Goulding, C. 234
GP, General Practitioner 134, 135, 149
Granovetter, M.S. 5, 60, 61, 122, 234
Grassroots Organisations 209
Greed 99, 103, 104
Grillo, R. 70, 234
Gujarat 55
 Gujarati 44, 50, 160
Gujar Khan 55
Gurdwara 184, 214, 247

H

Hajj 176, 180
Halal 55, 64, 88, 89, 90, 91, 117, 176, 190, 248
Hall, A. 222, 234
Hand on the Sun 144, 239
Hanging Out 42, 86, 132, 142, 147, 196, 197
Haram 88, 89, 90, 91, 105, 140, 176, 182, 190, 248
Harrington, B. 42, 234
Harrison, M. 49, 92, 102, 219, 222, 234

Herbert, D.E.J. 65, 66, 71, 225, 230, 235
Herzfeld, M. 41, 235
Hijjab 124, 176, 178, 180, 247. *See also* Purdah
Hindu 160, 179
Hirschi, T. 37, 38, 107, 132, 235
Hizb-ut-Tahrir 90, 180
Hoggett, P. 208, 235
Honeyford affair 64, 65, 66
Honour 34, 56, 84, 114, 119, 132, 137, 138, 152, 160, 171, 220, 224, 225
Hooper, S. 235
Hope, T. 71, 151, 235
Household, Pakistani 54, 55, 58, 85, 86, 92, 113, 116, 130, 140, 142, 143, 153, 159, 170, 172, 176, 181, 221, 225

I

Ice-Cream War 169
Identity 10, 14, 15, 16, 17, 20, 29, 30, 31, 33, 35, 36, 37, 42, 63, 67, 71, 92, 109, 131, 141, 175, 200, 210, 219, 220, 223, 229, 235, 238, 239, 242
Ijtihad 220
Ilahi, N. 52, 235
Imam 84, 151, 152, 166, 168, 177, 180, 187, 190, 193, 194, 195, 200
Immigrants 12, 29, 52, 55, 57, 236, 244
Imtiaz, A. 28, 35, 36, 37, 38, 109, 126, 127, 128, 130, 131, 138, 147, 224, 235
Indians 3, 18, 19, 20, 24, 34, 49, 52, 104, 160, 163, 168, 203, 219, 221, 223, 230, 241, 244
Inner City 48
Intergenerational gap/difference. *See also* Generation gap
Irfan, S. 161, 235
Islam 30, 31, 32, 33, 38, 57, 60, 108, 115, 116, 117, 118, 120, 121, 122, 128, 139, 160, 168, 173, 174, 175, 176, 177, 178, 179, 180, 181, 185, 189, 190, 192, 195, 197, 207, 213, 222, 224, 231, 232, 233, 234, 235, 237, 238, 241, 243, 245, 246, 249
Islamists 2, 35, 129
Islamophobia 32, 85, 102

J

Jacobson, J. 235
Jaddu 173, 247

Jan-Khan, M. 95, 235
Jat 66, 247

K

Kafir 90, 105, 124
Kalra, V.S. 12, 25, 26, 30, 31, 52, 62, 63, 69, 96, 162, 192, 231, 235, 236, 239
Kameti 63, 221
Karachi 32, 227, 231, 232
Kashmir, Azad 44, 53, 55, 57, 58, 66
Keighley 32, 174, 222, 244
Khanum, S. 105, 149, 236
Khidmat 94, 108, 112, 117, 122, 156, 248
Khuthba 194
Kinship 33, 58, 61, 229, 242, 243
Kismat 121, 122
Kivisto, P. 196, 236
Knight, S. 106, 209, 236
Krase, J. 77, 213, 236
Kundnani, A. 71, 109, 125, 209, 236
Kureishi, H. 64, 224, 236

L

Labelling Theory 74, 77
  Labelling 3, 4, 5, 8, 10, 25, 35, 42, 75, 89, 91, 103, 127, 130, 132, 147, 182, 209, 212, 216
Labour Migrations 52, 62, 63, 106, 132, 236
Labour Party 64, 106, 209, 245
Ladla 127
Lafanga 126, 132, 138
Lawrence Inquiry 69, 101, 238
Lederman, D.L.N. 29, 150, 236
Lee, R.M. 213, 236
Leeds Road 84, 85, 147, 190, 193, 200
Leeds University 2, 229
Lena Dena 60, 166
Lewis, P. 30, 44, 51, 65, 180, 190, 222, 225, 237
Lien, I.L. 28, 33, 34, 35, 38, 237
Life

Double Life 36, 98, 127, 130, 131
Karim Life 90
Life-Cycle 117, 179, 192
Local Institutions 6, 94, 196
Lombroso, C. 7, 8, 9, 10, 24, 234
London 13, 14, 15, 47, 154, 156, 163, 166, 167, 193, 200, 227, 228, 230, 232, 233, 234, 235, 236, 237, 238, 239, 240, 241, 242, 243, 244, 245
Lumb Lane 64, 205
Lutz, H. 135, 138, 237
Lyon, S.M. 165, 168, 225, 236, 237

M

Macdonald, J. 52, 237
Macey, M. 14, 28, 30, 31, 32, 33, 38, 39, 42, 50, 51, 67, 68, 70, 185, 202, 219, 233, 237
MacPherson, W. 69, 101, 238
Madrassas 38, 55, 117, 151, 174, 175, 184, 185, 190, 191, 192, 196, 206, 211
Mafia 28, 29, 59, 144, 146, 147, 223
  Mafia Mentality 144, 148
Makkru 88, 89, 90
Malik, Z. 109, 222, 238
Malinowski, B. 9, 10, 24, 25, 74, 77, 238
Mamadouh, V. 120, 238
Mandir 184, 214
Mangla Dam 52, 57
Manningham 31, 59, 62, 64, 66, 68, 219, 222
Marriage
  Arranged Marriage 51, 59
  Forced Marriage 94, 99, 135
  Marriage Cure 162, 164, 165, 183
  Transcontinental Marriage 43, 51
Masculinity 13, 14, 16, 30, 35, 104, 125, 145, 220, 227, 228, 234
Masjid 193. *See also* Mosque
Mason, J. 236, 238, 244
Mawby, B. 27, 28, 29, 32, 33, 49, 54, 55, 62, 71, 102, 168, 238
McGhee, D. 12, 238
McLoughlin, S. 41, 42, 47, 49, 55, 58, 59, 63, 64, 105, 115, 117, 178, 179, 189, 192, 193, 224, 235, 238, 239
Media 3, 4, 5, 11, 13, 16, 73, 75, 99, 118, 125, 135, 149, 167, 184, 194, 198,

Index

206, 207, 210, 222, 242
Mehmood, T. 144, 239
Melossi, D. 10, 239
Men, Young 1, 6, 14, 31, 35, 36, 37, 38, 66, 68, 69, 78, 82, 102, 104, 114, 124, 125, 126, 127, 131, 133, 139, 143, 144, 147, 148, 149, 162, 174, 196, 210, 221, 225, 228, 232
Merton, R. 103, 239
Metcalf, H. 41, 58, 239
Migration
　Chain Migration 52, 54, 55, 56, 57, 58
　Migration Policies 56, 62
　Migration Process 22, 27, 28, 29, 57, 61, 62, 244
Miller, L.L. 24, 75, 233, 239
Minority Ethnic Groups, Knowledge of 3, 4, 8, 11, 12, 17, 18, 23, 24, 25, 28, 30, 38, 45, 51, 69, 74, 147, 200, 208, 210, 223, 226
Mirpur 36, 52, 55, 56, 60, 62, 89, 115, 116, 131, 154, 160, 221
　Mirpuris 28, 31, 49, 55, 56, 57, 59, 64, 65, 90, 117, 123, 147, 160, 229, 241
Modood, T. 14, 17, 23, 24, 25, 30, 62, 95, 96, 101, 106, 120, 223, 224, 239
Moral Education 151, 231
Moral Panic 2, 11, 14, 70, 71, 75, 78, 85, 124, 125, 136, 147, 148, 165, 166, 225
Mosque 37, 38, 55, 64, 65, 72, 90, 116, 119, 151, 156, 174, 175, 176, 177, 185, 186, 187, 188, 189, 190, 192, 193, 194, 195, 196, 199, 200, 210, 211, 214, 215, 238, 239. *See also* Masjid
　Abu Bakr Mosque 193
　Mosque as Community Centre 192, 193, 211
　Pilrig mosque 38
Mothers 92, 110, 124, 127, 132, 136, 158, 161, 162, 166, 181
Multiculturalism 3, 51, 66, 236
Muncie, J.M. 74, 77, 240
Murphy, D. 41, 64, 240
Murtuja, S.B. 240
Muslim 1, 2, 4, 13, 14, 31, 33, 35, 51, 55, 64, 65, 66, 67, 72, 80, 83, 85, 89, 90, 105, 107, 113, 114, 115, 117, 118, 124, 130, 134, 135, 138, 139, 143, 148, 155, 160, 161, 174, 175, 176, 178, 180, 181, 182, 185, 191, 192, 195, 199, 200, 206, 209, 213, 215, 220, 224, 227, 228, 230, 232, 235, 236, 237, 238, 239, 240, 242, 243, 244, 247
　British Muslim 2, 180, 228
My Son the Fanatic 219

Myth of Return 49, 228, 231

N

Namaz 91, 117, 173, 174, 176, 177, 185, 192, 194. *See also* Salat
National Front (NF) 64, 68, 222
Niche, Economic 63, 96, 97, 104, 155, 158
Nikkah 124
Norms 10, 29, 33, 36, 37, 42, 60, 73, 93, 108, 121, 126, 127, 128, 129, 131, 150, 151, 158, 224
North West Frontier Province (NWFP) 55

O

Occidentalist 3, 11
Oppression 17, 18, 19, 20, 28, 120, 125, 210, 223, 226, 237
Orford, J. 31, 83, 167, 174, 195, 240
Orientalist Approach 34, 135
Oslo 28, 33, 34, 35
Ouseley Report 1

P

Pakistan 33, 43, 44, 48, 49, 51, 53, 54, 55, 56, 59, 62, 63, 66, 82, 83, 97, 110, 113, 130, 138, 140, 154, 155, 158, 159, 162, 163, 164, 165, 167, 170, 171, 189, 190, 200, 201, 220, 221, 227, 235, 236, 237
Pakistani 1, 2, 3, 4, 5, 6, 14, 20, 24, 25, 27, 28, 29, 30, 31, 33, 34, 35, 36, 38, 39, 41, 42, 43, 44, 45, 47, 48, 49, 50, 51, 52, 54, 55, 56, 57, 58, 59, 60, 62, 63, 64, 65, 67, 68, 69, 70, 71, 72, 73, 75, 76, 77, 78, 80, 81, 83, 85, 88, 90, 91, 92, 93, 94, 95, 96, 97, 98, 102, 104, 106, 108, 118, 121, 125, 126, 127, 128, 130, 132, 133, 134, 135, 136, 138, 139, 142, 144, 147, 148, 149, 150, 154, 159, 160, 161, 163, 164, 165, 168, 175, 176, 178, 179, 181, 184, 189, 196, 198, 200, 203, 206, 207, 208, 209, 210, 211, 212, 213, 215, 216, 219, 220, 221, 222, 223, 224, 225, 227, 229, 230, 231, 232, 235, 237, 240, 241, 242, 243, 244
Pankhurst, D. 208, 240
Parents 5, 15, 33, 35, 37, 38, 43, 79, 84, 85, 91, 92, 97, 98, 102, 103, 105, 106, 107, 108, 109, 112, 113, 114, 116, 118, 121, 127, 130, 131, 133, 137, 145, 147, 150, 151, 152, 153, 154, 155, 157, 158, 159, 161, 164, 165, 166, 168, 173, 174, 179, 180, 181, 184, 186, 191, 195, 198, 199, 204, 214, 223, 224, 225
Parental strategies 136, 154

Participant Observation 4, 18, 19, 41, 84, 134, 212, 213
Partition 54, 57
Passivity 93, 125, 136, 145, 148, 149, 178
Pathans 49, 55, 82, 90, 221
Pathologisation 3, 15, 16, 25, 38, 45, 210
Pearson, G. 80, 82, 83, 86, 97, 110, 135, 163, 240
Phillips and Bowling 7, 8, 11, 12, 13, 14, 16, 23, 24, 25, 28, 30, 39, 208
Pike, K. 27, 39, 40, 220, 240
Police 12, 21, 25, 30, 31, 35, 44, 64, 67, 68, 69, 70, 80, 82, 119, 141, 169, 170, 172, 185, 188, 197, 201, 202, 203, 204, 205, 206, 210, 211, 214, 215, 217, 222, 224, 236, 242, 245
  Policing 8, 11, 12, 67, 69, 150, 184, 202, 205, 212
Polish Migration 54, 106
Politics 21, 36, 42, 48, 59, 99, 140, 154, 207, 208, 220, 228, 230, 231, 233, 235, 236, 237, 238, 239, 242, 243, 245
Pollution 88, 89, 91, 137, 149, 222
Positivism 10
  Positivistic Approach 9
Practitioners 45, 83, 91, 106, 122, 167, 192, 195
Prevention 28, 35, 51, 56, 58, 71, 91, 94, 108, 109, 137, 149, 151, 168, 175, 180, 183, 200, 206, 208, 209, 211, 214, 235, 239
Prison 12, 31, 68, 69, 105, 107, 114, 167, 176, 184, 198, 200, 201, 203, 215, 224, 245
  Armley Prison 107, 114, 200, 215
  Prison Chaplain 107, 114, 200, 215, 224
Prophet 66, 178
Pryce, K. 8, 17, 18, 19, 20, 36, 219, 241
Punjab 58, 220, 225
  Punjabi 49, 50, 54, 55, 225, 229, 246, 247
Purdah 124, 238. *See also* Hijjab
Purification 89, 175, 176
Purity 88, 137, 222, 233, 244
Putnam, R.D. 60, 61, 62, 73, 196, 230, 241

Q

Quraishi, M. 28, 31, 32, 33, 40, 241
Quran 51, 83, 90, 117, 138, 140, 155, 173, 174, 178, 179, 181, 182, 186, 190, 214, 222, 225, 249

R

Race 3, 4, 7, 8, 9, 11, 12, 13, 14, 15, 16, 17, 18, 19, 21, 23, 24, 26, 27, 28, 30, 33, 39, 47, 65, 73, 75, 208, 212, 219, 227, 228, 229, 230, 231, 232, 233, 234, 235, 237, 238, 239, 241, 242, 243, 244
  Race Relations Industry 14, 15, 17, 21, 23, 229
Racialisation 3, 13, 14, 75, 241
Racism
  Biological Racism 101
  Cultural Racism 10, 12
  Historical Racism 102
  Institutional Racism 30, 69, 101, 102, 106, 204
Radio 90, 195, 227, 243
  Sunrise Radio 90
Rajput 225
Ramadan, T. 116, 195, 241
Rawalpindi 55
Rebels 38, 129
Reciprocity 10, 42, 58, 107, 138, 150, 166
  Reciprocal Exposure 4, 212
Reconversions 175, 176
Rehabilitation 35, 154, 163, 164, 180, 200, 216
  Home-Made Rehabilitation 176
  Village Rehabilitation 183
Reintegration 71, 175, 176, 231
Reintegrative Shaming Theory 25
Religion 5, 13, 20, 22, 27, 28, 29, 30, 31, 32, 36, 37, 45, 65, 66, 72, 76, 80, 88, 90, 107, 108, 115, 116, 117, 118, 120, 122, 128, 139, 156, 172, 173, 174, 175, 176, 178, 179, 181, 182, 183, 190, 195, 200, 210, 219, 224, 228, 233, 234, 235, 237, 239, 243
  Religion vs Culture Debate 31, 32, 88, 107, 115, 116, 122, 172, 181
Reputation 37, 56, 76, 85, 87, 117, 138, 147, 153, 156, 160, 193
Respect 3, 12, 15, 21, 34, 45, 57, 75, 96, 102, 106, 137, 144, 146, 169, 177, 188, 209, 215, 220, 222, 225, 236
  Respect agenda 209
Restaurants 97, 98, 106, 110, 164, 195
Retrieval 151, 162
Riots
  1995 Riots 15, 30, 31, 66, 202, 243
  2001 Riots 1, 2, 44, 67, 68, 69, 71, 85, 126, 208, 213, 219, 222

French Riots 70
Rosenhan, D.L. 132, 241
Rowe, M. 12, 241
Rude Boys 36, 128, 132, 138, 139, 140, 141, 143, 144, 147, 148
Rude Girls 131
Rukhia 173
Rushdie affair 1, 14, 28, 30, 36, 65, 66, 67, 225
Russell, K.K. 7, 8, 11, 23, 25, 241

S

Saeed, F. 165, 224, 225, 241
Said, E.W. 34, 241
Saifullah-Khan, V. 57, 59, 73, 160
Salat 117, 192. *See also* ; *See also* Namaz
Samad, Y. 14, 65, 66, 71, 230, 241, 242, 245
Sanctions 29, 71, 88, 150, 166, 167, 168, 228
Sanders, T.L.M. 42, 242
Sarup, M. 30, 242
Scarman Report 12
Schools 51, 56, 64, 92, 99, 105, 106, 127, 134, 159, 184, 189, 198, 199, 200, 206, 211, 242
Secret, P.E. 12, 242
Segregation 44, 50, 51, 58, 63, 70, 228
  Self-segregation 70, 228
Self Defence 33, 64, 71, 144
Sengupta, K. 75, 242
September 11th 243
  9/11 15, 28, 32, 70, 127
Sermons 181, 185, 189, 211
Sex 84, 91, 189
Shah, B. 224, 242
Shaikh, S. 58, 242
Shallice, A. 8, 242
Sharif 140, 141
Sharifisation 138, 141
Sharma, S. 21, 24, 34, 45, 209, 242
Shaw, A. 14, 43, 52, 56, 58, 59, 63, 125, 242, 243
Shootings 79, 84, 215
Siddique, M. 31, 49, 54, 55, 56, 62, 64, 65, 221, 243
Sikh 106, 160, 203, 247

Simmons, J.L. 74, 243
Singh, R. 49, 50, 51, 54, 55, 57, 58, 62, 64, 65, 67, 95, 96, 105, 243
Smith, A.D. 65, 228, 243
Snooker Centres 143, 197
Social Control
 Communal system of social control 151, 152, 159, 168
 Formal social control 172, 174, 198, 208, 212
 Informal social control 148, 149, 150, 154
Sons 92, 97, 105, 106, 113, 116, 132, 152, 153, 154, 155, 162, 167, 188
Spalek, B. 30, 232, 233, 238, 243
Sport 142, 180, 194
Stability
 Biraderi Stability 80, 130, 183
 Community Stability 36, 82, 92, 128, 131, 227, 229
Status 11, 15, 21, 25, 34, 44, 68, 101, 103, 112, 125, 137, 140, 141, 154, 165, 175, 178, 210, 213, 220
 Status competition 165
Stigma 82, 101, 136, 142, 157, 165, 166, 234
Strain Theory 102, 103, 141, 175
Strauss, A. 243
Streets, Keeping off 66, 78, 107, 142, 143, 144, 185, 194, 196
Structural Constraints 12, 22, 25, 95, 120, 210
Subcultures 16, 76, 125, 127, 139, 210, 224
 Subcultures Studies 132
Sufi 34, 237, 246, 249
Sylhetis 49, 50

T

Tableeghi Jamaat 38, 93, 121, 122, 156, 223
Taboo 2, 3, 8, 11, 14, 15, 16, 19, 25, 27, 28, 45, 46, 74, 166, 208, 212, 241
 Taboo of criminological research 7
Taj, M. 67, 243
Take-Away 98, 141
Tatum, B.L. 8, 16, 17, 19, 20, 21, 23, 28, 36, 95, 103, 120, 210, 223, 226, 243
Taweez 90, 172, 173, 174, 183
Taxi
 Private-Hire Taxi 63
 Taxi Business 63, 81, 106
 Taxi Drivers 63, 81, 97, 166

Taxi Hire 81
Taxi Ranks 62, 63, 96, 236
Television 90, 147, 195, 196, 201, 245
Terence, S. 21, 230, 242, 243, 244
Terrorism 75, 85, 185
  Terrorist 31, 75, 163, 242
Textile Mills 56, 62, 63, 96, 236
Ties
  Horizontal Ties 93, 108, 110, 111, 112, 114, 122
  Vertical Ties 108, 111
Trust 41, 42, 73, 105, 108, 111, 150, 179, 212, 239, 242, 245

U

Ulema 237
Umma 4, 71, 72, 185, 238
Umra 108, 176, 180
Unemployment 37, 50, 51, 98, 100, 221, 222

V

Vartan Bhanji 60
Victimization 11
Vigilantes 35, 129, 139
Vilayat 57, 140
Vine, I. 66, 243
Violence
  Private Violence 30, 83, 84, 91, 99, 125, 170, 171, 193, 237. *See also* Domestic Violence
  Public Violence 13, 28, 31, 33, 51, 67, 69, 71, 79, 85, 120, 205, 210, 237

W

Wallman, S. 30, 244
Wardak, A. 28, 37, 38, 58, 59, 71, 102, 107, 125, 127, 128, 129, 149, 155, 160, 213, 244
Webster, C. 28, 32, 33, 35, 36, 38, 51, 70, 71, 75, 80, 81, 82, 109, 124, 125, 126, 127, 128, 129, 139, 147, 244
Welfare State 62, 102, 110, 111
Werbner, P. 8, 19, 21, 22, 25, 28, 41, 47, 52, 53, 59, 63, 72, 75, 94, 125, 135, 140, 165, 223, 244
West 4, 21, 66, 115, 119, 120, 122, 181, 186

West Bowling 146, 197
Williams, F. 56, 207, 230, 245
Wilson, D. 31, 245
Wilson, J.Q. 9, 74, 77, 245
Women, Young 5, 111, 124, 125, 133, 149, 166, 178
Woolcock, M. 61, 245
Wootton, B. 9, 245

Y

Yasmin 225, 245
Youth 14, 16, 18, 21, 28, 33, 45, 51, 53, 61, 65, 93, 99, 102, 104, 105, 107, 109, 113, 118, 119, 120, 124, 126, 127, 129, 132, 133, 142, 147, 148, 174, 175, 180, 181, 182, 183, 189, 190, 191, 195, 196, 197, 198, 206, 210, 211, 227, 232, 234, 237, 240, 243, 244
  Young People 43, 51, 65, 68, 78, 84, 99, 100, 103, 108, 110, 111, 117, 121, 122, 124, 132, 134, 135, 136, 156, 177, 179, 181, 193, 199, 206, 211, 223, 225, 226, 244
Yuval-Davis, N. 137, 228, 236

Z

Zamindaar 225
Zat 140